WORDS
FOR TODAY 1994

Notes on Bible Readings

GW00703320

HBRA

INTERNATIONAL BIBLE READING ASSOCIATION

Cover photograph – Indian Mother and Child
(*Tear Fund*)

Published by:
The International Bible Reading Association
Robert Denholm House
Nutfield
Redhill RH1 4HW

ISBN 07197-0816-8
ISSN 0140-8275

Typeset by Avonset, Midsomer Norton, Bath, Avon
Printed and bound in Great Britain by Cox and Wyman Ltd, Reading

SCHEME OF READINGS 1994

FROM THE EDITOR

Greetings to our many readers worldwide, from the staff of IBRA and all who have written this year's notes. 'May God our Father and the Lord Jesus Christ give you grace and peace' (Philippians 1.2). As Paul would go on to say, we give thanks to God for your faith and remember you in our prayers. We rejoice that we are members of one family throughout the earth and pray that these notes will help you and ourselves to grow in faith.

Introducing new writers

Welcome to our many contributors, some of whom you know. And there are many new ones, bringing a wealth of insights from their wide experience and different cultural backgrounds.

Introducing new ways

You will have seen the new title on the cover and noticed other changes. Although we shall continue to study some books of the Bible, or sections of books, as in the past, we shall explore some of the themes of our lectionaries (especially the new Four Year Lectionary (JLG2). Readings from JLG 2 are marked with an asterisk * and come somewhere within about 10 days before or after the Sunday on which they are appointed to be read. We hope you will be helped by these links with Sunday's worship.

Maintaining our tradition

Many of you have valued the opportunity to study books of the Bible. This year, we shall study Amos, Hosea, Ruth, Jeremiah Acts 13-21 and 1 Peter together with Mark's Gospel, which is, used in most themes. We shall focus on each of the four Gospels in turn, with supplementary material from other Gospels when necessary.

The prayers

We are grateful to publishers who have permitted us to use prayers from a variety of sources. But we would like some new prayers for the future. Wherever you live in the world, if you have written a prayer that you think we might include, then please send it addressed to me – but don't expect to see it in print until at least 1996! By the time you read this, most of the 1995 notes will be edited and ready for typesetting! I can't promise to publish them all, but will do my best to include a wide selection.

Action

Our prayerful reading of the Bible should change our attitudes, so that we respond to the world around us in new ways. You will not have time to put every suggestion into practice, but we hope that you will consider each one carefully and that, as the year goes by, you will have made some new ventures in faith.

Introducing MARK – (the Gospel for study in 1994)

Imagine that you are a Jewish Christian living in Rome. Since the year AD64, the Christian community has been bitterly persecuted, including the apostle Peter. In the year AD70, the Jews in Judaea staged a massive stand against the Romans. Jerusalem was destroyed and its streets and Temple were awash with the blood of faithful Jews, maybe including some of your family and friends. Take time and read the Gospel of Mark straight through from beginning to end. It is written with such a lively, direct style and eyewitness quality that you will find it hard to put down. Try to hear what it says to you from a perspective of violence and persecution.

For its first readers, it tells the good news of the powerful Son of God, confronting and overcoming the powers of evil. It unfolds the surprising choices of the Son: in obedience to the Father, he is the human, vulnerable Son of man, the suffering Servant, who prepares his disciples to accept the cost of discipleship, to take up the cross and follow him.

Looking ahead

Please write and tell us what you find helpful and what is not. Preparing these daily readings is a two-way partnership. We need your help.

May you discover the living presence of Christ as you read and know that the Spirit leads you into all truth.

Maureen Edwards

Maureen Edwards – Editor

ACKNOWLEDGEMENTS AND ABBREVIATIONS

We are grateful for permission to quote from the following versions of the Bible:

NIV New International Version (Hodder & Stoughton) © 1973, 1978, 1984 by International Bible Society Anglicisation © 1979, 1984, 1989

NJB New Jerusalem Bible (Darton, Longman & Todd Ltd) © 1989

REB Revised English Bible (Oxford and Cambridge University Presses) © 1989

GNB Good News Bible

JB Jerusalem Bible

RSV Revised Standard Version

*Lectionary readings (JLG2)

Other IBRA BOOKS 1993　　UK prices

LIGHT FOR OUR PATH　　**£3.25**
　shorter notes for adults

FINDING OUR WAY TOGETHER　　**£2.95**
　Bible Study Handbook for group leaders
　(see page 46)

PREACHERS' HANDBOOK　　**£2.95**
　sermon outlines (see page 128)

DISCOVERING THE BIBLE　　**£2.25**
　for teenagers

THE STORY OF JESUS　　**£8.95**
　for young people and adults

BIBLE TRAIL　　**£2.50**
　for children

BIBLE STORYTIME　　**£2.75**
　for young children (all 6 £15.00)　　each book

LOOKING AT THE CROSS　　**£3.25**
　(see page 251)

LOOKING AT EASTER & ASCENSION　　**£3.25**
　(see pages 25 and 251)

LOOKING AT PENTECOST　　**£3.25**
　(see page 251)

LOOKING AT ADVENT　　**£3.25**
　(see page 251) (all four £11.95)

EVERYDAY PRAYERS
MORE EVERYDAY PRAYERS　　**£3.75**
FURTHER EVERYDAY PRAYERS　　each book
　(see page 84) (all three £10.75)

All prices include postage for the UK

A SURPRISING SAVIOUR

Notes, based on the Revised English Bible, by
Pauline Webb

*People meeting Pauline Webb for the first time often comment, 'It's a surprise to meet the face behind the voice!' She is best known as a frequent broadcaster on BBC's **Thought for the Day** and **Pause for Thought** and was, for eight years, Head of Religious Broadcasting for BBC World Service. She has travelled widely, as an officer of the Methodist Church Overseas Division and as a Vice-Moderator of the World Council of Churches.*

A friend of mine who had been an agnostic for many years, eventually, towards the end of her life, became a Christian. When I asked her what finally convinced her, she replied, 'Life has been so full of surprises that I've come to believe there must be a God who keeps things up his or her sleeve. So I think of God as being like a person who loves me and never ceases to amaze me the more I get to know him.'

There's a book called *God of Surprises*, written by a Jesuit priest, Gerard Hughes (published by Darton Longman and Todd 1985). It would make excellent background reading to our theme, particularly chapters 10 and 11. The author uses three guidelines we could apply to our reading about Jesus:

● remember that he is human, like us;

● reflect that we are meant to be like him;

● realise that deep within us we can have the same spiritual resources as were available to him.

If we follow these guidelines as we read the following passages, we may be in for some surprises!

✳ *Surprising God,*
disturb our minds with new thoughts of you,
direct our feet into new paths of faith,
and delight our hearts with new hopes of heaven.
Through Jesus Christ our Lord.

January 1-8 Surprising anger

Saturday January 1   LUKE 2.41-52 *

A surprising teenager

Gerard Hughes points out in his book *God of Surprises* that
Luke 2.49 is the only recorded saying of Jesus from the first
thirty years of his life. What does that say to us about Jesus
himself as both listener and teacher? What warning does it
carry for us about our anxieties for others and our inability
sometimes to realise how important it is for them to make their
own discoveries of faith? And what does it show us about the
resources available to us as we embark on our own exploration
of the Scriptures?

Teenage boys today, as in Jesus' time, are expected, at a
special Bar Mitzvah ceremony, to become 'sons of the Law',
able both to read from and to expound the Torah to their elders.
Sometimes modern young people surprise their elders by the
unsuspected depth of their understanding and maturity, if this is
not stifled by over-protective parents. It has been said that 'a
boy becomes a man when a man is needed'. We should never
underestimate what God is doing in the life of others, especially
of teenagers.

✳ *Open our eyes, O Lord,*
  that we may see new truths in familiar words.
  Help us to perceive how your promises are being
  fulfilled
  in our lives and the lives of others.

Sunday January 2   MARK 2.23-28

A surprising lawbreaker

There is a striking contrast here between carefree disciples
strolling through the cornfields on a peaceful Sabbath day, and
the stern Pharisees clearly looking for some way of trapping
Jesus. It is not likely that the disciples plucked the ears of corn
out of any deliberate defiance of the Law. It would seem a
natural thing to do as they brushed past it and admired the ripe,
golden fullness. But the Pharisees turned the occasion into one
of legalistic confrontation.

Jesus calmly responded, appealing to their own tradition.
Oddly, his reply misquotes 1 Samuel 21.1-6, where the high

priest referred to was Ahimelech, not Abiathar. He also omits any reference to the conditions on which David was allowed to eat sacred bread. But, in a surprising master stroke, he quotes back to his critics his version of one of their own rabbinical sayings: 'The sabbath is delivered unto you, and you are not delivered to the sabbath.'

People in authority are sometimes tempted to use legalistic arguments to ensnare others, even when they unwittingly commit only minor transgressions. But the Son of man came to show a more humane way of treating one another, with understanding, compassion and a sense of proportion.

✳ *Lord save us from being so strict with others*
  or with ourselves
  that we miss out on enjoying your good gifts to us.

Monday January 3   MATTHEW 12.9-14

'The better the day, the better the deed'

For the devout Jew, the Sabbath is the most joyful day of the week, a day for affirming life as well as for praising God. The fourth commandment was 'Remember to keep the sabbath day holy'. It was only later, through centuries of oral tradition, that a whole catalogue of rules grew up to protect its holiness. Some of these were plainly ludicrous, and Jesus deliberately challenges one of these extraneous laws to emphasise that the sacredness of human life is as important as the sacredness of a holy day. To the question he is asked in verse 10, the correct answer according to the Law would have been, 'Yes, if a person's life is in danger. Otherwise, No.' To the question Jesus poses in return, there were various opinions in the rabbinical schools. Some would have said that the lawful thing would be to bring food to the animal, or at least to make it comfortable. So Jesus emphasises that compassion is always lawful and that nothing should be esteemed as of greater value than human life.

✳ *Lord, help us to understand*
  that any day becomes holy when good deeds are done
  in it.
  So may we honour you this day
  by the way we treat both our fellow human beings
  and all creatures, great and small, for your name's sake.

Tuesday January 4

Storm in the Temple!

How different is this second visit of Jesus to the Temple from his first! Then, as a young boy, he astounded the scribes by his scholarship. This time, a grown man, he alarms the money-changers by his anger. It is an anger expressed physically as well as verbally. Animals are driven out, tables overturned and people rebuked. What was it that made him most angry? – the exploitation of the poor, the greed of the money-changers, or the desecration of God's house? Perhaps, to Jesus, all these three factors together added up to blasphemy.

'Do not turn my Father's house into a market.' The young boy Jesus had delighted to be in his Father's house, doing his Father's business. So it comes as a shock to him to see that house turned into a market.

There is a sense in which today we see the whole world being turned into a market. The 'market economy' with all its dealing in currencies and its fluctuations in values affects us all and is destroying the lives of millions of our fellow men and women. How angry do we become about it? What can we do to reclaim God's world-house for all God's people?

✳ *Lord, come into the temple of my heart this day,*
and cleanse from it all that desecrates
this dwelling-place of God.
Make me as angry as you are over my sins
and the sins of our society.
Make me as ready as you are
both to condemn and to forgive them.

Wednesday January 5

Blunt speaking

This chapter is the last in Matthew's Gospel that records Jesus speaking out publicly, to the whole multitude. It is probably a collection of sayings, arranged, as Matthew so often does, in one continuous discourse. It is not a condemnation of all Pharisees. Many of them were good and upright people, whom Jesus counted among his friends. But it was those who misused religion who angered him so much, particularly when they excused unjust actions and unfair attitudes with pious platitudes. People might be scrupulous about small details of religious observance, giving to the Temple a tenth of all their produce, even to the smallest herbs. But if they were unscrupulous in their treatment of others, Jesus condemned them in no uncertain terms.

Notice in verse 23 what Jesus regards as 'the weightier matters of law'. He refers to Micah 6.8 as the standard for true religious life. Which sins do religious people tend to condemn most readily today? How much prominence do we give to justice, humility and reverence as the most important moral values? How often do we speak out against hypocrisy, greed and self-indulgence?

✴ *Lord, grant that we may speak plainly and act honestly.*
Help us to reflect our worship of you
in the respect and justice we show to all people.

Thursday January 6   **MATTHEW 10.34-39**

A test of loyalty

The first words of this message come as a shock. But remember the words of Simeon to Mary when he saw the infant Jesus and prophesied that a sword of sorrow would one day pierce her heart (Luke 2.34). Note too Jesus' own warning that those who take up the sword will perish by it too (Matthew 26.51-52). So here he seems to be saying, not that the purpose of his coming was to bring a sword, but that the consequence of it would cause pain to those who loved him and provoke violent reaction from those who saw him as a threat to their own power. He is warning his disciples that if they follow him, they too will find themselves involved in controversy, even possibly within their own families. They will also be treated as enemies of the State and become victims of persecution. All this will test their loyalty.

In this passage, as in yesterday's, there are echoes of the prophet Micah (7.6). Only a commitment beyond the family as an end in itself enables us to find the true values of family life, just as only in self-giving, to which Jesus calls us, do we find our true selves.

✴ *Lord, help me not to shrink from controversy*
but to struggle through it
to the full integrity of following you.

The Servant with the sharp tongue!

This is one of the 'Servant Songs' describing the One whom God will send to save Israel. The prophet may have been reflecting on his own sense of vocation as God's messenger, or he may have been envisaging the kind of Messiah Israel needed to lead them out of exile, or he may have been speaking of the whole nation. Whoever he is referring to, note the qualifications Isaiah considers necessary for such a calling: a sense of destiny from one's earliest days, a sharp tongue, a swift wit and a deep spirituality. A vocation does not depend on either false modesty or over-confidence. The Servant seems, in this passage, to have neither. What he does have is the conviction that God has been with him from the days of his birth, even through pre-natal influences, and God is leading him on to fulfil an even greater purpose.

How would you describe the way God has prepared you for your work in life? How ready are you to welcome God's plans for your future?

✳ *My every weak though good design,*
    O'errule or change, as seems thee meet;
Jesus, let all my work be thine;
    Thy work, O Lord, is all complete,
    And pleasing in thy Father's sight;
Thou only hast done all things right.   *Charles Wesley*

Never currying favour

In his lively book, *St Paul and his Letters* (published by Darton Longman and Todd), Hubert Richards quotes a second century description of Paul as 'small of stature, balding, bow legs, eyebrows meeting, nose slightly hooked.' This unflattering physical portrait is not much relieved by the personal portrait Paul paints of himself in this, the earliest of his letters, the Epistle to the Thessalonians. Wherever he had preached so far, he had suffered insult and injury but he had never watered down his message to avoid upsetting people. Does he sound like the kind of person you might feel inclined to invite to your church as your new minister?

Paul knew that the people of Thessalonica were under attack for their faith and that slanderous rumours had been spread about him. This was no time for honeyed words. He wanted to tell them frankly, though lovingly, what it costs to take Christ seriously. There is no such thing as an easy discipleship. Are we too often more ready to hear and to preach 'the comfortable words of the Lord Jesus' rather than the uncomfortable ones?

✳ *Lord, help us to share with others not only our words,*
but our very selves,
with all our faults and with all your love.

January 9-11 *Surprising humility*

Sunday January 9   **MARK 1.9-11 ***

Identifying with ordinary people

Take time today to picture the scene on the bank of the River Jordan. A fiery wayside preacher has gathered around him a motley crowd of people: some hanging on his every word, others ridiculing this wild man from the desert. Then through the crowd comes the solitary figure of Jesus. John had already spoken of him in awe, as One far more worthy of honour than he is himself. Yet Jesus comes, wanting to be treated as one of the crowd, going down into the waters of baptism with the others, identifying himself with their sins.

I was once in Ethiopia at the time of the Festival of Timkat. It was the custom in those days that on the Feast of the Epiphany, the Emperor would go out into the streets, there to be publicly re-baptised, as a sign of his humility before God and the people. Then all the people too would be sprayed with the water of baptism, so that they might share in this annual cleansing.

We are not told whether anyone but Jesus saw the sign of God's favour resting upon him. We do know that he did not boast of it, but took himself away quietly to ponder all that it would mean for the rest of his ministry.

✳ *Lord, make me realise that I am one of the many*
needing your forgiveness,
but help me to recognise too
that you have a special purpose for each one of us.

Monday January 10

Serving us

Archbishop William Temple said of this passage, 'We rather shrink from this revelation. We are ready, perhaps, to be humble before God; but we do not want him to be humble in his dealings with us.' We want our heroes to remain on their pedestals, so that we who aspire to be like them may hope one day to share in the honour and privilege they enjoy.

Read this familiar passage very carefully, trying to see it from the point of view of each of the main characters in the story. What do you think this unexpected action of Jesus meant for Peter, for John, for Judas, for Mary (who must surely have been somewhere near her Son on that last evening)? With which of them do you identify yourself most readily?

Christ's humility shows itself in his readiness to serve us. Ours shows in our readiness to receive his service. It is said that it is better to give than to receive. But it is sometimes harder to receive. It puts us in the debt of the one who gives, and robs us of the pride of being in the position of giving to others. Who are the people from whom you receive the most in terms of humble service and menial tasks? How often do you give them the honour they deserve?

✳ *Won't you let me be your servant,*
Let me be as Christ to you?
And pray that I may have the grace
To let you be my servant too.   *Richard Gillard*
from The Servant Song (Maranatha, USA)

Tuesday January 11

Seeing the Kingdom in the smallest child

The point of this passage goes far beyond an expression of love for the little ones. Nowhere else in the Gospel is Jesus described as 'indignant'. Offence against children always made him angry. The Kingdom belonged to them. Some scholars suggest that verse 15 is a later addition by a scribe, to try to explain why Jesus, unlike most men of his time, took notice of children. The main point of the story is our attitude to them, particularly in their vulnerability. We give them little importance; Jesus sees them as inheritors of the Kingdom. So he publicly blesses them, with gestures in which some commentators see a prefiguring of a later ritual of infant baptism. But whether that is so or not, the story is a stern reminder to us all that children are not 'the church of tomorrow'; they are part of the Church of today. It depends on the witness of that Church as to what kind of tomorrow they will inherit.

✱ *Lord, save me from any action or word*
   that would put a stumbling block
   in the way of one of your little ones.

For personal reflection or group discussion

When have you been surprised by Jesus' response to a person or situation? What have you learnt from the moment of surprise?

In what ways do we need to change that others may find the quality of our lives challenging?

January 12-17 Surprising disciples

Wednesday January 12   **MARK 1.16-20 *; JOHN 1.43-51**

Ordinary people

Why on earth do you think that, for his first disciples, Jesus chose a group of fishermen? What particular qualities could they have had to equip them to share in his ministry? They seem to have been a close knit group whom Jesus had probably known for some time. But clearly the moment when they decided to leave all and follow him was deeply etched in their memory. Notice how Mark, who was probably writing down Peter's own reminiscences, records the eye-witness detail that Simon and Andrew were casting their nets at the time, whilst James and John were mending theirs. When Jesus said he would make them 'fishers of men', what expertise and experience could they bring to such a task?

Turn now to the second reading for today: John 1.43-51. Here we see how the call was extended to people with other kinds of experience. Only Philip was called by Jesus directly. The others came at the bidding of their friends or families. Yet when they found Jesus for themselves, it was as if he had been searching for them all along. It is the kind of experience which Francis Thompson records in his poem, *The Hound of Heaven*.

Still with unhurrying chase,
  And unperturbed pace,
Deliberate speed, majestic instancy,
  Came on the following Feet,
  And a Voice above their beat -
'Naught shelters thee, who wilt not shelter Me.'

Like the poet, Nathanael eventually found Christ, only to discover that Christ found him long before he recognised who it was who was pulling at his heart strings.

✳ *Lord, I thank you for those whose influence first led me into your company.*
Show me if there is someone in my immediate circle to whom I should be particularly commending your call.

Thursday January 13   **MARK 5.1-20**

The eccentric outsider

It is a pity that this extraordinary encounter is so often referred to as 'The Story of the Gadarene Swine'. What was important to the Gospel-writer was not what happened to the pigs but what happened to the man, a fanatic brought to his senses when he met Jesus. Until then, he had been shunned by people who were afraid of him. But note that verse 8 suggests that Jesus took the initiative in convincing the man that he could be cured. Thereby he won the man's extravagant allegiance. Jesus turned this adulation into a personal relationship by asking the man's name. He did not dismiss his reply as nonsense, nor did he treat the man's request for proof of the healing as bizarre. As far as possible, he met his patient's expectations and gradually calmed his fears, easing him back into normal living. Presumably it was Jesus or the disciples who provided the man with clothes to wear and a place to sit.

What can we learn from this story about our own attitudes to those who seem disturbed in mind or eccentric in their behaviour? How far are we able to see beneath the deranged personality someone to be respected and helped back to recognition in the 'normal' world? What is the criterion of normality?

✳ *We pray today for those who care for people suffering from mental illness, that they may never lose respect for their patients nor fail to see their full potential.*

The foreign woman

Like so many of the women who followed Jesus, this woman is nameless. The Gospel writer obviously did not consider it necessary for her to to be personally identified. Maybe he did not even know her name. But he does record three things about her which are all important in her becoming a disciple.

● She is a foreigner, and although the story seems to reinforce the special place of Israel in God's plan for the world (verse 22), it is also made clear that people of other races and faiths are approved of God in the sincerity of their worship.

● There is emphasis on the fact that she is an attractive woman, about whom there has been much gossip, but Jesus, without any hint of condescension or condemnation, engages her in deep theological conversation, accepting her at her own value and not at other people's.

● Jesus recognises that she wants to be needed, as we all do, and he begins his relationship with her by asking for her help, not offering his. But she knows her real need, as he does too, and so she eagerly joins the company of those who follow him.

✳ *Pray for any women or men you know who come from a different culture from your own.*
Pray for humility to learn from them the wisdom of their heritage, and for sensitivity to share with them the depths of your own spiritual experience.

Gossiping neighbours

The word 'gossip' originally meant a friend, especially one related by spiritual ties, like a godmother. So it implied a person of holy conversation. But, like so many good words, it degenerated in meaning. The Concise Oxford Dictionary defines it now as 'a news monger of rumours or tittle-tattle', and adds laconically, 'especially women'. So it is refreshing to note how often in the New Testament it is through the gossiping of women that the gospel story is spread.

The first Christian evangelist whose words were ever recorded was a widow of eighty-four, who went out to tell her neighbours that she had seen the infant Christ (Luke 2.38). Now in this story, the Samaritan woman cannot keep her news to herself. She must tell her neighbours and so the whole community comes to seek out Jesus. The disciples completely fail to realise the new opportunity this whole contact opens up, just as they fail to acknowledge that Jesus does not depend upon them alone for support and sustenance. Nor are they the only ones working for the Kingdom. God has chosen some surprising allies for us, often people whose worth we fail to recognise. Yet, in spite of what Jesus says, the men disciples do not learn to trust what gossiping women tell them (Luke 24.11)!

✳ *Jesus help me this day in all my conversations*
to speak words of hope and encouragement to others,
and teach me how to listen for the good news
others have to share with me.

Sunday January 16   JOHN 3.1-11; 7.50-52 and 19.39-40

A middle-aged admirer

There is a play by Harold Pinter called 'A Slight Ache'. It depicts a middle-aged man sitting in his garden, apparently having achieved all the comfort he needs in life. But he is haunted by a tramp standing at his gate, about whom there seems to be a mystery this man cannot penetrate. The play reminded me of Nicodemus, a respected, honourable citizen, yet one with 'a slight ache' in his heart, a longing for a whole new grasp on life's meaning. The effect of his encounter with Jesus goes on haunting him all the rest of his days, and although he can never bring himself to public discipleship, he gives secretly of both his substance and his support in the cause of Christ.

Yet Jesus had assured him that, even at his age, he could make a fresh start, if only he was prepared to throw his customary caution to the wind, and let the Spirit take him wherever it will. Later he does tentatively take a risk on Jesus' behalf, but there is too much at stake and he dares not lose his reputation. So in the end, though he still wants to honour this strange prophet, he does so secretly when, as he thinks, Jesus is safely in the grave.

✳ *Disturb the complacency of my life, O God*
and help me with the passing years
to become ever more ready to learn new truths
and to risk new ventures of faith.

The weak and foolish

Paul could hardly be accused of flattering the congregation at Corinth! His words here are spoken partly in anger with people who have become quarrelsome and divided among themselves. He wants to warn them against thinking that they know all there is to know about the faith. But even as he reminds them of their humble origins, it is as if the wonder of what God has done with such simple people overwhelms him, and he sees even their limitations as a sign of God's grace.

We can sometimes harbour romantic illusions about what the Church should be like, a company of saints in shining armour! But then we meet some local congregations and we become disillusioned. It is never a good thing to live with illusions. The reality about the Church is much more splendid. It is among this frail, struggling, sinful community of folk that we find heroes and heroines of the faith who outshine and outshame those whom the world admires for their power, their wealth and their strength. The gospel speaks its word of liberation, not through the powerful but through the oppressed. May God make us humble enough to receive it from them!

✴ *God, who has chosen the weak and the foolish,*
help me to be glad that I am one of them.
Save me from false pretensions or delusions of grandeur
and teach me that your grace is sufficient for me,
that your strength is made perfect in my weakness.

For personal reflection and group discussion

Think of opportunities you might have to draw others into conversation – in the supermarket, at the hairdressers, taking children to school, on the bus . . . See the passage in John 4.1-6 as a guide.

ACTION

Meet somebody who fits the description in any one of the above sub-titles and discuss together your different experiences as followers of Christ.

THE BODY OF CHRIST
Week of Prayer for Christian Unity

Notes, based on the Revised Standard Version, by
Lavinia Byrne

Sister Lavinia Byrne of the Institute of the Blessed Virgin Mary works at the Council of Churches for Britain and Ireland, where she is associate secretary for the Community of Women and Men in the Church. She is author of **Women before God, The Hidden Journey** *and* **The Hidden Tradition,** *all published by SPCK.*

The Week of Prayer for Christian Unity speaks to the deepest aspirations of the Christian community. Year by year, for a week in January, we pray that the wounds of history which have divided the Body of Christ may be healed. This prayer is not offered to God in any triumphalist way; Christian unity is not about 'them' joining 'us'. It is about all of us trying to grow closer to the God in whom we live and move and have our being, who is imaged for us most perfectly in Jesus Christ, whose Spirit we are all invited to share, whatever our Church affiliation.

> *Let us pray:*
> *God who calls all to unity in the friendship of Jesus,*
> *give us loving hearts and wills*
> *as we pray for the unity which he desired.*

Tuesday January 18   **JOHN 15.1-17**

At the heart of Jesus' farewell discourse to his friends, recorded in John's Gospel, comes a powerful image: 'I am the true vine.' The image he chooses is about growth, which happens organically, from within the very substance of the vine. Nourished by the sun, by rain and chemicals which feed it from the soil in which it is planted, the vine forces its way into the light. We have here an image of growth which gives us a powerful understanding of what it means to belong to Jesus.

If you have ever looked at a vine, you will know that there is no distinction between the vine and its branches. From the moment it emerges from the soil, the vine begins to spread. It is its branches. To belong to Jesus is to be part of the true vine.

For this reason, we can pray in complete confidence because, when our wills are united with his, we will pray as part of the living vine. So this week above all others, we pray to know what the call to oneness in Christ might look like in our own day and our own times.

✳ *God who made us to enjoy each other in the life of the vine which is Christ,*
give us a desire to pray for the unity which is your will.

Wednesday January 19   1 JOHN 4.13-21

'Anyone who lives in love lives in God.' The words of John's First Letter are compelling. They also repay careful attention: because what John does not say is that 'Anyone who lives in God lives in love.' None of us can be self-satisfied; Christianity puts a fundamental requirement in place which means that we will be judged by and for love, not by and for our professions of religious virtue, or even by our claims to faith. So that our faith in Jesus has to be about a conspiracy of love, not a conspiracy of fear.

Can you make a list of people from other Churches whom you know? Can you name their churches? Have you ever prayed with them, worshipped with their congregations? What do they learn about Christianity from you? What can you learn about Christianity from them?

✳ *We pray to the God of love,*
that in all we are and say and do,
we may witness to the power of this love in our lives,
and so to our faith in the God revealed to us in Jesus.

Thursday January 20   EPHESIANS 2.11-22

The author of the Letter to the Ephesians makes a chilling point. We were once aliens; we have only been brought close through the blood of Christ. What does this mean in practice?

One thing is certain: religious or confessional superiority is totally out of order. Christ is the source of our forgiveness and redemption. For this reason, our author employs the image of the Temple as a sign of holiness. We are being built into a new household for God. The work of building is God's, not our own, and God will fashion us into one holy temple.

In present-day Israel, the place where the Jerusalem Temple stood, is a holy place which draws together Jews who gather at the Western or Weeping Wall, Muslims who come to the Temple Mount to visit their magnificent Mosque there, and also Christians who come on a pilgrimage to visit sites associated with Jesus. As we pray for Christian unity, let us do so in ways which respect those who seek God in the other major living world faiths.

✳ *Let us pray to the God of Abraham and Sarah,*
the God of Isaac and Rebecca,
the God of Jacob and Rachel,
for a spirit of trust and reconciliation.
May the spirit of the Gospels drive out fear and hostility
as we seek to find God's holy will
for the human family throughout the world,
especially in countries where
Christians and Jews and Muslims live together.

Friday January 21　　　　　　　　　　**EPHESIANS 3.1-13**

What does it mean to be a 'prisoner of Christ' or a 'servant of the gospel'? The vocabulary used in this passage is ambiguous, as it has a distinctly historic feel to it. We are uncomfortable with language which suggests hierarchies and power relationships; we are happier with the language of equality. None of us is entirely happy with the thought of being a prisoner of a servant. These are words which have few honourable associations for us.

So what is the mystery which Christ proclaims? It is precisely the liberty we most desire, a liberty which is a mystery or infinite treasure because it makes us all members of the body of Christ. In Christ, we are offered the true equality of belonging. Nowadays it is very difficult for people to feel that they belong to anything. We are deeply scarred by the kinds of greed or apathy which set whole communities against each other. Let us pray for global healing between nations which have made servants of each other and prisoners of debt; let us pray for world unity.

✳ *We pray for the world-wide community of nations,*
for unity and healing between us all.
We pray that, as parts of the body we call planet earth,
we may be fearless in building up
the body of Christians everywhere,
poured out in forms of service which bring dignity
to those who give as well as to those who offer them.

From the macrocosm of global unity amongst the nations, we move to the demands of unity as we experience them in the microcosm of our personal quest for integration and wholeness. We would do well to remember that unity is about ourselves as well as about the Church, the major faiths and the world.

So we pray that our hidden selves may grow strong. And this poses a further question of course. What does my hidden self look like? How much time and attention do I ordinarily give to my hidden self? Or have I a lurking fear that any time spent on myself is time wasted or misplaced?

Try to give an honest answer to these questions and then pray to the God of light and of shadow for strength and a sense of your own glory.

✸ *God of power and might and glory, shadow and shade,*
give me a sense of my own glory,
made as I am in the image and likeness of your glory,
for your glory and not for shame.
Hide me in your shadow as I seek to know my hidden self
and then call me out into your merciful light
for the glory of your name.

Sunday is the first day of the new week and so we do well to stop and examine the deep spiritual motives which drive us to hear the call of Christ. The words 'selflessness, gentleness and patience' speak to our profoundest aspirations. Would that they were always the driving force in our ecumenical dialogues! Would that the language of competitiveness or doctrinal or sacramental superiority could be driven out by the imperative of the gospel!

Try drawing up a list of the five qualities you most admire and the five defects you most despise in other people. Think really seriously about these and write them down. Then pray:

✸ *I come before the God of disclosure and honesty,*
who calls me to truth in Christ, whose Spirit is unafraid.
I come before the God of selflessness,
gentleness and patience
who will be selfless, gentle and patient with me.

Now turn again to the lists of five qualities and defects you named in other people. Turn very simply to God and ask for help in identifying them in yourself.

Monday January 24 **Ephesians 4.7-16**

Every Christian community is challenged by the idea that the gospel asks us to welcome difference. God gives different gifts. The ecumenical requirement put in place by this chapter's subtlety alters our thinking: Christians are not asked to be identical with each other; we are not to be clones. Instead the real challenge of the gospel is directed towards our ability to recognise each other's gifts.

How difficult do we find it to accept that some may be gifted as apostles, some as prophets, some as evangelists, some as preachers, some as teachers? How do we discern these gifts? What training or encouragement are in place in our churches for the recognition of these gifts? How comfortable are we with the idea of giftedness? Or are we secretly rather opposed to gifts, preferring a kind of banality which renders the gospel innocuous?

✱ ***We pray in thanksgiving to the God of all gifts,***
who makes each of us different
and asks us to welcome each other in trust and love.
We thank God for the great evangelists,
saints and hymn writers,
missionaries and teachers of our own and every age.

Tuesday January 25 **EPHESIANS 6.10-18**

On this last day of the Week of Prayer for Christian Unity, the struggle assumes cosmic proportions. We are invited to join forces against the cosmic powers that constitute the 'spiritual army of evil in the heavens' Each of us will construe this in our own way. Each of us has a different bit of the justice agenda firmly in place in our hearts and imaginations. At our most passionate, we will be certain that the entire credibility of the Christian endeavour rests upon the Churches' response to justice and peace, to sexual equality, to racial equality, to ageism, homelessness and debt.

The challenge is addressed to us all. Am I prepared to allow the gospel to speak to issues which belong to the public domain? Or is the gospel a private truth? In our answer to this question will rest a whole host of other concerns.

✳ *Let us pray for those who work for the coming of the Kingdom in the certainty that the Lord's Prayer is addressed to NOW as well as to the future. Let us pray for Christian unity in the words of Revelation 20.22: 'Amen; come, Lord Jesus.'*

For personal reflection and group discussion

How many Christians of other traditions do you know? What is at stake when we pray for Christian unity? How can we value difference?

Do we aspire to Christian unity in a way that opens or closes Christians from the world's living Faiths?

How can we take the agenda of social justice seriously, given that so many groups in society are disadvantaged and divided?

ACTION

Try to discover what links exist locally with the wider fellowship of your national Council of Churches. How can you put the wider ecumenical questions about good inter-faith relations, global and social concerns to your local church and parish?

LOOKING AT EASTER & ASCENSION

This new book in the *Looking at . . .* series by Brian Haymes, reflects the glory of the resurrection and Jesus' ascension.

● *UK price:* **£3.25** (see page 251 for **Special Offer**)

LET EARTH AND HEAVEN COMBINE

Notes, based on the New English Bible, by

Trevor Hubbard

Trevor Hubbard, chairman of the IBRA Committee, is a Baptist minister. Prior to his retirement he was General Superintendent of the North Western Area of the Baptist Union of Great Britain.

We often separate parts of our life: some we label 'work', 'home', 'leisure', 'church'. What we do at work sometimes seems to have little relevance (except for the pay!) to what we do at home; or our leisure to the church. Life cannot be compartmentalised in this way; each part relates clearly to the rest . . . No more can human experiences of life be divorced from the divine. God is involved in the whole of it – happy and sad, good and bad. These notes attempt to show that there is no place where God's Kingdom cannot be found 'in our midst'.

> *There is no place on earth O God,*
> *where you are not present.*
> *In these moments of reflection,*
> *open our minds to your truth*
> *and our hearts to your presence*
> *through Jesus Christ our Lord.*

Wednesday January 26   **1 CHRONICLES 29.1-19***

'Everything in heaven and on earth is thine.' To that sentiment we pay lip service, though for much of our time we deny it in practice. The prevailing philosophy of our age seems to be 'What I possess is mine to use as I wish.' Paul echoes the lofty concept of David, 'You do not belong to yourselves; you were bought at a price' (1 Corinthians 6.20).

The vast riches of the king were handed back to God who had given them. By such example the rest of the people were encouraged to make similar gestures. And the accumulated wealth was used to build a Temple whose opulence was breath-taking! Such wastefulness, some would say, when the money could have been used to help the poor who were there in David's time, as they are in ours!

If we need church buildings, we ought to bring to them our highest and our best. For they ought to say something about the grandeur and majesty of God. Yet David is quite clear that building temples is no more important than being the kind of person whose life reflects the glory of God.

✳ *they minister in a sanctuary which is only a copy and shadow of the heavenly.* (Hebrews 8.5)

Therefore let our church buildings, be they tin tabernacles or cathedrals, reflect the worth we attach to God.

Thursday January 27   PSALM 24

Why worship God? Would not the thought and time we spend in worship be far better used to help those in desperate need? What can human words add to the glory of God? Even our loftiest language cannot comprehend God's majesty. God is sufficiently wonderful not to need our words of praise. When the Hebrew pilgrims walked in procession up Zion's hill to the Temple and there in question and response worshipped, were they wasting their time – and God's?

The worship of God is an expression of how we value God and the world in which we live. It is that mystic rite in which we claim forcefully that earth is linked to heaven, and mortals such as we to God. It enables humankind to see the real significance of their lives in the light of the majesty of God. In worship, flawed human life catches some reflection of God's radiance.

Of course, if we were to wait until our motives were as impeccable as the Psalmist suggests, we would wait for ever! Thank God that Jesus came to make us what he is and, in offering us forgiveness, transform our soiled lives.

✳ *Eternal Light, Eternal Light,*
   How pure the soul must be . . .

There is a way for all to rise
   To that sublime abode; –
Christ's offering and his sacrifice . . .   Thomas Binney

27

Friday January 28   JEREMIAH 7.1-11

Do you refuse to walk under a ladder? Some say it might bring bad luck! Some people wear a charm, even a cross on a chain, as a token of good luck. In the RAF I used to carry a small New Testament in my breast pocket! They are superstitions in which, no doubt, we do not really believe, but also acknowledgments that powers beyond ourselves help shape our destiny. The contemporaries of Jeremiah were faced by hordes of Chaldean invaders. Jerusalem was threatened, but the presence of the Temple seemed a sure sign that the city was impregnable. Was not the sanctuary a token of God's certain presence and power to save them? It had become for them a talisman and saved the city from neither siege nor violent destruction.

Two ways can give us confidence:

● The integrity of a good life. Worship must be matched by deeds. Leslie Weatherhead was fond of calling the Kingdom of God, the Kingdom of right relationships. For honest living is not only refraining from doing wrong, but actively promoting justice.

● The presence of God is not confined to places but discovered wherever God's people walk in integrity.

✳ *God is our shelter and our refuge, a timely help in trouble . . .*
The Lord of Hosts is with us,
the God of Jacob our high stronghold.   *Psalm 46.1,7*

Saturday January 29   GENESIS 28.10-22

Some places hold life-long memories for us; the village where we were married; the graveside where a parent is buried; a park or compound where we played with the children. Place names can be evocative of such memories, like Bethel, 'the house of God'. They stand as a constant reminder of the places where heaven meets earth.

Jacob was trying to escape to the sands of the desert where his forefathers had lived:

● He was running away from problems of human relationships, a brother out for revenge after being deceived. Peace comes, however, in rebuilding what has been broken, not in pretending it had never happened.

● He was running away from responsibilities. He had an important part to play in the work of God. His destiny lay in being where God wanted him to be, not hankering for the faded glories of the past.

God sometimes stops us in our tracks and challenges us to complete what God had begun in us. Such experiences are Bethel for us – the house of God.

✳ *The angels keep their ancient places;-*
Turn but a stone and start a wing!
'Tis ye, 'tis your estranged faces,
That miss the many-spendoured thing.

Francis Thompson

Sunday January 30 World Leprosy Day   MARK 1.40-45 *

Social ostracism, for whatever reason, is evil. It happens in too many societies, in terms of race, culture and religion. The leprosy sufferer was cut off from the society of 'well' people, because they thought that contact with him, however slight, carried the risk of infection. But Jesus reached out his hand. The gesture itself was healing. The man knew he belonged again.

Sometimes, we take up that same stance of aloofness within the church. We wrongly imagine that holiness means keeping the world at arms length. For Jesus, it meant getting deeply involved, 'up to the elbows'.

In Thailand, Mr Lamom, who has suffered leprosy since he was a youth, was not rejected by his family. He suffered numbness in parts of his body so that if injured, he felt no pain. His family made charcoal and one day he fell into the ashes and burnt an arm. He did not feel that pain and not until his arm became badly infected was he taken to Manorom Christian Hospital. By then it was too late. His arm had to be amputated below the elbow. Worse followed when he developed cancer in the other arm which required a whole arm operation. He was a determined man. He now has an artificial left arm with a strong gripping hook attached to his body by wires. He opens and closes the hook by moving his left shoulder. He lives alone, still makes charcoal and in addition has taken up carpentry! His strong faith in God, confirmed by human hands that touched and healed in spite of the putrescent odour of gangrene, gave him his motivation. This once stricken man is a shining light for Christ in his village.

Think of situations in the place where you live where Christians keep people who are different at arms length. Men and women of other faiths? Those suffering from AIDS? How can we touch their lives and heal them – and, through that action, be healed ourselves?

✻ *My hands are numb and broken.*
I am blind;
And I can neither feel nor see
My little pot of violets;
So I bend to kiss
The wee, sweet flowers
That mean so much to me.

Mumei, Japan © Leprosy Mission

Monday January 31   1 CORINTHIANS 6.12-20 *

Christ's hands touched the man whose body was scarred by leprosy. The divine had touched human life and healed it. God became man when Christ assumed human flesh at his incarnation and thereby hallowed human life for ever. What we do with our bodies is therefore important.

● They express our personality. We call it 'body language'. What a person does with her hands, for example, can betray deep emotions that she may seek to hide. In ballet, the bodies of dancers express a wide range of human emotion. Do you find such expression meaningful for you?

● They can be abused. What comes highest on your list of sins? Is it sexual sin or gluttony – or what? In what ways are you most conscious of abusing your body – driving it too hard?

● They can be used to glorify God. In many churches today body language has become a part of worship: the raised hands; the use of dance; the kiss of peace. Do you find yourself at home in such outward expressions of worship?

✻ *Use this prayer as one of commitment to Christ:*
With my body I honour you, all that I am I give to you,
and all that I have I share with you within the love of
God, Father, Son and Holy Spirit.

Marriage prayer from the Alternative Service Book

Tuesday February 1   REVELATION 21.22-27

'Earth's crammed with heaven,
      And every common bush afire with God...'

So wrote Elizabeth Barrett Browning. In our reading, the reverse is true! Heaven's crammed with earth! The poet said that those who did not appreciate the presence of God in the midst of human life sit around and pluck blackberries; there will be no fruit gatherers in heaven! For God is at its heart.

Heaven will always carry the reminders of earth whose splendours and riches are absorbed into its glory. Heaven and earth are linked through all of time and eternity.

But some of the trappings familiar to human eyes will not be needed. There will be no need of our sacred buildings which are but symbols of the presence of God. Nor is there need for bread and wine at the eucharistic feast. The broken body, raised and exalted to God's right hand, needs no further sign. Nor will the tokens of man's insecurity be needed; there will be no locked gates for all that makes for safety will be found in the God who is our shelter and our home.

✳ *We praise you, our God,*
for every glad experience within human life
that reminds us of your presence with us.

For personal reflection or group discussion

Read again Genesis 28.10-22. How do you understand the experience at Bethel? In what ways is your community a reflection of the tensions present in Jacob's life? How can a sense of God's presence in the midst of our lives change our outlook? and that of our community? As you reflect on these questions, look through your local or national newspaper and relate what you have learnt to the problems reported there.

ACTION

Where does contemporary life contradict the values of the Kingdom? Could you create an action group from your church and other churches to deal with the issue?

PUTTING THINGS RIGHT ON EARTH
(The book of AMOS)

Notes, based on the Revised English Bible, by
Brian Haymes

Brian Haymes, Principal of the Northern Baptist College, Manchester, is author of the 'Looking At' series published by IBRA and is currently President of the Baptist Union of Great Britain.

Amos, an eighth century prophet, worked as a herdsman and fig-grower, which meant he was not a professional prophet. He did not do the work for payment. He was a 'called' man.

He lived in a time of national prosperity. Both Israel and Judah had expanded their boundaries and were politically strong. Many saw this as a sign of God's blessing but Amos saw a different picture. He saw a people on the way to judgment because justice, commerce, worship, all were corrupted and the nation was sick without realising it.

Amos was no revolutionary but, like the other prophets, called people back to their roots in God's covenant. You cannot put things right on earth while things are not right with God.

> *Living God, disturber and saviour of your people,*
> *open our eyes to the truth of your Word,*
> *the state of our lives*
> *and the condition of our nation,*
> *that with faith and hope*
> *we may pray:*
> *your kingdom come,*
> *your will be done on earth as in heaven.*

Wednesday February 2   **AMOS 1.1-15**

This is a disturbing beginning to the book. Our first thought of God is in terms of comfort, strength, a shepherd, a father. Amos' encounter with God is like the roaring of a lion (verse 2). Here is terror beyond human power to tame. Amos is deeply aware of the wrath of God. Something has gone wrong enough to provoke God to raise up the prophet.

The theme of God's wrath is uncomfortable. It sits uneasily with thoughts of God's love. Yet the fact is that we are only angry about what we care for. The opposite of love is not hate or anger but indifference: it is saying, 'I couldn't care less.' But there is something going on here about which God cares. God's wrath is an expression of God's love.

And so God speaks (verse 3). The message originates, not with Amos, but with God. Accusations are made about the nations, mostly the enemies of Israel. The God of Amos has a concern for international politics. The nations may not acknowledge God's sovereign rule but they too are subject to the law, and the wrath of God. It is easy to imagine Israel gloating over their neighbours' sins. But then it is always easier to see the speck in another's eye while ignoring the log in your own!

✷ *Living God, we praise you for the love*
that longs and cares enough to put things right on earth.

Thursday February 3   AMOS 2.1-8

The list of nations and their war crimes continues with Moab and then Judah. You can almost hear the people of Israel cheer as Judah is named. There is little love lost between the two kingdoms. Now, as Judah surely deserves, there comes the judgment of God!

Seven nations are mentioned, the perfect number, and possibly the hearers of the sermon think that is the end but, to their surprise and discomfort, God has a word against Israel.

The crimes listed are not of war and international injustice but part of Israel's own national life: exploitation of the poor, of women, of economic and social oppression. A people whom God set free has been taken into slavery again, by their own leaders. They take comfort in their claims to a special relationship with God, but the way they live exposes their unfaithfulness.

It is a terrible thing to presume upon the mercy of God, as if God's call on our lives has no moral or social implications. Where are people exploited and oppressed today? Of what 'crime after crime' might we be guilty?

33

✳ *Give us, Lord, the courage and faith*
   to be honest about ourselves before you.

Friday February 4

It is a hurtful experience to have your love taken for granted. Many a parent knows that pain when children act thoughtlessly but, in truth, we are all guilty. Then something happens and we remember what people have done for us, what they mean to us, and how much they love us. Much pain is caused because we forget to remember.

Israel is gently reminded of what God has done. God was the one who set them free from slavery, led them in difficult days and brought them to be a people in their own land. You can almost picture the people nodding as God asks whether this is not the case (verse 11).

God bears the burden of all this sin. God is not uncaring. The peoples' wrongs weigh heavy. It is not in spite of the fact that they are God's people that judgment will fall, but because of it. There will be no escape for anyone. It is a chilling and disturbing thought that love can take this form. If only the people would remember what God has done! To forget leads to a loss of identity. That is true for Israel and for us.

✳ *Thank God for every instance when we are reminded*
   of what God has done for us in Christ.

Saturday February 5

Amos' message pricks the bubble of popular easy piety. No one likes to hear that from a preacher. Who does Amos think he is anyway? In a series of rhetorical questions, all of which play on the idea of there being no effect without a cause, Amos argues that no one can prophesy without God speaking first.

Verse 7 may have behind it the idea of the 'Heavenly Court'. God sits with messengers, who hear God's plans and are privy to God's purposes. Thus the prophet, who overhears all this, is not making up his own message. God has spoken. What else can the prophet do? The Lion has roared, who is not frightened (verse 8)? Amos is one who has been called. His message may be devastating for Israel but he can do no other than speak it out because it is the word of God.

Many people claim to speak for God and it is not easy to test their authenticity. One 'test' may be reluctance. Amos does not find it easy to give such a message. Who wants to be unpopular? But he cannot do otherwise. He must tell out what he has heard. He claims nothing for himself but everything for God.

✴ *Loving God, help us to hear and receive*
even your uncomfortable word.

Sunday February 6   AMOS 3.12 to 4.5

Martin Buber, a great twentieth century Jewish theologian, said, 'There is nothing like religion to mask the face of God.' There is a way of being busy with religious observances, attending public worship and parading our religion before others that, in God's name, keeps us from true encounter with God! Jesus identified this danger (Matthew 6.1-18).

The rich women of Israel, with their husbands, were very proper in religious attendance. But the reality of their lives was that they oppressed the poor by their greed. Their rich, expensively furnished homes stood in sharp contrast to the situation of their fellow Israelites. They loved to go to worship and thought they were pleasing God. But the demands of God go deeper. The calling of God is more penetrating. Their religion was busy but superficial. It contributed to rank injustice. So, doubtless to their great surprise, judgment would come and Amos pictured them and their children being reduced to ruin and taken into exile.

Worship that is separated from the ethical demands of God is a dangerous business, in Israel and anywhere else for that matter.

✴ *Lord, may our worship and our social living*
be one hymn of praise.

Monday February 7   AMOS 4.6-13

A French philosopher once said that when he died, God would forgive him, for that was God's business. That is a terrible statement of misunderstanding. It takes neither our sin nor God's grace seriously. It shows no sense of the pain there is for God in bearing our glibness and sin, as if our disregard of the relationship cost God nothing. The cross will always stand as a sign of what it costs God to go on loving us all.

Israel is charged in this passage with taking God for granted. There is, for us, the difficult thought of God sending famines, droughts, plagues and earthquakes to warn the people of their disobedience. In spite of all, still they do not return. So the prophet calls the people to prepare to meet their God. We should not read this as a threat but as another powerful call to repentance, to turn again and recognise the covenant love of God. Dietrich Bonhoeffer warned Christians of this day of cheap grace. The grace of God is always costly to God, but free to us. How can we ever presume upon that mercy? How can we ever take God for granted? A true godly repentance will always show itself in deeds of trusting obedience.

✳ *Father, we wonder how and why you go on loving us as you do.*
This is love amazing and divine.
Thank you.
Thank you.

Tuesday February 8   AMOS 5.1-15

In T.S. Elliot's play 'Murder in the Cathedral', the women of Canterbury act as a kind of chorus. Their speeches have a sense of impending doom about them and they speak out of their own experience of 'living and partly living'.

This passage from Amos begins with a funeral dirge over a nation not yet dead but only 'living and partly living'. The way they have set for themselves is leading to their destruction. There is an element of tragedy here because the rich and powerful are becoming more prosperous, more powerful and do not realise that they have gained their position by unjust means. They are guilty. It would be wiser at such a time for them to keep quiet about themselves (verse 13).

God wants them to live – but that will mean they must change their ways and seek justice. They claim God is with them but their social immorality and injustice show only how far they have gone from God. They are living and partly living. Full and true life will come only with a recognition of the ways of God – and living in trust of God's mercy and in obedience to God's covenant law.

✳ *Thank you for Jesus, the way, the truth and the life.*

God 'spurns' and 'takes no pleasure' in empty ceremonies. God will not accept the offerings, nor listen to the songs. The popular religion of Israel is under judgment and there is no escape.

What does God want? Justice and righteousness are the answer (verse 24). We picture justice as a static figure, blindfolded, with a sword and balance in her hands. But this is too impersonal a picture for what God wants. Justice and righteousness are what people are called to do. It is a matter of seeking and acting rightly, expecially towards those who are needy or who are being cheated. Israel's stress on the external ceremonials of religion cannot cover up the deep sickness in her life.

The people say they long for the Day of the Lord, believing it will bring them blessing and glory. But Amos turns this idea on its head. Do they not realise that the Day of the Lord will be judgment, gloom, darkness? It is because they have no fear of the Lord that they have every reason to fear the coming day. It is only when we come to the New Testament that we have grounds to look forward to the Day of the Lord, for that will be the coming of Christ and his Kingdom. Yet Christians must beware also of presuming on God's mercy, lest we substitute easy religion for doing the will of God.

✳ *Lord, may your kingdom come,*
   may your will be done on earth.

For personal reflection and group discussion

In the light of what you have read so far in the book of Amos, look through your national newspaper. What are the most disturbing stories and why? What would Amos have to say in God's name to your society? Write a prayer of confession and think about what you might do to respond.

Jesus tells a story about a wealthy man and a beggar who sits at his gateway (Luke 16.19-31). Everyday Dives must see Lazarus lying there with his sores. Or does he? Perhaps he is too preoccupied with his own concerns.

The leaders in Israel have become wealthy. They have all the trappings of affluence in their homes. What is wrong with that? Nothing, if they also have a passion for the wellbeing of all their fellows citizens, a desire that the prosperity of the nation be shared. But Israel's leaders are indifferent to the cry of the people. They seem to believe that their nation will not fall. Amos reminds them that greater cities than theirs have been overtaken. The confidence of the leaders is misplaced. Their luxury and status will not save them from the coming desolation.

Amos gives some incongruous pictures: horses running on rocks, oxen ploughing water. That's not natural! But then, in Israel, justice has become injustice! That's not what God intended. Israel's social order is upside down. They might think that natural but God thinks otherwise.

✳ *Father, open our eyes,*
bring us to our senses,
help us do what you want.

Friday February 11 AMOS 7.1-9

Locusts have eaten the harvest. Heat and drought continue. All in Israel see the evidence. But there is a difference between sight and insight. In a vision, Amos sees the possible coming judgment of God. He intercedes for the people. He does not cut and run. He is given to share something of God's own passion for the people. He prays for them and the prayer is heard.

In his third vision, the plumb line, there is no disguising that Israel is out of true. This time, the prophet does not pray. It is too late. What is called for is repentance. The people must turn to God. Nothing else can turn aside the coming judgment. Short of repentance, there is an inevitability about the response of God to a disobedient people.

There is a heavy seriousness about this passage. For the nation to repent would mean great social and economic changes: no more oppression, no more disregard of the poor. But the inner motive for that lies in a deeper sense of the grace and goodness of God.

✳ *Lord, may our nation show the fruits of true repentance.*

The relationship between politics and religion is often a touchy subject. Most governments want all the support they can get and resent it when the Church starts to be critical. Then, they say, the Church should stay out of politics. But sometimes, although it is not the intention of the prophet or the Church to make a political point, it is heard as a serious challenge to the political powers that be.

Amos has been very critical of the policies whereby such deep social injustices and economic divisions have entered into the life of the nation. It seems that he has even dared to speak such words in the King's chapel. Presumably the King expected more comfortable, less disturbing and subversive words than the prophet spoke.

Amos is not into party politics. He has been called from his everyday life to deliver a message. He does not do this kind of thing professionally, for money, but because God requires it. And if the King should take offence and banish him from the royal pulpit, so much the worse for a monarch who wants to hear only what comforts him and not the word of God that can save him and the nation from the judgment that is coming, as surely as summer fruit ripens. But then this attitude is not limited to the politically powerful. None of us likes the word of rebuke and challenge, even if it comes from God!

✳ *Lord God, we pray for all who have political power.*

If people have difficulty in seeing how religion and politics relate, what about religion and business? In Israel, there were business people who were at least religiously observant. They kept the Sabbath – but their minds were elsewhere. And despite their religious duties, their ethics were far from godly. So they cheated their customers. And worse, they took their fellow Israelites into slavery again.

One of the saddest sayings of Jesus is 'Truly I tell you: they have their reward already' (Matthew 6.2, 5, 16). He speaks about those who want above all else the things of this world and their tragedy is that they achieve them! They have their reward. If our hearts are set on what does not satisfy, then an emptiness will come. Amos tells of a coming hunger for the word of God. The plans that Israel made have become ashes in their mouths.

They committed themselves to unjust economic policies. Their tragedy is their success. But what are the goals of our life? What have we set our heart upon? Are we satisfied or do we hunger and thirst for righteousness?

✳ *God of mercy, may we know the blessedness of those who long to see right prevail.*

Monday February 14   AMOS 9.1-10

This is another awesome passage. Picture Amos back in the shrine, standing by the altar. Then comes this literally devastating word of God, an earthquake of a word. People may try to run from the judgment but there is nowhere to go. This coming desolation will be complete. God's moral law cannot be flouted with impunity. A religion that does not lead to moral acts and just living is a sham that God sees through in a moment.

God rules not only over Israel, God's chosen people, but the Egyptians, the Philistines, all the people who are Israel's enemies, on whom they think the judgment of God should fall. But it is these very same people who are are being used in God's purposes. Amos' hearers must think their whole world is being picked up and shaken to bits. Dare we think of God's purposes being worked out in our history?

And dare we hope in the goodness, the never failing covenant love of the Lord? After all the true judgment spoken, is there a future for us? In Christ, Yes!

✳ *Disturbing God,
though mountains quake and seas roar,
and the nations are in turmoil,
help us to trust and obey your call.*

Tuesday February 15   AMOS 9.11-15

A friend needed urgent surgery. Something had gone seriously wrong in his body and was steadily eating his life away. It was a drastic situation calling for bold decisive treatment. An operation was necessary. The diseased part had to be cut out and destroyed. Of course, for all the care of doctors and nurses, there would be pain, anxiety and anguish. Thank God, the operation was a success. The surgery virtually gave him more life.

Had that been the case with Israel? The situation was serious and God had to act painfully that the people might be made whole again. Amos' last words are ones of hope and restoration. What is the ground of that hope? It is not some easy optimism that all will turn out for the best. Amos does not offer a sentimental 'happy ending'. His hope rests in God, a covenant-keeping God of mercy and love. Can God's people turn again, for if they do, then, 'on that day', righteousness will flourish on the earth. All peoples will know justice, peace and security. It will be all that God wants. It will be God's kingdom. God has made that pledge. That is the ground of hope.

✳ *Thank you Lord, that by prophets and obedient people, you never stop putting things right on earth.*
May we serve your purposes of peace and justice today.

For personal reflection or group discussion
What is the relationship between communion and community? between worship and making public protests against injustice? How can our prayers, offerings, praises and preaching be part of 'putting things right on earth'?

ACTION
Find out what one of the international agencies is doing to promote world justice (for addresses see below). Ask them how you can encourage your church to share this work.

Introduce a friend to

WORDS FOR TODAY

For the **1994 book**, send us only **£2.00** (including postage), together with your friend's name and address, and we will do the rest. *(This offer is only available after June 1, 1994 in the UK.)*

LENT 1

ENTERING LENT

Notes, based on the Good News Bible, by

Simon Barrow

Simon Barrow is an Adult Education and Training Officer in the Anglican Diocese of Southwark. He works with inner-city churches and has a practical concern for the link between spirituality and social issues.

Lent is a remarkable gift to the worldwide church. It is a time of soul-searching, of renewal and of forgiveness. It provides a special opportunity to change those things which most damage ourselves and others. Above all, it is a season for re-experiencing the healing presence of God in our everyday lives.

How sad, then, that Lent has become, for many, a matter of formal ritual and routine combined with a dab of guilt. A recent opinion survey in Britain showed that most people thought of Lent merely as a time for trying (often failing!) to give up small luxuries – like sugar in tea.

This is a deeply impoverished view of the liberating possibilities which Lent offers – especially in a world where many have no 'luxuries' to give up. But what are the alternatives? What does it all mean? Here is a chance to prepare for Lent anew.

> *Loving God,*
> *may Lent become for us a time*
> *of new beginnings, not dead-ends;*
> *of renewal, not guilt;*
> *and of liberation, not captivity.*
> *In the name of Christ.*

Ash Wednesday, February 16   **ISAIAH 58.1-10 ***

True worship

For some years, a small group of Christians have gathered each Ash Wednesday to pray outside the Ministry of Defence in London. They mark one another with the sign of the Cross as a token of personal repentance. Then they mark a Cross in ashes on the Ministry building, making a public call on the British government to combat world poverty instead of producing weapons of mass destruction. Often they have been arrested.

Such powerful symbolic action naturally causes controversy. Parliamentarians have accused Christian peacemakers of 'meddling in politics' instead of 'devoting themselves to the worship of God'. Yet it is uncomfortably clear from today's reading that the biblical prophets saw true worship and the cause of justice, especially the cause of the poor, as inextricably linked.

The last ten chapters of Isaiah date from about 538 BC, when the Persian king Cyrus had delivered the Israelites from captivity in Babylon and ordered the rebuilding of the ruined Temple of Zion. But these changes, signalled earlier in Isaiah, were long coming. Disillusion set in. The mass of people were still economically exploited, yet the ruling national group (who were also responsible for public lamentation and fasting) remained greedy and selfish (see Isaiah 56.9-12).

With shattering force, Isaiah responded to this iniquity by making it clear that God would not be bribed by devotional practices which were contradicted by neglect for the poor. Even renouncing food and personal comfort does not 'make a good impression' on God – unless it is done to serve the needy neighbour.

What lessons would Isaiah have for your church and nation? What is true worship? How can we link personal and corporate repentance? These are real challenges for Lent.

✳ *God of love,*
help us to match the praise of our mouths
with the justice of our deeds.

Action

List some features of your society which contradict the message of God's love for all. Which one will you ask your church to act on?

Thursday February 17   1 CORINTHIANS 9.19-27 *

True freedom

Today's reading is about the kind of freedom which is obtained, not by license, but through devoted service and self-discipline. In a hedonistic culture this is not an easy message to grasp. It may be misconstrued as puritanism or even masochism. But that is not the intention. For in verses 19-23, Paul describes the genuine fulfilment he finds in bringing the good news to fruition among people of very diverse convictions and backgrounds. He is not ashamed of his share in the liberating activity of God.

The background to this passage, which echoes provocatively in our own pluralistic age, is important. At a time when the membership of the Early Church was becoming predominantly Gentile instead of predominantly Jewish, Paul resolutely refused to be bound by either group or to be paid by the Corinthian congregation (see 9.15-18). This gave him the freedom to relate to everyone.

Paul would do nothing to contradict his faith in Christ, but he could still take seriously the beliefs of those bordering on pagan rites. Such faith in the universality of the Christ-like God requires adaptability, but not expediency, for God is at work in all.

Commitment to the gospel also demands the training, endurance and skill of a serious runner or boxer (verses 23-27). This, not the accolade of the winner, is the basis of the comparison. As in Romans 8.21, Paul desires nothing less than the salvation of the whole creation. His seriousness and determined flexibility are invaluable but hard-won, like all Lenten gifts.

✳ *God of grace,*
give me the strength and openness
to serve you in all
and through all.

Action

List ways in which you and your church need greater discipline (or training) and adaptability. Discuss these points with others in the congregation.

Friday February 18   **MARK 2.18-22 ✳**

True living

As will become clear from tomorrow's reading, Jesus recognised the real value of abstaining from nourishment to help 'clarify the mind and direct the will' *(David Tripp)* in some crucial situations.

What is equally clear from today's passage is that, unlike John's followers, Jesus was no routine ascetic. He believed in celebration just as surely as he opposed stifling 'religion', a word which means 'to bind' and which is all-too-readily substituted for the good news.

Verse 19 reminds us of the delightful profligacy of the wedding at Cana. Verse 20 does not appear in Matthew or Luke and may be a later addition, since the Early Church reintroduced fasting to a greater degree than Christ's followers ever practised it.

Jesus' emphasis was on joyful living – but not gluttony – as the norm, and abstinence for particular purposes. As if to rub in the point, he went on to depict the gospel as 'new wine' and suffocating religious ritual as 'old wine-skins'!

But given the increasing divide between those who gorge and those who starve in our world, do you think fasting (perhaps tied to giving, prayer and protest) could assume a greater role in modern Christian discipleship? Can we rejoice and be in solidarity with those who suffer?

✳ *God of life,*
   help us to enjoy your gifts
   and struggle ceaselessly
   to ensure that they are shared by all.

Action
Think of a way you can fast to raise money for the hungry and to raise others' awareness of this problem.

Saturday February 19   **Mark 1.12-15 ***

True repentance
In biblical terms, the season of Lent derives from Jesus' own period of fasting for forty days and nights, through which he resisted the subtle temptations of evil. Though our lives may be very different, the struggle against the seductive powers-that-be (whatever they are in our situation) is an inescapable call of the Spirit (verse 12) for which God will equip us (verse 13).

If we avoid the painful choices between good and evil, life and death, how can we opt for life? For example, have not those who hide from reality in hedonism and trivial consumerism already let evil and death off the hook? In global terms, is not the apathy of the rich minority the reason for the misery of the poor majority?.

But if we face the really tough choices together, we discover, in the footsteps of Christ, that the good news is assured. God is for us, and everything is 'worth it'.

In a word, the challenge – for Lent, for all time – is (verse 15) 'repentance'. To repent means to experience transformation, to turn around completely, to start walking in a totally new direction: from death and sin to life and union with God and each other. And the time? Now. What a terrifying yet glorious calling.

✳ *God of liberation,*
shake us to the foundations
and show us the way to life
and freedom for all Creation.

For personal reflection and group discussion
Read again the actions suggested for each day and decide how you will use them personally or as a group.

ACTION
List the things which need changing, even turning upside-down, in your life and the life of the church. Where will your strength and resolve come from?

RESISTING POPULARITY

Notes, based on the Revised English Bible, by
Lesley Husselbee

Lesley Husselbee is the Secretary for Ministries of the United Reformed Church in the United Kingdom. She is also President of the National Christian Education Council.

Most people like to be liked by others. Many of us will go out of our way to use placating words or actions to ensure that other people accept us. We want to gain respect, but seeking popularity often has the opposite effect.

We know that Jesus was tempted to show that he was the Son of God in ways which would make him popular with everybody. What if he had thrown himself off the cliff, or changed stones into bread? This would certainly have made him popular, but he rejected such methods. Instead, he seems to have gone out of his way to take the unpopular path, which led to misunderstanding, suffering and death. But it was only by this path that he could fully demonstrate the nature of God.

Wise and loving God,
show me when I should stand up for what is right,
even if it makes me unpopular.
Give strength and courage
to those who resist popularity
to follow you.

First Sunday in Lent, February 20　　　　**MARK 2.1-12**

Certainly many in the crowd were impressed by Jesus' healing of the paralysed man, but a significant group, teachers of the law, were not. It was essential to Jewish faith that only God could forgive sin, so, in their eyes, Jesus was committing blasphemy. Pharisees believed that if someone was sick, then either they, or one of their family had sinned. Jesus said in effect: 'You say that I have no right to forgive sins? You believe that if this man is ill he is a sinner and cannot be forgiven? Very well, watch this!' Experts of the Law were caught out. The man

47

was cured, so he must be forgiven. This meant that Jesus' claim to forgive sin must be true. What's more, they reasoned, if this kind of thing went on, all orthodox religion would be shattered and destroyed. In this incident, Jesus had, in fact, signed his own death warrant, and he knew it.

It has never been easy for Christians to challenge orthodoxy in the Church. When he nailed his protest to the door of the church in Wittenberg, Martin Luther challenged the hypocrisy of the sixteenth century Church for seeking after power and wealth instead of the Word of God. Like Jesus, he had to stand trial. In more recent times, Christian thinkers in Latin America have worked and spoken out for the liberation of the poor, but a large section of the Church feels threatened. What is God saying to us today about the priorities of our faith?

✳ *Lord, give me courage to challenge injustice.*
Support those who risk hurt and danger
by daring to serve you.

Monday February 21   MARK 2.13-17

Who are the outcasts in your society? How much do you know about them? Have you even tried to get alongside them?

If he had been seeking popularity, Jesus would have chosen to socialise with those who were well-thought-of in his society: the rabbis, the pharisees, the wealthy, the respectable. Instead, he chose prostitutes, exploiters, thieves, ordinary workers, children and women – the non-respectable.

I wonder why we like to choose like-minded, and greater-status people to be our friends? Perhaps it is because we hope that something of them will rub off on ourselves. Perhaps we are afraid that if we join the 'sinners', then we will 'catch' their adultery, homosexuality, drug abuse or foul language. But that is to see only in stereotypes. Jesus appreciated the loveliness behind the 'bad' labels and because he saw the good, those sinners were able to become just that.

Jesus was misunderstood of course. He went where he was needed most; where people knew that he had something of value to give. Taking the popular social path would not have been the best way of sharing and showing God's love.

✳ *Pray for the outcasts in your neighbourhood,*
and for those who befriend them.

Some ministerial friends tell me that, if there is something especially important that they want to say to the members of their church, they will invite a friend to come in to say it. Why? At home, people are so used to hearing them that they stop listening. After all, 'a prophet never lacks honour except in his home town, among his relations and his own family.'

It must have hurt Jesus very much indeed to find that he could not say the really important things about the nature of God in his home town of Nazareth. To his neighbours and family he was just 'Jesus the carpenters's son'. Nobody expected very much of him. No doubt Jesus would have liked to have been popular in his own town, but he knew that if he was to be heard, he had to go elsewhere.

Has it occurred to you that God is speaking to you through the ordinary things around you that might be obvious to an outsider? Maybe you have got so used to them that you have 'switched off', you are just not listening to what God has to say. Try today to see one 'new' thing in your surroundings. What is God saying to you? What does God want you to do about it? Don't let Jesus be a prophet lacking honour in your home.

✳ *Lord give me eyes to see and ears*
   to heard your word for me today.

Pharisees expected that when the Messiah came, there would be some spectacular sign. They failed to see what was obvious to Jesus, that there were signs of God at work all around. Of course, it would have been tempting for Jesus to concoct some powerful and popular sign like changing stones into bread or flinging himself off the Temple to be caught by angels, but we know that he resisted this. He wanted people to see God for themselves and to choose for themselves by faith.

Do you expect God to send a sign to you today? Some people try to bargain with God. 'If you make my baby son well', they say, 'I'll come to church'. But God doesn't work that way. Things don't always go better for Christians. Sometimes Christians can pray and pray for a sign to show them the direction in which God is leading them, and that direction just doesn't seem clear. In this passage, Jesus said, 'No sign shall be given.' And yet we also know that God can speak to us in unexpected ways, like the way the little boy's lunch, later in this chapter, became food for five thousand people.

✳ *Pray for people who feel that God is distant from them. Ask God to come near.*

Thursday February 24   JEREMIAH 31.27-34 *

Jeremiah promised a time when there would be a special relationship for all people with God, when sins would be forgiven. Christians have taken this 'new covenant', to refer to the coming of Jesus. So why didn't Jesus tell everyone that he was that special person, foretold by Jeremiah, who would bring about this special relationship with God? His disciple, Peter, got close to understanding this, but Jesus insisted that it should be kept a secret. Why? It would have certainly made him popular. But would people have believed it, and even if they did, was it as easy as this? God does, through Jesus, promise forgiveness of sins, but we have to make a contribution too. We have to have faith in him.

At the beginning of the passage, Jeremiah tells his people that they must take responsibility for the wrongdoing of their nation. They must not just blame their ancestors, as was the custom in the past. Perhaps there is a sense in which we, too, must acknowledge our part in damaging the world and hurting other people, if we are to accept God's forgiveness. That isn't always popular, but it is what Jesus showed us was needed. The Cross comes before Resurrection.

✳ *Lord, show me where I have hurt you and others, and forgive me.*

Friday February 25   HEBREWS 2.1-18 *

The problems of the new Russia may be difficult ones as the countries begin new ways of life, but the kind of persecutions that were present in the old Soviet Union were, in many ways, far worse. For a soldier to refuse the military oath of allegiance to the Soviet state had always been a crime. Two brothers from Sharlyk refused with the words: 'We have not refused to serve in the army which goes with Christ, with God. But to serve in an army which is against God and Christ, that we cannot do and will not do. We are Christians.' It was winter. Wearing summer clothing, they were made to set out on a 150 km journey to Orenburg on foot. Both of them froze to death on the way.

Why did they do such a seemingly foolhardy thing? They did it for Jesus, who did a similarly foolhardy thing. Jesus, the popular leader, who was cheered as he entered Jerusalem on Palm Sunday, was arrested, and then abandoned by his friends and, it seemed, by God too. Jesus, who was jeered at and accused by the crowd, allowed his popularity to evaporate. The writer to the Hebrews explains that Jesus had to suffer in order that he could emphathise with and help anyone else who suffers for his sake, like the two brothers; like you and me when we stand up for him.

✳ *Lord, help people who suffer today*
to know that you understand,
and that you are with them.

✳ *Pray for any you know who are in trouble.*
From Candles in the Dark, Mary Craig
(Hodder and Stoughton)

Saturday February 26   MARK 3.19-27 *

Just imagine how Jesus felt when, just after he had begun his ministry and had called his disciples, he went back to his own town, only to find that his own friends and family were so embarrassed by him that they explained him away by saying, 'He has taken leave of his senses!' People in the crowd who had been healed cheered him; but his own thought he was mad! After all, in their eyes, he had left a well-paid job to become a wondering vagrant and was attracting all kinds of undesirables. His neighbours even said that he was possessed by Satan. Jesus' response was that, far from supporting the Devil, his task was to do all that he could to erradicate evil from the world.

Have you ever been misunderstood in a similar way? Do some of your friends and colleagues think you are mad to read your Bible or go to church? Do you have difficulty in explaining the nature of God to people around you? If so, take comfort from Jesus' experience, and ask God for support.

✳ *We pray for those Christians who try to share their faith*
with people who laugh at them,
or who persecute them;
for those who speak out against evil,
that God may give them courage and support.

For personal reflection or group discussion

Read again Mark 2.13-17. Why do we like to choose like-minded people or those of greater status to be our friends? What does this passage say to us about the people we should get to know? What does it have to say to us about being popular?

Second Sunday in Lent, February 27   MARK 8.27-33 *

The time had come for Jesus to find out if his careful teaching had borne fruit: hence the question to his disciples. When it dawned upon Peter that Jesus was the Messiah, he was so excited that he couldn't take in what being 'Messiah' really meant. Why didn't Jesus give the disciples longer to enjoy the idea? Why didn't he bask in the popularity and fame that news of it would have brought?

Jesus knew what the disciples had difficulty in coming to terms with: that being the Messiah, did not mean earthly glory. It meant great suffering, rejection and death. The disciples remonstrated with him, as most of us would have done on hearing his interpretation of the future. And then, Jesus acted in an almost harsh way, almost as if he would have liked to believe that suffering was not ahead.

How can we, as Christians, best help people who have just heard tragic news? How can we come to terms with the fact that being a Christian does not necessarily make life easier? Jesus did not use platitudes; he patiently lived alongside his disciples in those last few days which led to Jerusalem and the Cross.

✶ *When the woes of life o'ertake me,*
hopes deceive, and fears annoy,
never shall the cross forsake me:
lo! it glows with peace and joy.   *John Bowring*

Monday February 28   2 TIMOTHY 1.8-14 *

Here we have Paul, that great early Christian missionary and preacher, imprisoned, awaiting a death-sentence, and telling Timothy, his young disciple, not to be ashamed of him or, more importantly, of telling others the good news of Jesus. For

Timothy, loyalty to the gospel was unlikely to bring popularity; it was much more likely to bring trouble.

At the outbreak of the Second World War in Germany, Dietrich Bonhoeffer could have avoided trouble by going to the USA to lecture, or staying with his national church and keeping quiet. Instead, he did neither of these things. He spoke out against the immorality of the Nazi policy to exterminate Jews, the handicapped and any non-Aryans. On 5th April, 1943, he was imprisoned and, just after Easter, 1945, he was executed. As Bonhoeffer accepted death, he wondered often why he could not have been saved to help in the reconstruction of Christian life in Germany after the war. But this, too, he accepted. As he wrote, in his poem 'The Death of Moses':

✳ *Now, Lord, thy promises have been fulfilled,*
to me thy word has been for ever sure . . .
God, quick to punish sin or to forgive,
thou knowest how this people has my love.
Enough that I have borne its shame and sacrifice
and seen salvation – now I need not live.

> Dietrich Bonhoeffer
> From The Narrow Path Bible Readings with
> Dietrich Bonhoeffer (Darton, Longman and Todd)

Tuesday March 1   **2 CORINTHIANS 4.1-6 ✳**

Try an experiment. Light a candle, and place it somewhere in the daylight, or where there are bright lamps around. Now place the candle in the darkest place you can find. Which shows the light more clearly? Look at the candle for a few minutes, and think about God's presence.

Many Christians that I know have become very discouraged, because people around just don't want to know about Jesus. To their neighbours, the Christian story is an out-moded fairy-tale, and they are far more interested in self-advancement, or struggling to make ends meet than wanting to listen to God. And yet, my Christian friends know that their darkness will be dispersed, if they will only accept the light God offers.

The candle flame burns with a beauty all of its own. It doesn't need people to embellish it or compete with it. Perhaps that is why Paul, writing to Christians in Corinth, told them not to put the spotlight on themselves, but on Christ. So how can we proclaim Christ without proclaiming ourselves? Think of one way in which you could make it more possible for your neighbours to understand his love?

✳ *We pray for those who quietly share Christ*
with people who experience trouble, despair or apathy.
Help them to get alongside,
to listen and emphathise,
so that light may shine in their lives.

Wednesday March 2   **MARK 9.2-10 ***

Here was the ideal opportunity for Jesus to really prove to everyone that he was special – the Son of God – and he failed to capitalise on it. There, up on the mountain, he had appeared in shining glory with key figures from Jewish history – Moses, representing the law, and Elijah, the prophets. It was a wonderful chance for him to demonstrate how the Messiah had come to bring the New Covenant to his people. And what did he do? He told his disciples to keep the experience a secret until he had risen from death. Why?

Jesus did not go up the mountain to glorify himself to others. He wanted to make sure that his decision to go to Jerusalem and accept the Cross was the right one, and here, God affirmed this. It also gave Peter, James and John something to hold on to. They must have found it hard to come to terms with the idea that the Messiah had to die. Now they had heard God's Son acknowledged by God. It was as if God had ordained him for his journey to the Cross. But, for the moment, the disciples did not understand what being the Messiah entailed. Jesus knew that they could only tell other people when they comprehended what death and resurrection really meant.

✳ *Loving God, forgive me for wanting you to operate*
in the way I want.
Help me to trust that you understand much more fully
than I can comprehend
what is best for the world,
and help me to have patience to wait for your timing.

Thursday March 3   **EXODUS 24.12-18 ***

If we are to develop our friendship with someone we care about deeply, then we need to make time to be with them. The friendship is much richer if we can listen to them, share our joys and sorrows, laugh together, and, sometimes, get angry with each other. The same is true if we want to get to know God more deeply. Most Christians find that their faith grows if they can take time out each day to be with God – to read the Bible, to listen, and pray. Some Christians, like Mother Julian of Norwich, or Thomas Merton, find that they have been called to separate themselves totally from other people in order to do this; others try to find a daily quiet time alone with God, even if it is only time waiting at the bus stop, or doing household tasks.

Moses could have used his experience of the dazzling light of God's presence on the mountain to boost his own popularity, but instead, his immediate reaction was to stay there alone for forty days and nights. Like Jesus in the wilderness, he had a great need to spend time in the quietness, getting to know God.

✳ *Ever-present, caring God,*
  help me to spend more time with you;
  to be more aware of your presence,
  and to listen to what you are saying to me.

Women's World Day of Prayer, March 4   PSALM 69.1-9

How would you feel if you were persecuted or ostracised for speaking the unpalatable truth? Many in that situation would tell you that they swing from periods of certainty to times of deep depression, darkness and even rebellion. Psalm 69 was written by such a person. It expresses the intense anguish of one who loved God, Jerusalem and its holy Temple, but who found persecution hard to bear.

The Psalmist, probably a disciple of the prophet Jeremiah, must have struggled to persuade his people not to rebel against Babylon and so to save Jerusalem from destruction. As with Jeremiah, they laughed at him and ostracised him, so that at times, even God's presence was hard to find. He probably wrote this psalm after the destruction of Jerusalem in 587BC, when King Nebuchadnezzar's armies captured Jerusalem's intellectuals and artisans and took them off to Babylon to forced labour. He reflects also what it feels like to be oppressed.

The religious struggles over Jerusalem have not stopped. In recent years, Palestinians and Arabs have fought for the city. During the Gulf War, a modern Babylon aimed missiles towards Israel. In 1992, Israel evicted Palestinians over the border into the no-man's land between Israel and Lebanon.

But there are signs of hope. Today's Women's World Day of Prayer worship material comes from Jerusalem. The theme is **Go, See and Act**. Together, they demonstrate that out of the suffering of contemporary Israel and Jordan, can come peace, just as, 2,000 years ago, Jesus took the unpopular route of suffering and death on a cross so that all of us might be saved. If that peace and salvation sometimes seems a long way off, remember that God can act with just a few loyal people. Those few add up. Today, thousands of women all over the world are praying together. Just think what God can do with such a force. As the psalmist says, 'Lord God of Hosts, let none of those who hope in you be discouraged through me' (verse 6).

✳ *Pray for those who work for peace in Israel, Iraq and Jordan, and for all Christian women who pray together today.*

Saturday March 5   PSALM 69.10-21

Everything seemed to be going wrong for the psalmist. He had tried to keep on worshipping God, but other people sneered at him, and we can just imagine their singing drunken songs about him. Worshipping God had certainly not made him popular! If he had wanted to be popular, he would, no doubt, have had to renounce God and join the sneerers.

Have you ever come close to feeling as despairing as the psalmist? How have you reacted when things seem to have gone from bad to worse? Has it ever seemed as if God has deserted you, and if so what have you done about it?

What impresses me about the psalmist is the way he did not give up, even although God did not seem to have answered his prayer. He knew that God would answer him, but it would have to be in God's good time. I have found it encouraging to read the lives of saints and prominent Christians. Many of them speak of a time of 'the desert of the soul', and they have gone on to say that God's will did become clear, in God's own good time.

✳ *Patient God, help me to wait patiently for you,*
especially when I am full of despair,
and feel that you are not there.
Uphold all who despairingly wait for you today.

Have you ever felt really angry with someone else? If so, how have you expressed it? Did you speak to the person, or, perhaps, have you rehearsed what you would like to say to him or her over and over in your head?

In the first part of this passage, the Psalmist does not seem a very nice person at all. No matter how his enemies might have deserved it, his heart is full of revenge. He gleefully lists all the things he would like God to do to them. And then the mood changes. The psalmist is full of praise to God. He knows, deep in his heart, that God will restore the people to Jerusalem, even if that will take time.

Time is a great healer, especially when we are angry. We just have to trust and give God time. We also know that because Jesus took the unpopular path to suffering and death, we can now be forgiven by God, through his glorious resurrection.

✳ *Forgiving God, help me to be forgiving too.*
Show me how I may begin to mend broken relationships;
and strengthen those who find it difficult to forgive.
Help me to resist the temptation to be popular
rather than taking the harder path of doing your will.

For personal reflection or group discussion

Read again Mark 8.27-33. Why did Jesus want to keep the news of his messiahship a secret? What made Peter and the other disciples reject what Jesus had to say to them about his suffering and death? How can this incident help us to reflect upon our own experiences of undeserved suffering?

ACTION

Find out about the work of people who support the persecuted and wrongly imprisoned, like Amnesty International. Could you do anything to help, such as write letters to people in power?

THE ARMS OF LOVE

Notes based on the Revised English Bible, by

Rosemary Wakelin

*Rosemary Wakelin is a Methodist minister in Norwich (UK), best known for her **Prayer for the Day** on BBC and her clear challenge to the attitudes of British Christians regarding the role of women and the use of inclusive language.*

Until recently, we have only had access to male interpretations and commentaries on the Bible. So nearly all insights came through male eyes, little being made of the feminine part of God's nature, the significance of women in the Gospel story or what women could contribute through their very different experience. By concentrating on only part of the evidence, we have missed out on other vital insights and received a distorted image of God. Women are now being heard, however, so at last feminine experience is being placed alongside the masculine to the enrichment, not only of women but perhaps even more of men, for it liberates the crushed and undervalued femine side of their own personalities and holds out the possibility of wholeness, in God's image, for all of us.

> *God our mother,*
> *you hold our life within you;*
> *nourish us at your breast,*
> *and teach us to walk alone.*
> *Help us to receive your tenderness*
> *and to respond to your challenge*
> *that others may draw life from us,*
> *in your name.*   Janet Morley, All Desires Known (SPCK)

Further reading

All Desires Known, Janet Morley (SPCK)
The Hidden Tradition, Ed. Lavinia Byrne (SPCK)
Our God has NO Favourites, Primavesi/Henderson (Burns and Oates Ltd)
Through the Eyes of a Woman, Wendy Robins (YWCA)

The verses which go before this story tell of Zechariah receiving an angel visitor with doubt and fear. After all, he is the priest in charge – what do you do with something as unprecedented as an angel with an impossible message? – he is struck dumb. Nor is the message he receives as dynamic as that received by Mary: John's mission is to be short term; that of her child will last for ever. Though awed and wondering how it can happen, Mary responds with the perfect Christian answer, 'All of me belongs to God. Let it happen as you say' – thus opening the way, by her trust and obedience, for God to come in to his world. God's activity is not confined by human values and conventions. Mary's courage and faith in saying 'yes' enables a new beginning and breaks down the manmade barrier between heaven and earth.

It is amazing that when God wants to reveal himself to humankind, he puts his confidence in the motherly care of an inexperienced, (possibly) teenage girl to nurture and influence his beloved. 'The folly of God is wiser than human wisdom, and the weakness of God stronger than human strength . . . He has chosen things without rank or standing in the world, mere nothings, to overthrow the existing order' (1 Corinthians 1.25,28). Read 1 Corinthians 1.18–2.9 for Paul's amazing commentary on the way God works.

✻ *O God,*
  you fulfil our desire
  beyond what we can bear:
  as Mary gave her appalled assent
  to your intimate promise,
  so may we open ourselves also
  to contain your life within us,
  through Jesus Christ.

                              Janet Morley, All Desires Known (SPCK)

Tuesday March 8   **LUKE 1.39-45**

Mary hurries off to her cousin Elizabeth to share her extraordinary news and to rejoice with Elizabeth at her pregnancy. The two women meet with exuberant joy (shared by the unborn John) and Elizabeth pours out her wonder and excitement at what God is doing through both of them – surely the only proper response to recognising God's activity.

The first lines of this lovely song (verse 42) have been linked with Roman Catholic devotion and have been consequently avoided by Protestants, which is a pity. The role of Mary, a real woman, cannot be over-estimated. God trusted her to get it right – and she did! So while Zechariah, unable to control what was happening, remained dumb (perhaps Luke means him to be a symbol of the old order – the elaborate Judaism which proved unable to be open to the new thing that God was doing), the two powerless women got on with the business of cooperating with God and exulted and rejoiced. Both had reason to be amazed, but disregarding any social or physical consequences, they embraced what God was doing in them and rejoiced in each other's part in the grand design.

✴ *O unknown God,*
  whose presence is announced
  not among the impressive
  but in obscurity:
  come, overshadow us now,
  and speak to our hidden places;
  that, entering your darkness with joy,
  we may choose to cooperate with you,
  through Jesus Christ.

Janet Morley, All Desires Known (SPCK)

Wednesday March 9   LUKE 1.46-56 *

These verses are the famous 'Magnificat', the song of Mary. What is less known is that this song is attributed to Elizabeth by some witnesses (see the footnote in the REB). Whoever said it, it is an outpouring of gratitude, joy in God's goodness and confidence in God's promises. Luke interrupts the action of the story to insert this commentary on what is really happening, drawing on rich sources of the Old Testament, and so linking what is happening now, in the coming of this special child, with all God's previous activity through the story of Israel. Compare it with the words of Hannah's song in 1 Samuel 2.1-10 (and, if time permits: 1 Samuel 1.11; Job 5.11,12,19; Genesis 17.7 and Psalm 113).

Echoing as it does the insights of previous generations into God's nature and priorities, it is also a sort of pre-manifesto for Jesus' ministry, carrying the upside-down ideas which later proved so threatening to the powerful who opposed Jesus. 'Upside-down' suggests 'wrong way up'. Maybe we need to look at that. Perhaps it is human beings who have got it all the wrong way up. Jesus was right: the way God wants things to work is completely different from the way we usually do things! When are we going to catch up with him?

✴ *Pray for insight and the courage to catch up with Jesus.*

Thursday March 10   MARK 3.31-35 *

This is a strange story, striking a jarring note in Jesus' apparently heartless reception of the news of his family's arrival. On another occasion (John 7.1-9), his brothers tried to persuade him to go for a higher profile, and later, when Jesus was the centre of controversy, they tried to take him home on the grounds that he was mad! These odd references suggest that Jesus' family, though concerned for him, had little understanding of what his ministry was about. Today's passage is reminiscent of BBC's TV programme 'Bread' – the Boswell family going as a body to retrieve one of their number! But we read the Bible with 20th century eyes, forgetting that the Gospel writers were writing theology for persecuted Christians, to help them understand the amazing truth about Jesus and his Church.

So let's look again. Jesus is teaching in the middle of a crowd. His ministry is flourishing. This interruption represents the 'old order' of every generation – the 'mother and brothers' from whom he came. So Jesus looks at the people around, who are drinking in the good news of the new Kingdom – the new relationship with God – and identifies them as his family. This was wonderfully encouraging to those first, hard-pressed readers, desperately needing to hear confirmation of their relationship with God in Christ. It's wonderful news for us too!

✴ *Thank God that in Christ we become his family.*

Friday March 11   JOHN 19.25-27; ACTS 1.12-14

The crucified Jesus sees, among three or four women, his faithful mother who has followed to the last, and (alone among the Gospels) this writer refers to the one man who dared to follow to the cross, 'the beloved disciple'. In his own agony, Jesus is aware of their need and gives his heart-broken mother into the filial care of his beloved friend, and his shattered friend into the motherly care of his beloved mother.

But John is also writing theology. Here at the cross are representatives of the old and new Israel whom he places in one another's care. Mary is to see her place in the context of the New Covenant where God's activity, begun in Judaism, is to continue; she is to nurture and protect it as her child. 'The beloved disciple', who represents the new order, is told to embrace and sustain the 'mother' Judaism.

In the Acts, we see Mary as already part of this new community. The tragedy is that Synagogue and Church separated irrevocably: two great religions, each incomplete without the other, became estranged. We need to remind ourselves that it was baptised Christians who perpetrated the Holocaust.

✳ *Thank God for what we have received through 'mother Judaism.' Pray for the coming together of all peoples into the family of God.*

Saturday March 12   ISAIAH 49.13-23

The imagery in this passage is very feminine. Zion, like other Hebrew city names, is feminine and she is seen as a forsaken wife. Although called upon to rejoice, she is desolate and doubting, believing that God has left her, so the prophet gives God's strong reassurances. Not only does God love her, but with more faithfulness than even the strongest expression of human love – that of the mother for her child. She is so precious that, like a lover, her name is tattooed on the palms of God's hands. For Christians, this reflects another image – the risen Christ showing Thomas his hands and feet, bearing the prints of love, 'those dear tokens of his passion' (Charles Wesley).

In Old Testament days, prosperity and peace meant rebuilding destroyed cities and an abundance of children – all this is promised, so much so that they will complain there is not enough room! The triumphalism and desire to see enemies utterly humiliated is very human and still much in evidence, so we need to remember that although there are wonderful insights into God's nature in the Old Testament – especially in Isaiah – it took the message of the cross to demonstrate God's different understanding of how humans should relate. Enemies 'licking the dust' is 'light years' away from 'Father forgive them'.

✳ *And thou Jesus, sweet Lord, art thou not also a mother?*
Truly thou art a mother, the mother of all mothers,
who tamed death in thy desire to give life to thy children.
St Anselm

This passage continues with female images, used elsewhere in Isaiah, of both Zion (49.15-16; 54.1; 65.23) and God (42.14;46.3) as mothers. The birth image reverses the curse of Eve, for now Zion, with God's help gives birth. With no prolonged agony she has her son – the nation is reborn. And motherhood is about great joy and celebration, about sustaining children with an abundance of milk and the comfort of the breast. Prosperity is about delighting in plentiful milk and the security of being carried on the hip and dandled on the knee! Verses 7-11 refer to Zion's motherhood, but translators suggest that verses 12-13 are talking of God's experienced motherly care.

All this makes a change from the far more common military or powerful images of God and reminds us of how much we have missed by neglecting the experience of half the human race, made in God's image. Maybe, now we have reached the inevitable 'Mutually Assured Destruction', we will make more strenuous efforts to draw on other wisdom, with solutions to human problems other than killing. It helps when we see God as Lifegiver, painfully and carefully bringing us to birth and sustaining us with his own life – and exulting in the joy and satisfaction of motherhood!

✴ *So Jesus Christ who sets good against evil is our real mother. We owe our being to him – and this is the essence of motherhood! – and all the delightful, loving protection which ever follows. God is really our Mother as he is our Father.*   Julian of Norwich

---

For personal reflection or group discussion

Go back over this week's notes and underline any ideas or insights which have been new to you, difficult to accept or which have deepened your faith. Read again the verses of Scripture that accompany them and reflect carefully on their truth. In a group, share your reactions.

ACTION

Whether you are a woman or a man, decide to do something which will affirm the contribution of women to the life of your church.

LENT 4
THE PAIN OF LOVE

Notes, based on the Revised Standard Version, by
Clare Amos

*Clare Amos is the Director of the ACTS Centre, a Christian
resource and educational centre for laity and clergy, sponsored
by the Anglican Diocese of Southwark.*

Does love hurt? What is our vision of God? In Christian tradition,
so often God has been viewed as remote, 'up there', far from
the reality of human suffering. The hymn, 'Immortal, invisible,
God only wise', with its line, '. . . naught changeth Thee',
expresses this succinctly. But nobody can seriously explore the
Bible without realising that this is an incomplete picture of God
who suffers with his people in the Old Testament and is
enfleshed on their behalf in the New.

The glory of the God of the Bible is that he is Love and, as
Love, he hurts for us. This is our God, a God for those who live
in the Century of Auschwitz and Hiroshima and so much other
evil on a cataclysmic scale. We can respond to this God
because we know that he has first responded to us.

> *Love that gives, gives evermore,*
> *Gives with zeal, with eager hands,*
> *Spares not, keeps not, all outpours,*
> *Ventures all, its all expends.*
> W H Vanstone

Monday March 14   **LAMENTATIONS 3.1-9 ***

Protest is, or can be, a part of faith. That is the message of
Lamentations - and many other parts of the Old Testament.
Protest at our human condition, protest when we feel life is
unfair, protest even when we feel God is unfair. Lamentations is
not a polite and tactful book: it springs out of the raw experience
of the people of the Old Testament. Jerusalem and its Temple
had been destroyed, the aristocracy had been deported to exile
in Babylon. Those remaining in the land, who included our
writer, suffered famine and deprivation. Why? The answer of the
prophets and historians was that God had punished the people

for their sins and faithlessness. But that did not ease the pain; it only deepened it. Was there any hope for a future relationship between God and the people of Israel? Was there any possibility of forgiveness and contrition?

Those are the questions our writer is throwing at God here. With images that seem to come from the siege of Jerusalem and the taking of prisoners, he describes his physical and material plight. But the focus of his anguish is that his relationship with God seems to be fractured: 'he shuts out my prayer' (verse 8). Yet this anguish is itself the ground of hope. In Psalm 22, utter despair is redeemed as the psalmist addresses God as 'my God.' Here the fact that he is still calling out to God is the beginning of renewal: for you only cry out to a God who you believe may – one day – perhaps listen.

✴ *Out of the depths I cry to you O God,*
  Lord, hear my voice.   *Psalm 130.1*

Tuesday March 15   **LAMENTATIONS 3.18-33 ***

Who would imagine that words of the cherished hymns, 'New every morning is the love', and 'Great is thy faithfulness' come out of the heart of this powerful, questioning piece of poetry. There are many surprising things about Lamentations, not least the fact that it is an 'acrostic', in which the verses in turn begin with successive letters of the Hebrew alphabet. Such passion and literary precision do not seem to us to belong easily together – but the writer of Lamentations marries the two – and increases the power of his writing.

Here we are at the mid-point of the book. It began with protest, and seems to end in despair: and yet in these verses, for a moment, everything seems to change. Life seems dark, without a glimmer of light for now - and yet we can remember what God has done for us and our ancestors in the past. God's love is indeed steadfast. The words used to describe God here – 'compassion', 'faithfulness', 'mercies' – all suggest a God who cannot easily sit by, unmoved by people's suffering. Their pain becomes his pain too. And there is a strange, prophetic hint in verse 30, 'he gave his cheek to the smiter'. Originally, it was the face of a captive inhabitant of Jerusalem. Many years later, it becomes the cheek of God, standing abused and smitten for the healing of Jerusalem's people.

Wednesday March 16   **LAMENTATIONS 3.46-57**

To acknowledge our grief in weeping is not a part of Anglo-Saxon culture. We are ashamed of tears and regard them as a sign of weakness. Women perhaps are allowed to weep, but men must show their masculinity by not giving way. The Bible and people of other cultures know better. Tears are both necessary and health giving and can be seeds of transformation. Joseph needed to weep before he could be reconciled to his brothers. Christ himself wept before he raised Lazarus from the dead.

There are many links between these verses and Jeremiah 8.18 to 9.19, and perhaps Jeremiah's reflections can help us to interpret this passage. Who weeps for devastated Jerusalem? In Jeremiah, the tears are shared between people, prophet and God. The grief of the people moves God to tears. Here in Lamentations the writer weeps both with and for his people. God does not – quite - weep, but does draw near to say 'do not fear'. God cannot take away the pain but can share it with us.

The ultimate answer to the pleas of Lamentations is found in the Gospels. The writer's fear is reflected in the fear of the disciples who travelled with Christ to Jerusalem. But it is also taken up and transformed by Christ's own fear in Gethesmane. The writer's insistence, that he will not stop weeping until the Lord looks down from heaven and sees, receives a response beyond his imagining. God comes down and himself weeps over the beloved Jerusalem (Luke 19.41-44).

* *Those who sow in tears shall reap in joy.*   *Psalm 126*

Thursday March 17   **MARK 3.1-6**

The Passion casts its shadow a long way back in the Gospel of Mark – at least as far as this story of healing, where human suffering is relieved, but at the cost of the first hint of Christ's own pain. It is an encounter that will be repeated over and over again in the rest of the Gospel, between those who are threatened when traditional laws and customs are side-stepped, and the love of God which is illogical and vulnerable enough to break all its own rules.

The keeping of the Sabbath was painted by God into the very fabric of creation (Genesis 1), and was a cornerstone of the laws given at Sinai. But it was given for human blessing not human bane, a core part of God's liberation of a people enslaved to those who worked them until they cried. Yet it seemed that for some, the Sabbath itself had become a hard task-master, with boundaries as rigid as the walls of the slave camps the Israelites had endured in Egypt. Ironically, but not accidentally, Jesus was grieved 'at their hardness of heart' – language reminiscent of the hard-hearted Pharaoh of Egypt. Hearts of stone cannot tolerate the risk of the Spirit's freedom – it might upset the political status quo of the Herodians, collaborators with Rome, as well as religious niceties cherished by the Pharisees.

✳ **Lord, let not our hearts grow hard in this city,**
this place,
this world.

Friday March 18   MARK 9.30-32: 10.32-34 *

In our readings from Lamentations, we ended with the words 'Do not fear'. It is strange then, that fear is a central theme in today's readings and throughout the Gospel of Mark. It is with fear that the Gospel concludes even in the time of resurrection (Mark 16.8). From the moment of the Transfiguration, Jesus was striding speedily and purposefully towards his destiny, aware that Jerusalem was the place where so many of God's messengers had perished. His disciples struggled on behind, barely able to keep their master in sight as he raced on far ahead of their understanding.

But their bewilderment was laced with fear; fear for Jesus, and themselves. Like a drumbeat or a death knell, the prediction of the death of the Son of man is repeated in these chapters of the Gospel. Who was this mysterious Son of man? Why did Jesus talk about him in the third person? Perhaps the title reminds us of Christ's role as the 'new Adam', the man who represents all men and women. So the solemn words about this figure who will suffer grievously, yet then rise to glory, may not be just a prediction of Christ's own passion. They may also be a challenge to Christ's disciples, who hesitantly travel in Christ's way. We, who wish to become part of the Body of Christ, the new Adam, must be prepared to share in his pain, if we wish to share in his glory.

✳ *Let us journey even in heart and mind to Jerusalem, the
city of suffering and glorification. Let us give everything
that the Kingdom may come.*

After 'Rule for a new Brother'

Saturday March 19   MARK 10.35-45 *

But should not this suffering on earth be rewarded with special
and prime seats in heaven? As Jesus and the disciples are
nearing Jerusalem, those fearful disciples are beginning to get a
glimmer of what lies ahead – and in case they are not sure,
Jesus spells it out clearly: they can indeed share in his baptism
and in his cup. For those who knew their Old Testament,
'drinking the cup' suggested a painful and poisoned drink,
quaffing the fruit of human sin which had been mixed with God's
anger. The symbolism of baptism, going down into the darkness
of the waters, called to mind the darkness of death. To be
baptised with the baptism of Christ was to be baptised into his
death (see Romans 6.3). James, John and the others have
moved one step forward in their understanding – only to slip two
steps back! 'Let's transfer our quest for power to heaven itself,'
they say!

In Mark 8-10, an interesting pattern emerges. Each time
there is the slow and messy learning of something new: Peter
opens his eyes to realise that Jesus is the Messiah (8.29), the
disciples learn that prayer is necessary to share in Jesus' work
(9.29), and discover that children may find it easier to become
disciples of Christ than those who are weighed down with the
world's riches (10.15,23-27). Each time Jesus then predicts the
suffering of the Son of man. And each time one or more
disciples spectacularly put their foot in it! Peter tries to 'rebuke'
Jesus (8.32), they have an argument as to who is the greatest
(9.34), and now they ask for special treatment. Sometimes
learning about the pain and cost of love, is painfully slow, both
for those who are learning, and for Jesus who is our teacher.

✳ *My God, I love Thee; not because
I hope for heaven thereby . . .
but as thyself hast loved me,
O ever-loving Lord.*   *Latin, 17th century*

For personal reflection or group discussion

Read again Lamentations 3.1–9. When have you felt like this? Or can you think of others who have expressed these feelings? Read Psalm 22 and reflect on the meaning in the light of the notes for March 14.

Fifth Sunday in Lent, March 20   **PHILIPPIANS 2.5-11 ***

These words were perhaps sung by the Early Church as part of a hymn to Christ, and have been used in many modern hymns. They are stirring, yet difficult to interpret. Try and read them in several different Bible translations. You will see how each translator has changed the flavour. But underlying the description of Christ in verses 6-8 seems to be the story of Adam, who was created in the likeness of God and sought, quite literally, to 'grasp' the knowledge of good and evil – only to be expelled from the garden lest he should live for ever. This disobedience led from the life of the garden to death. Now Christ has set in train its reversal. He, the new Adam, has counteracted Adam's disobedience by his obedience to death – and gained life, not just for himself, but all Adam's heirs.

In last week's readings, we saw that mysterious figure – the Son of man – who lived out what humanity was called to be, setting his face towards Jerusalem. To understand this passage, and the path to the passion in the Gospels, it is important to realise that in the Bible humanity and divinity are not poles apart. Our problem is not that we are too human, but that we are not human enough. Christ was the perfect pattern for humanity – and as such restored the original glory that is humanity's privilege, to be in the image and likeness of God.

✳ *We confess we have marred your love*
   and wounded your image in us.

Monday March 21   **MARK 14.32-42 ***

Back in chapter 10, Jesus seemed an almost inhuman figure as he raced towards Jerusalem in the conscious knowledge of the destiny that awaited him there. In case we think he did not know normal human fear and despair, Mark makes it clear that the 'cup' Jesus was required to drink was one that, humanly

69

speaking, he wished to avoid. Yet in the garden, Christ shows himself as the pattern for our humanity: in Eden, the first garden, Adam had eaten in disobedience to God; in Gethesmane, this second garden, the New Adam pledges his obedience to and trust in God to reverse Eden's failure. The intimate word he uses, 'Abba', 'Father', cherished by the Early Church as a precise memory of an actual word spoken in Aramaic by Jesus, underscores his depth of trust and commitment.

God, who meets us in Jesus, does not demand that we should be unafraid. Jesus, the pattern for our humanity, clearly knew fear, as Mark is telling us here. But God asks us to trust him in the midst of fear and pain, and promises to be with us, holding our hand, as a father holds his son (Hosea 11.3-4).

✱ *Father, may I hold your hand when life is dark around me?*

Tuesday March 22   MARK 14.43-52 *

As Gethesmane draws to its close, Jesus' isolation is emphasised. Although Peter, James and John are there while Jesus prays, their insistent sleep suggests they neither know nor care about the depth of his struggles. They all flee, even a young man who has to leave his clothes behind to do so. Is the young man Mark himself? Some think so, while others see him as symbolic of those in the Early Church who would one day be baptised into Christ's death - but not yet. In any case, that role of the Son of Man, the faithful servant of God who had to suffer, is narrowing down. Perhaps all humanity is being called to share the task, but for now at least, it seems to be only Jesus who is prepared to acknowledge the call. And the treacherous gesture of Judas, betraying his friend by a kiss, an intimate token of human affection, further serves to remind us of how horribly alone Jesus has become. One of the deepest wounds Christ suffers is the pain he knows as he finds his trust, love and friendship are being betrayed.

✱ *Vulnerable God, through the pain of your passion,*
teach us to cherish those who are weak
and vulnerable and lonely today.

Wednesday March 23   MARK 14.53-65 *

God, who loves and cherishes his human creation, is vulnerable. Love cannot exist without the possibility of being hurt. We know that from our own experience. In the Passion of

Christ, we see in sharp focus, as if refracted through a prism, what is eternally true in God's relationship with human beings. By our blows and rejection, we so often wound the One who loves us to the end and to his own pain.

From the moment of his arrest, Jesus says and does very little. Others speak and others do to him. You can discover this for yourselves if you read the passion story dramatically: you do not need your best speaker to portray Jesus – you had better keep him for Caiaphas or Pilate!

Our experience also teaches us that the easiest thing to do if someone hurts us is to return the blow, either physically or metaphorically. If we cannot retaliate, then our instinct is to 'pass on' the hurt and transfer it to another. The remarkable feature of this trial of Jesus is his virtual silence: he is absorbing into himself all the anger and evil the world can throw at him and refusing to allow it to spread further.

✳ **Be still, my soul, and be silent with the Lord.**

Thursday March 24   MARK 14.66-72 *

The pain of betrayal, and the pain of false accusation, is now followed by the pain of denial. Peter, Mark's hero and perhaps his mentor, is a hero with feet of clay. So often throughout the Gospel, he has said the wrong thing at the wrong time; frequently saying too much – and now, when it matters – not enough. Yet those who first read this Gospel probably knew that Peter had recently met a martyr's death, crucified upside down in Rome during the persecution instigated by the Emperor Nero. He had had the chance to escape – but this time had refused to deny his friend and Lord. Mark is a Gospel for those of us who, like Peter, need a second or third chance – or perhaps even more. Peter's bitter weeping is a painful moment of contrition, a first step on that journey that will end in the streets of Rome. Our sorrow at our failings is a searing moment when pain can begin to lead towards healing.

Peter's denial means that Christ starts his journey to crucifixion absolutely bereft. Surrounded by the crowds, he is, in reality, alone, the only man who is prepared to live and die the role of the Son of man. In the next chapter, the story of the crucifixion will be interpreted in the light of Psalm 22. If you read the first half of that psalm one thing stands out: it is the account of a man so deserted by his fellow humans that he even wonders if God has deserted him too. There will come a moment when the one will become many and a solitary cross in Jerusalem will reach out to embrace the whole earth, the past and future (see also Psalm 22.22 to the end). But that is the other side of Easter. For the moment Love's pain is suffered absolutely alone.

✳ *God, may I begin to share - just a little – in bearing the weight of the world which you hold up alone by your aching arms.*   *After the style of W.H.Vanstone*

Friday March 25   ROMANS 5.1-11

What the readings of the last few days have expressed in narrative form, is spelt out systematically by Paul. Christ died for us when we were still 'weak' and 'enemies'; he died for cowardly Peter and even for treacherous Judas. He died alone, so that we might never have to be alone again – but be reconciled and at one with God. He was the one who died, yet as 'Son of man' he calls all human beings to share rejoicingly in his sufferings that we too may share in his glory (verses 2-3).

Sometimes in Paul's letters, God seems distant from Christ's Cross and sufferings on our behalf. It is as though God is a solemn judge presiding over a heavenly law court in which various legal niceties have to be observed. But not so here: Christ's death is simply and purely described as God showing his love for us. Perhaps what is in his mind at this point is the story of Abraham and Isaac (it clearly is in Romans 8.32). In the Cross of his Son, God the Father suffers even more than the pain Abraham suffered as he led his only son towards the mountain of sacrifice.

At the beginning of the chapter, it is not clear whether we should read 'we have peace with God', or 'let us have peace with God.' Perhaps the ambiguity is necessary or providential. The depths of our alienation from God were too great and long-standing to be completely undone in a moment. In the Cross, the potential for peace is given: but it is only as we come to appreciate the pain God has endured on our behalf that our own hearts of stone are gradually melted into flesh.

✳ *May the peace of Christ begin to enfold and change us.*

Saturday March 26   Psalm 70

Here we have, very simply and succinctly, the two halves of biblical faith set out together to make one complete whole.

There is lament, a passionate cry for help, and there is thanksgiving. They belong together and both are necessary. So often we cherish the one and neglect the other.

Perhaps we Christians have tended to 'lose the lament'. We regard it as impolite to God to be quite so insistent on our needs. But the God of the Gospels is a God who wants and asks for honesty in relationships – with each other and with him. He is prepared to hear our laments, to suffer our sufferings with us, and even, on Good Friday, to lament our lament for us.

But verses 4-5 are also necessary. The purpose of life is the praise of God, sang ancient Israel. Life can only gain its fullest meaning when God is praised from the depths of our hearts. God is our salvation (verse 4) and deliverer (verse 5). Is it providential that these words remind us of the core meaning of the name 'Jesus', – 'saviour'?

Today, the day before Palm Sunday, is known as 'Lazarus Saturday' by Eastern Christians. It commemorates Lazarus who is brought to life again (John 11) and perhaps also the poor man who dies in the parable (Luke 16.20). Psalm 70 could indeed be Lazarus' prayer: the words of all the world's poor who go hungry while the rich are fed, but who have the faith that God will vindicate them – the source of their salvation and even of life.

✳ *O people of God, let us hope in the Lord,*
for with the Lord there is mercy
and with Him is plenteous redemption.

After Psalm 130.7-8

For personal reflection or group discussion
Reflect again on Philippians 2.5-11 in the light of this week's readings. Try to make a list of the reasons God might have for choosing to become so vulnerable.

What challenge does this make to us? Why do we find it so hard to respond?

ACTION
Resolve to respond to a challenge you have avoided because it may make you unpopular.

LENT 5

TRIUMPH AND TRAGEDY

Notes, based on the Good News Bible, by

Ernie Whalley

Ernie Whalley is a tutor at the Northern Baptist College in Manchester, United Kingdom, and a minister in the South West Manchester Group of Baptist and United Reformed Churches.

Wherever we live, and in whatever age, human suffering hits us hard. The question 'Why?' comes to our lips, especially when innocent suffering is involved. Nor do we escape from these questions when we belong to the community of Christian faith.

In all our thinking, though, we are led back to Jesus and above all to the last days of his earthly life. Here we see the cost of God's love for the world. God's saving love meets us where we are and brings us salvation. Here we find the clue to the divine presence amid innocent suffering. May the story, as told particularly through Mark's Gospel, speak to us all this Holy Week as we join Jesus on his final journey.

> *Living God, we come to you this Holy Week,*
> *just as we are.*
> *Help us to glimpse again*
> *the cost and wonder of your love in Jesus,*
> *so that we may respond in trust and hope.*
> *May we find fresh meaning and purpose,*
> *in the name of Jesus Christ our Lord.*

Palm Sunday, March 27   **MARK 11.1-11 ***

Crowds soon gather when something unusual is going on. Curious faces draw together all sorts of people from many backgrounds and viewpoints. When Jesus entered Jerusalem for the last time in triumph, the religious leaders were all around with their threatening glances, as they saw the one who undermined their prestige and authority. Mark gives particular prominence to the disciples of Jesus.

The time had come for Jesus to make a public statement of his messiahship. The conflict with religious leaders, which had been brewing for some time, was now set to proceed to a climax as Jesus came openly to the Holy City. Here was prophecy dramatised on the streets for all who had eyes to see. The one 'who comes in the name of the Lord' was revealing the nature of his kingship, not on a war horse but on a colt of peace.

The road to peace, that gospel 'Shalom', is one which requires courage now as it did then. Such a demonstration of peace means that people have to take sides.

✱ *Lord, show us the way to peace*
and grant us courage to follow you.

Monday March 28   MARK 11.15-19 *

Any image of Jesus being a 'meek and mild' character is shattered by this story. Jesus the disturber was not just using words but physically turning over tables. Why? What was he really trying to turn upside down?

At its heart, this story is about worship and how to make it accessible to all peoples. The desire to bring 'worthship' to the living God was being thwarted by the economic policies of the Temple establishment. Jesus was reacting against the Temple tax. This tax had to be paid in the one currency, Temple shekels, and pilgrims from all over the world, were at the mercy of the rate of exchange. The Temple treasury was making easy money. The poor felt this most. Even the cost of doves, the sacrificial offerings of the poorest, were subjected to inflated prices.

This was a dramatic prophetic act, not on the public street but in the heart of the worshipping community.

✱ *In what ways are we hindering people, especially the*
marginalised, in the worship of God?
Is our church really open to all?

Tuesday March 29   MARK 14.12-31 *

To eat a meal with friends is an occasion of great meaning and joy, wherever we live. If the host is about to leave the area, the shared meal has added significance. In one sense, the meal we call the Last Supper was typical of those a rabbi would eat with his disciples. But there are other additional elements here, especially in the words. With their remembrance of Passover as the backcloth, the disciples were made aware of God's saving acts for the people. A new 'covenant' was being inaugurated through the self-giving of Jesus. The disciples, amid all their differences, were invited to eat together at this last meal with their master.

The sharing of bread and wine plays a very significant role in most of our Christian traditions. Yet whether it is shared in great Cathedrals or in homes and hospitals, the cost of divine friendship is celebrated and we receive strength for our journey. Beyond words, we proclaim the grace of God and renew ourselves to serve in the ways of God.

✱ *Lord, as we share bread and wine in our church,*
  draw us closer into one body.

Wednesday March 30   MARK 15.1-15 *

'It's not fair!', we cry out when we sense we have been treated unjustly. As we approach the last days of Jesus' life, we see the various elements of injustice building up.

● False accusations are brought in the trials of Jesus as his enemies conspire to get rid of him.

● A renowned bandit, guilty of murder, is set free rather than Jesus, the innocent one.

● Jesus is whipped. This was carried out with a leather thong which had pieces of lead and bone tied onto it. Usually this would make the victim unconscious.

A crowd, possibly including the supporters of Barabbas, is manipulated to demand the crucifixion of Jesus. The time for words is ending. Words have little meaning after a while for those who will not listen. Jesus is silent. In the face of tragedy, silence can be the most appropriate and powerful of reactions.

✱ *Pray for those who are in prison*
  both the guilty and the innocent.
  Pray for their families.

Maundy Thursday, March 31
                    MARK 15.16-20; ISAIAH 50:4-9 *

It is striking that the Gospels give the most detailed account of any crucifixion in ancient literature. Death in this way was a common occurence, in the days of Jesus, specially reserved for political crimes, violent offences and disobedient slaves. It was a public event designed to protect peace and prosperity for the majority. Yet it offended the reputation of Roman civilisation, so there are few descriptions of it. The Gospels describe the horror in graphic form.

As we read the story of the crucifixion and ponder, we are confronted with its evil. Today's reading includes the preparations for this most painful form of death:

● the physical effect of the crown of thorns and the beatings on the head;

● the mockery of being saluted, taunted and spat upon.

The depths to which human nature can sink are brought before us, as our beaten and bruised Saviour begins his final walk. Yet he takes the pathway that leads to forgiveness for the whole world. Here is the hope of new life for all.

✳ **Behold, the Lamb of God, who takes away the sin of the world.** *John 1.29 (RSV)*

Good Friday, April 1   MARK 15.21-47 *

The question 'why' is often on our lips. At times we may feel abandoned. On this day of days we hear again the one who cried, 'My God, my God, why did you abandon me?' Those who have been close to Jesus are now watching from a distance. He has refused the drugged wine. He faces crucifixion fully aware of its pain. He is among sinners, even in his death. In death, as in life, Jesus identifies with the most wretched in society, even though they too hurl insults at him. In our bafflement and doubt, we see the one who takes upon himself the very worst evil and suffering can do. And he does it for us.

There is something different about this death. An army officer, no doubt familiar with crucifixions, senses it and makes a confession of faith.

The scandal and tragedy of it all comes to us today. Yet, at this place of the greatest anguish, here is God – Emmanuel.

Read slowly Mark 15.21-47, the passage for today, imagining the scene.

✳ *Were the whole realm of nature mine,*
    That were an offering far too small,
Love so amazing, so divine,
    Demands my soul, my life, my all. Isaac Watts

77

Saturday April 2   **HEBREWS 4.14-16; 5.7-9 ***

In 1985, 55 people died in a fire in a football stadium in Bradford, England. At the Memorial Service, a cross was made out of the charred timbers and placed on the platform. One of the speakers, pointing to it, said to the grieving relatives and friends, 'I can only live with this in the light of the cross'. Two years later in that same stadium, Desmond Tutu, Archbishop of Capetown, referring to the painful struggle of his own people in South Africa, spoke of solidarity in suffering.

The cross of Jesus Christ connects with human experience today all over the world. Jesus, the great high priest, is the bridge between God and humanity. Because of his own suffering, Jesus the divine Son literally 'suffers along with' all who suffer, wherever they are. We live by the promise of divine grace which is ours at the point of our greatest need. Thanks be to God!

✳ *Thanks be unto thee, O Lord Jesus Christ:*
  for all the benefits which thou hast given for us;
  for all the pains and insults which thou hast borne for us.
  O most merciful redeemer,
  friend and brother,
  may we know thee more clearly,
  love thee more dearly,
  and follow thee more nearly;
  for thine own sake.   *St Richard of Chichester*

For personal reflection and group discussion

Who are the forgotten ones in your community? Read again Mark 15.21-47. How would Jesus react to them? What would he do? What would he say? Remembering that you are called as disciples of the crucified and living Jesus, what does it mean to 'carry the cross' in your community?

ACTION

Crucifixion is one of the marks of discipleship. In the light of the cost of God's saving love in Jesus, prayerfully consider one aspect of your life which needs to be adjusted.

EASTER 1
CHRIST'S VICTORY

Notes, based on the Revised Standard Version, by
M Gnanavaram

M Gnanavaram is a priest from the Madurai-Ramnad Diocese of the Church of South India. He is now on the staff of the Tamilnadu Theological Seminary, Arasaradi, Madurai, South India, where he teaches New Testament. At the time of writing, he is involved in New Testament research in Wycliffe Hall, Oxford (UK).

The dramatic story of the resurrection of Jesus is attested to in the synoptic, Johannine and Pauline traditions of the New Testament. Every New Testament author presents this story in accordance with the life setting of his readers. Therefore in this week's meditations, we will attempt to relate the resurrection of Jesus to the everyday life of the people by

- considering what the text says;
- examining how it was relevant to those believers of the Old Testament and the first Christians;
- relating that message to our present context both at personal and social levels;
- ending with a short prayer for the day.

Dear God, our Father and Mother,
open our hearts to your word.

Easter Sunday, April 3   **Mark 16.1-8 ***
          (cf also Matthew 28.1-7; Luke 24.1-12; John 20.1-10)
Jesus rises from the dead
          'Do not be amazed; . . . he is not here'
This is the important phrase to remember on Easter Sunday. Jesus has been raised. He could not be confined to the tomb. For the religious and political leaders, the tomb was a symbol of the defeat of Jesus' movement, and victory for them. Some

knew and accepted that Jesus was innocent and righteous (Mark 15.39; Matthew 27.54; Luke 23.47; John 19.21; John 3.2; Acts 2.22). Religious and political powers of oppression joined together and tried to crush the movement of the kingdom. It was the greatest injustice that the righteous Son of God was crucified (Acts 3.13-15). So Jesus' resurrection is a symbol of victory over injustice and oppression by both political and religious authorities.

What did it mean to the early disciples? Their fear was removed (note the angel's words, 'Do not be afraid' Mark 16.6). They were empowered to go and tell the good news. The disciples, who locked the doors of the house for the fear of the Jews (John 20.19), became courageous enough to stand outside and preach the good news (Acts 2.14ff).

What does this mean to you today? If you are afraid at a personal level, God says to you, 'Do not be afraid.' If you fear the unjust structures of this world, do not be dismayed. There is hope of victory over injustice and for a righteous world order in the resurrection of Jesus.

✻ *Lord, we thank you for giving us hope in hopelessness.*
We remember innocent people who are oppressed
by unjust political and religious authorities.
We pray for those places where religious fundamentalism
is used by political opportunists
to threaten the lives of innocent people.
Give us strength to work for their liberation.

Monday April 4 **Mark 16.9-18**

(cf also Matthew 28.16-20; Luke 24.13-35; John 20.24-31)

The power of the resurrection

'In my name they will cast out demons'

Jesus appears to his disciples and gives them authority over deadly things (Mark 16.18) such as demons, snakes, sickness and death-giving powers of destruction, and authority to preach the good news of liberation to the whole creation (Mk 16.15; Matthew 28.19-20; John 20.22-23). This is not the oppressive authority which operated in Jesus' crucifixion, but a liberating authority which transforms dehumanised people into human beings.

We read about the power of the resurrection in the life and ministry of the apostles and ministers in the Acts and the Epistles (Acts 2.4; 19.6; 28.5).

There are many situations where human beings suffer because of dehumanising powers. They are political, socio-cultural, economic and religious in nature. Christ's resurrection gives us power and authority to work against these death-giving powers (Luke 4.18-19; John 20.21; Philippians 4.13).

✴ *Thank you Lord, that you give us power in our*
powerlessness.
Give us wisdom to use your strength
to work for your glory in the service of your kingdom,
for the freedom of your people
who suffer because of death-giving powers.

Tuesday April 5   1 Corinthians 15.1-12 *

The hope of future resurrection

'*How can some of you say there is no resurrection of the dead?*

This chapter is the first surviving witness to the resurrection of Jesus outside the Gospel tradition. Paul brings out the relationship between Jesus' resurrection and the ultimate resurrection of believers. His argument for a bodily resurrection should be understood against the background of Gnosticism and the Sadducees who did not accept a bodily resurrection (Matthew 22.23).

For Paul, the body is as important as the soul. 'Body' symbolises all matter, including experiences of history which relate to our whole life. Matter matters to God! Bodily resurrection is also the resurrection of the community, when God overcomes all enemies, death being the last enemy to be destroyed (1 Corinthians 15.24-26).

Our history of so many failures needs the hope of resurrection. God is concerned about our body, history and ecology. All the failures, irresponsibilities and incompleteness of our history will be set right.

✴ *Thank you, Lord, that all history is in your hands,*
and that you will complete our history
by the power of the resurrection of your Son Jesus Christ.
Help us to work with you
as you always work towards that completion.

John 5.17

Wednesday April 6

Resurrection and restoration

'I will turn the darkness before them into light'

In the 'Servant Song' of Isaiah 42, the author brings out a hope of restoration against the background of the sufferings of Israel in exile. God promises to bring them back to their land and give them joy and peace. It is God's messianic justice which will bring restoration (42.2-3). God will bring out prisoners from the dungeon, and release those who sit in darkness. He will turn the darkness before them into light (42.16). Like the resurrection of Jesus, these are impossible things for human beings, but not for God's mighty power.

The real experience of the Israelites was that God brought them from the land of Babylon. They praised God who restored their life in Israel. It was not a 'religious' experience but a historical experience.

This gives us enormous hope of restoration for our lives and encouragement to participate in the work of God for the restoration of justice to the marginalised and oppressed.

✳ *Dear God, our Father and Mother,*
we thank you that you are the God of compassion and justice;
for your promise to turn our darkness into light.
We pray for places where darkness prevails,
for political prisoners who are away from their homelands;
for countries where people experience instability and exploitation
because of the involvement of foreign powers.
We pray that you will bring justice and peace to them.

Thursday April 7

Resurrection and new life
(cf Col 2.20-3.17)

'So we too might walk in newness of life ... dead to sin and alive to God'

The resurrection of Jesus gives us new life both at personal and social levels. But to experience this, we have to experience crucifixion. For Paul, this is to consider ourselves dead to sin: to crucify the death-giving aspects of life (Galatians 2.19). At a personal level, life comes through our negation of death-giving ways and through the power Christ gives. Many Christians stop at this level, but socially, life comes only through the voluntary suffering we accept for the sake of justice for the oppressed, exposing the power of evil and making people aware of it. This is what Jesus did on the cross (Colossians 2.14-15; John 12.31-32).

This was the experience of the Early Church. They negated the death-giving aspects of life and affirmed life-giving qualities: love, equality and sharing.

If we are willing to experience new life through Christ, we have to crucify the death-giving old order and affirm the ways of the life-giving new order.

✴ *Lord, we thank you for new life*
through the resurrection of your Son Jesus Christ.
Give us courage and wisdom
to work with you in giving life to others.

Friday April 8   **Exodus 14.15 to 15.1 ***

Resurrection and deliverance

'I will sing to the Lord, for he has triumphed gloriously'

Today's passage speaks about the great deliverance of the Israelites by the hand of God. What is the relationship between this incident and the resurrection of Jesus?

In the Old Testament, sea and deep waters symbolise danger and death. The Israelites are saved from the sea as well as from the oppressive hand of the Egyptians. The history of God's salvation is repeated in the glorious triumph of Jesus Christ over against death in his resurrection. Both events are miraculous triumphs of deliverance.

For the Israelites, God's hand meant deliverance from danger and death. In Jesus' resurrection, the early Christians experienced deliverance from death and so they were not afraid of dying for their faith.

Sometimes we find ourselves caught in a problem and do not see any way out. God in his power can open up a way for us. God wants us to work with him for the deliverance of others who are caught up in dangers of death. Christ gives us his power in our ministry of deliverance.

✴ *Lord, we thank you that you deliver us*
from all sorts of perils and dangers.
Thank you for saving us from death.
Help us to work for the deliverance of others
who are caught up in dangers of death.

Resurrection and witness

'This Jesus God raised up, and of that all of us are witnesses'

In his first sermon on the day of Pentecost, Peter says that the experience of Pentecost itself is a witness to the resurrection of Jesus Christ. For this he brings scriptural evidence from the Old Testament.

The Early Church was a witness to the resurrection of our Lord Jesus (Acts 2.32; 3.15). How were they witnesses? By their resurrected lifestyle. It was a different lifestyle, rejecting conventions. It was a totally different model both in terms of religion, culture, society and economics (Acts 2.44-47; 4.32-37). In the same way, God expects us to witness to Jesus' resurrection through the challenging lifestyle of the church.

✳ *Thank you, Lord, for calling us to be your witnesses, for martyrs who gave their lives for rejecting unjust powers.*
Help us to witness to the resurrection of our Lord Jesus through our resurrected lives.

For personal reflection or group discussion

What are the death-giving aspects of your community or nation? What would 'resurrection' mean for your people? Where do you see signs of God's power already at work?

ACTION

How will you work with God to bring the different aspects of resurrection to your community and environment?

CHRIST'S PRESENCE

Notes, based on the New English Bible, by
John Carden

Having been a missionary, first in Pakistan and then in Jordan, John Carden worked most recently with the World Council of Churches in Geneva, compiling the Ecumenical Prayer Cycle **With All God's People***. Many of the thoughts and prayers relating to this week's theme arise out of these and other experiences of the World Church.*

A sense of Christ's presence is best accomplished by regarding these passages as a series of pictures for contemplation rather than as texts for detailed analysis. All are instances of the power of the Holy Spirit, and indicate the manner of God's continued presence with us. Although the Bible passages will take us back to the Jerusalem and Galilee of the days of Jesus and before, we must constantly make the connection between the manner of God's presence in those times and God's presence in the world of today.

> *Lord, help us not to dwell too much on the past,*
> *holding you to the Galilean hills and streets of*
> *Jerusalem,*
> *but to know you more and more*
> *as present Lord and Saviour,*
> *risen, ascended and always with us*
> *through the power of the Holy Spirit.*
>> *Adapted from a prayer by Jean Coggan,*
>> *from Care and Comfort, by Kenneth Leech (DLT)*

Sunday April 10   JOHN 20.19-23 *

With the disciples in the upper room

Many will be familiar with the story of Brother Lawrence, a 17th century French Carmelite, who found that he could experience the presence of God in his daily work in the kitchen as much as in his set times of prayer. 'I do nothing but abide in his holy presence,' says Lawrence (in his book, *The Practice of the*

Presence of God), 'and I do this by a simple attentiveness, and a habitual loving turning my eyes on him.'

Finding themselves stretched to breaking point in demanding situations in Asia and Africa, a number of present day disciples of Christ sought to apply this experience to their day to day lives. It was this simple truth of the gospel story – that Christ still stands in the midst of his disciples, offering peace, joy and forgiveness – that led to the formation of the ecumenical fellowship called 'Companions of Brother Lawrence.'

Members of the fellowship, now more widespread, seek to practise the habitual recollection of Christ's presence; learn to 'close doors' on some activities in order to engage fully in others; recognise their need for recreation, time for reading, writing letters and for sleep; and rejoice in God's help and forgiveness. All of these, surely, are means by which we too may grow in the assurance of the presence of Christ.

✴ *O God, here we are, all devoted to you:*
make us according to your heart.
  Brother Lawrence, from The Practice of the Presence of God,
  tr E M Blaiklock (H & S)

Monday April 11   JOHN 20.24-29 *

Encounter with Thomas

Christians in the Indian sub-continent firmly believe that, following his encounter with the risen Christ, St Thomas made his way to India where he preached the gospel, cared for the sick and needy, and was eventually martyred for his faith.

For Indian Christians, as for countless others, the assurance of the presence and blessing of God upon all those who have not seen and yet have believed – often referred to as 'the last beatitude' (verse 29) – has been a source of great comfort and strength. In this assurance, Indian Christians have borne a rich harvest of service, spirituality and theological reflection.

In recent years, however, in the forthright tradition of their founder, Indian church leaders have been asking serious questions about the institutionalism of their church, confessing that 'Over the last 75 years we haven't had an encounter with the people . . . We have pulled out of society, we have recoiled. All we show is our institutions, and we shy away from a real spiritual encounter.' Prompted by today's gospel account of the encounter between Jesus and Thomas, does this not raise questions about our own encounters, or lack of them, to which we also should address ourselves, especially in this Decade of Evangelism ?

✴ *O Christ, we come into your presence,*
and how beautiful it is.
There is no place so beautiful as the place where you are.
Prayer of a Mar Thoma Christian, South India

Tuesday April 12   JOHN 21.1-14 *

By the lakeshore

A collection of tumbledown shacks surrounded by patches of dirty sand, and well out of sight of the royal palaces and luxury hotels, Sinbad's Sea Restaurant seen by day is far from inviting. But at night, under a full moon and a string of fairy lights, its sordid reality is miraculously transformed. And so it was for the Palestinian children from the School for the Deaf on their annual holiday trip. After a fish supper that night, we all crammed into a small courtyard. Sitting on the ground, with the moon above and the sea lapping at the door, they relived the events of the day. Then, using sign language as well as words, the school's director began to tell them this story of Jesus' appearance to his disciples by the lakeshore.

Hearing it for perhaps the very first time, with flashing eyes, gesticulating hands, strange noises – using every faculty left to them – the children responded to his questions and eagerly asked their own. What sort of ship had the disciples used for fishing? What kind of fish might they have eaten? How did Jesus get there? Where was he now? Here was an interest which we, familiar with the story, rarely show.

Such was the response that night of these so-called handicapped children, that for me sitting among them, there was no question as to where Jesus was now.

✴ *Thank you, dear Lord, from the bottom of my heart,*
for our food and our clothes, and for everything.
Prayer of a Palestinian child

Wednesday April 13   JOHN 21.15-19

Encounter with Peter

Pakistani Christian convert from Islam, Bilquis Sheikh (in *I dared to call Him Father*, Kingsway Publications), tells of an occasion shortly after her baptism, when, having returned to her Muslim family for the funeral of a relative, she practised a small deceit. This, for her, represented a denial of her faith, and resulted in her losing the sense of Christ's presence with her. Following considerable heart-searching she identified her sin, asked for God's forgiveness, and experienced a regained sense of the presence of Christ.

Thereafter, whenever she did not feel his nearness, she would search backwards to discover how she had grieved him, confess her sin and ask forgiveness. Through this practice, she learned what she called 'the beautiful secret of repentance'.

The exercise of the beautiful secret of repentance and restoration seems a good way of describing the event recorded in today's reading. Most commentators agree that there is some connection between Christ's threefold questioning of Peter, and Peter's earlier threefold denial; but suggest that in the reiteration of the call to 'Follow me' there is also an invitation to Peter to search back, and remember other earlier calls to follow, and to be thankful for them.

✳ *O God*
I thank You
for my call,
recall; yes,
and many other calls beside.

Lancelot Andrewes and Albert S Newton
from The Ecumenical Prayer Cycle

Thursday April 14   EZEKIEL 34.7-16 ✳
The presence of Christ in the prophetic imagination

'Shepherds of the flock of Christ, pay attention!' warned the leader of a group of ministers out walking near Jerusalem. They had just encountered an Arab shepherd preventing his flock from straying too far by means of a handful of well-aimed stones! He went on to say that in western Christian imagination, the shepherd's role has been sentimentalised at the expense of some rougher aspects of the job.

Writing from a refugee colony in Babylon to fellow Jews in beleaguered Jerusalem, Ezekiel no doubt had this picture in mind when he shared with his wayward people his vision of redemption coming as a shepherd.

One Anglican priest, working in inner city London, models his ministry on this whole chapter, arguing that much pastoral ministry today is concerned solely with individual problems, whereas that in Ezekiel's vision is God-centred. It is a ministry of public care and leadership involving the whole community, and sometimes calls for a few well-aimed stones!

Let us therefore quite unsentimentally apply the rough, rich imagery of the shepherd to ourselves and our community, asking in what ways God is calling us to exercise this ministry.

✳ *O Christ, great shepherd,*
come to us your sheep who stray too readily;
and by whatever means,
the voice, the dog, the well-aimed stone,
guide us back into your way.

Friday April 15　　　　　　　　　　　JOHN 10.7-18 *

A caring presence

I once looked after a country congregation in which one of the church officers, a farmer, sometimes came to his church duties straight from nights of lambing. Conditions in the lambing shed were often cold and messy, and he came after a quick change smelling strongly of disinfectant! Asked how sheep were, when giving birth, he replied, with a mischievous glance towards the assembling congregation, 'They are like people; some make a fuss, and others just get on with it!'

More often than we realise, our language in prayer and worship is shot through with references to sheep and shepherds as a picture of the caring presence of God. For me, the presence of that 'shepherd' – along with his wife, also straight from caring for the young lambs – invested such words with a practical solicitude, a comprehensive caring function, which I had not really appreciated before.

A house group recently studying 1 Peter 5.1-4, suggested different ways in which they might mediate the presence of Christ as 'good shepherd' in their neighbourhood: ways like visiting the bereaved and those in prison, as Christian listeners or Samaritans, teaching children and helping in play-groups . . . Think of other equally down to earth ways, and pray:

✳ *Thank you, Lord, for counting me one of your sheep.*
Teach me, Lord, to count better, like you.
　　　　　　　　　　　　　Albert S Newton, Montgomery, Alabama

A judging presence

For many of us, accustomed to hearing this familiar passage in the context of Christian Aid or other services of social concern, the words which speak of Christ coming as judge (verses 31-33 and 41-46) are often unappreciated. But for those who live in poverty in the bastis of Calcutta, the shanty towns of South Africa and the favellas of Central and South America, the promise that Christ will one day come as judge, and pass judgment on the awful inhumanity and inequalities in society, is a source of great comfort.

A young British volunteer youth worker among the alcoholics, drug addicts and desperately disadvantaged young people of the violent South African township of Soweto, speaks of how for him in that situation, the judging presence of Christ has become an essential part of his creed. Referring to the people of Soweto, he says, 'The only hope they can find is in God and in the knowledge that God is ultimately a God of justice, who empowers his people to bring about justice now, and to speak out and stand out for love and reconciliation . . . In that struggle,' he concludes, 'faith becomes deeper and more real.'

✷ *Lord, we pray that when you come to us in the unloveable,*
the despised and the wretched of the earth,
we may know it is you.

For personal reflection or group discussion

Imagining you are one of the disciples, read again John 21.1-19. What are your feelings? How does the living presence of Christ challenge you?

'Look! Listen! Care!' In what ways may these imperatives help us to recognise the presence of Christ in our sisters and brothers?

ACTION

Apply the threefold summons to 'Look! Listen! Care!' to the week ahead and discover more of Christ's presence.

LOVED FROM THE BEGINNING
(The book of HOSEA)

Notes, based on the New Jerusalem Bible, by
Sheila Cassidy

Sheila Cassidy is a medical doctor caring for men and women with far advanced cancer. In 1975, she spent two months in a prison in Chile because she treated a wounded revolutionary. For the past ten years, she has worked in Plymouth (UK), initially as Medical Director of St Luke's Hospice, and now as Palliative Care Physician at Plymouth General Hospital. In her spare time, she writes, preaches and does a little religious broadcasting. In all these, she draws deeply on her own experience of God met face to face in torture, in solitary confinement, in an enclosed convent and, more recently, in working with the dying.

If you are unfamiliar with the Old Testament prophets in general and Hosea in particular, 'tighten your seat belt' because we are in for a wild ride. The prophets were men 'drunk on God', seduced like the wretched Jeremiah, so besotted with love for God that they had to speak God's word, whatever the cost. In a world (then and now) which likes to keep God either safely in heaven or conveniently locked in the tabernacle, Hosea, trembling, found himself speaking of God as 'lover', likening our relationship with the Divine to a marriage. Even now we blush to think of it. We can cope with a God of wrath and vengeance, particularly as we usually see God's retribution destined for someone else. We have grown to be very comfortable with the image of God as Father and can curl up happily on his imaginary lap when the going gets tough. But God as Lover – that's surely too much!

> *Father God, Lord of the universe,*
> *stretch our hearts and minds,*
> *for we are only little people.*
> *Fearful and conservative, we seek a smooth path*
> *to a safe and cosy God,*
> *who will keep us warm forever.*
> *Blow our minds with your mighty word,*

so that one day,
we may dare to accept and return
your jealous love.

Sunday April 17   HOSEA 1.1 to 2.1

Yes. You did read it correctly. This passage does begin with
God telling the prophet to go out and marry a whore, a
prostitute, a 'tart', or whatever word you prefer. Before you
weaken and give up at the very idea, or get put off with the
peculiar names of his children, try looking at it in this way. The
prophet is old when he writes, looking back on his life and trying
to see the hand of God in it. Slowly, it dawns upon him that,
once again, God has written straight with crooked lines, and that
those bitter early years, when his wife ran off, have much
deeper meaning than he'd ever realised. When, despite his grief
and humiliation at her affairs with other men, his love kept him
faithful to her, God was teaching him an amazing truth: if he, an
ordinary man could love an adulterous wife, forgive her again
and again, take her back, soiled and disgraced into his arms,
how much more patient and forgiving is God?

✱ *Amazing God,*
how can you forgive us, again and again,
and go on loving us
through thick and thin?
Show us once more
the depth of your compassion,
for we are very weak and foolish,
no better than our ancestors
or the man or woman next door.

Monday April 18   HOSEA 2.2-13

Here the prophet expands his imagery of the unfaithful wife and
we are left in no doubt of his fury against her. We see not the
compassion but the righteous anger, the jealous love of God.
He will catch up with his prostitute bride in a blind alley, rip from
her the jewels and furs given by her lovers, wipe from her face
the caked lipstick and mascara which so mar her original
beauty. Then, surely, as she stands naked and ashamed, the
curb crawlers will see her and, mocking her nakedness, reject

her. Then, and only then, will she realise her utter foolishness and, covered by his overcoat, cling once more to the husband she has rejected.

✳ *Lord, we too are weak and foolish.*
We too have betrayed your love,
running after all manner of false gods.
Strip us now of those riches which corrupt
and our lust for power and privilege.
Take us back, naked and ashamed,
to the house of your faithful love.

Tuesday April 19   HOSEA 2.14 to 3.5

The words 'I am going to seduce her and lead her into the desert and speak to her heart' have always been very important to me, because of my own very powerful experience of God in the arid desolation of solitary confinement, and of loneliness in the convent. I have always believed that God does indeed lure his wayward people into situations where they are so stripped, that they are totally open to him. The mystics, I believe, would concur with this interpretation. The 13th century preacher Meister Eckhart writes, 'The more helpless and destitute the mind that turns to God for support can be, the deeper the person penetrates God and the more sensitive he is to God's most valuable gifts' (*Tenth Talk of Instruction*).

My scripture mentor, however, says that the desert here represents the Israelites' idyllic covenant relationship with Yahweh in the desert. This was before they began to moan about the lack of melons and pomegranates and went off in search of more comforting, less demanding gods. However we choose to interpret this passage, it seems that we are more likely to hear what God has to say to us when we are stripped naked by fate, or at least 'travelling light'.

✳ *Lord our God,*
trembling,
we dare to ask
that you call us
into the desert
where we may once more hear you
whisper our name with love.

93

This passage begins with a chilling description of a nation gone wrong: a nation where God is ignored, justice replaced by persecution, the truth by lying and perjury, fidelity by adultery, and kindness by violence. It is a country where old people are mugged, women raped, and little children killed. Pension funds are embezzled, teenagers corrupted by drugs and fathers misuse their tiny children. The streets are full of litter, the seas poisoned by chemicals and seals die of an unknown virus. In short, it is a description of our own and many other nations, for we are a weak and misguided people who have grown up to take for granted the plunder of rain forests and traffic in cocaine.

Then, as we hang our heads and wonder what we could have done to make it otherwise, we hear that, this time, it is not we who stand accused but the priests and elders of our community. We, the people perish for want of knowledge, for lack of direction; we are hungry for God, dying for lack of his life within us – and we do not even know what is wrong with us.

And yet, pity our poor clergy, rightly expected to be teachers and pastors. Mostly they do their best: they are only men and women like us, dressed up in funny clothes and placed upon what can be a very lonely pedestal.

✳ *Lord, take pity on your people.*
Give us leaders of integrity,
priests of holiness,
and open our closed and greedy hearts
to the searing power of your word.

We might be forgiven for thinking, as did our Victorian ancestors, that God is against sex. With so much talk of adultery, whores and prostitution, is it any wonder that whole generations of pious people have been led to believe that the human body is unclean and that the act of procreation is an obscene necessity for the continuance of the race? Not so! The human body is a miracle of God's creation, the temple of his Spirit, the work of his hands. God made us, body, mind and spirit, laughter, love and longing. God loves us with a passionate, a jealous and everlasting love.

What then are we to make of Hosea? In order to understand these chapters, we must realise that the prophet is using sexual imagery and the sins of our ancestors were not so much carnal indiscretions as the worship of idols. They found the unseen God of the theophany at Sinai scary, his demands excessive. Like us, they wanted security, a comfortable life and a God who would stay politely where they put him. They tried to confine God to the sanctuary, built splendid temples in the hope that he would let them alone, but God isn't like that.

✳ *O scary, wonderful, jealous God,*
forgive our mean hearted ways.
Give us the courage to worship you
in spirit and in truth,
and to love your people
as you have loved us.

Friday April 22   **HOSEA 5.4-15**

I suppose this is the kind of passage which makes people afraid of God. Here we have the avenging, the Shiva side of God, with talk of rending his people like a lion. I don't pretend I find it easy to reconcile with my own image of a God of love and compassion. The Bible is full of these difficult passages, for our God is a God of paradox, infinitely mysterious, far beyond our puny understanding. It is not that God seeks out fallen human beings to punish them but that, when we pursue evil, we alienate ourselves from God. By worshipping false gods of money, power, lust, and violence, we dull our hearing and cloud our vision, so that we can no longer hear or see God. I know this from my own experience, for when I have drifted away from God, he has become so unreal that I have forgotten him. The scary thing for me is not the thought of the wrath of God, but the desolation of life without him.

✳ *Lord our God,*
please hold us tight,
even if we struggle
and never let us go,
for there is no joy,
no life
without you.

Saturday April 23   **HOSEA 6.1-11a**

This short chapter is pivotal to our understanding of the nature of true worship. God states quite clearly what he wants of his people: 'faithful love is what pleases me, not sacrifice: knowledge of God, not burnt offerings.' In order to understand the significance of these words quoted by Jesus in Matthew 9.13, we must remember that animal sacrifice, holocausts, and burnt offerings had come to be seen by the Jews as a sure way of atoning for sin. They had fallen into the perennial human trap of thinking that God can be appeased by ritual. It is the same mistaken thinking as that of a corrupt politician who goes piously to church in his best clothes on Sundays and formulates unjust laws or fiddles his taxes the rest of the week.

This message is not unique to Hosea, but was a favourite theme of the prophets: if your worship is not an outward expression of your love of God and sorrow for sin, then it is blasphemous. Spend a few moments reading Amos 5.21-24, Micah 6.6-8 and Isaiah 1.11-20, and then try rewriting them in modern language:

I hate, I scorn your youth festivals,
I take no pleasure in your synods . . .
Spare me the din of your choral evensong,
the drone of your boring plain chant . . .
Find somewhere to live for your homeless,
welcome the refugee . . .

✳ *Lord, our God,*
forgive the way we fool ourselves
in our relationship with you.
Give us broken and contrite hearts
that will be acceptable to your holy justice.

For personal reflection or group discussion
Reflect on the images of God in these first five chapters. How does such a God speak to you and challenge you?

Sunday April 24   **HOSEA 6.11b to 7.7**

When we think about violence in Central Europe, South East Asia or Latin America, it is easy to cry out in righteous indignation at the barbaric treatment of their prisoners of conscience. Men and women are stripped naked and tortured with electric shocks, pregnant women are eviscerated and bound men dropped live from helicopters. Terrible as these acts of cruelty are, there is something even worse, and that is the quiet conspiracy that goes on in the offices of the dictatorships. Executions are ordered with the single stroke of a pen and carried out without question. But there is yet another remove: in the board rooms of the 'developed' world, politicians and businessmen play dice with the lives of people ten thousand miles away as they support regimes which please them and sow dissension in those which don't. The ancient world had its own 'Watergates' and in this passage, the prophet condemns, in the name of God, the ministers of state who scheme and cheat, with their plotting hearts 'hot as an oven which the baker need not stoke.'

✴ *Lord of justice, Lord of the poor,*
Keep us honest and cleanhearted all our days.
Forgive the many times we too have cheated
and fill us with your own integrity,
so that we may shine like candles
in a naughty world.

Monday April 25   **HOSEA 7.8-16**

It is not easy for us who have no exact translation for the Hebrew word 'HESED' to understand God's grief and fury with the Israelites. 'Hesed' is translated as 'loving-kindness' or 'faithful love' and describes the love with which God made a covenant with his people. After the pyrotechnics on Sinai (take another look at Exodus 19 and 20), God made a covenant, a marriage type bond with his people, that he would be faithful to them, be with them day and night, through thick and thin, if they would have no false gods before him and be just and generous in their dealings with each other. All this ranting and raving on the part of the prophets, this calling of names – 'you "half baked cake", Ephraim'; 'you "silly witless pigeon"' – is because the people have betrayed the covenant. Our God, the God of Abraham, Isaac and Jacob, is not a watchmaker God who makes his world, winds it up like a clock and then goes off to have a nap. He is a jealous God, possessive, burning with love. He cannot just stand by aimlessly while his people make a mess of their lives. Always, always, God is calling us to repentance, luring us into the desert, to speak to our heart.

✴ *Lord our God, teach us, we pray*
the meaning of covenant love.
Help us to be good to the poor and the stranger,
to make time for lonely widows and delinquent orphans
that we may be worthy to be called your people.

Again and again, the prophet rails against the idolatry of the people of Israel and it is tempting to say to ourselves, 'Oh, not again! What has all this got to do with us – we don't worship idols, we've grown out of that sort of thing!' The truth is, of course that we worship idols without realising it: we spend our money on fabulous four wheeled beasts with flashing eyes and giant sea birds with terylene wings. We are far too sophisticated to worship the giant lingam, that primitive source of virility, so we get our sense of invulnerability by speeding over road or water, hair flying, oblivious of cyclists splashed, or rowing-boats swamped in our wake. We do not see the trudging pedestrians, mothers weighed down by Coke and Ketchup, walking home in the rain to feed their nicotine-stained, workless husbands and broods of bored and restless children.

✳ *Lord our God,*
   what should we do?
   We cannot personally feed
   all your hungry or house your homeless.
   Fill our hearts with gratitude
   and help us to live more simply,
   so that others may simply live.

I believe that this passage is one of the most beautiful and the most important in the Old Testament, indeed of the whole Bible. I long to show it to those who see the Old Testament portrayal of God as a harsh, unapproachable deity, in marked contrast to the 'gentle Jesus' of the Gospels. Frankly, I think that kind of talk is ignorant and misleading. The Old Testament has an amazing wealth of images of God, so that we may begin to understand the mysterious and catch a glimpse of the invisible. In Exodus, we meet God as the scary, all powerful, mysterious El Shaddai, God of the mountain, who will brook no idol. In Isaiah and the early passages of Hosea, we meet the same God and, mind boggled, are introduced to him as spouse, as lover.

In today's passage, we have a wonderful image of God as parent, an unbelievably tender picture of a father looking after his child, feeding him, lifting him to his cheek, teaching him to take those first wobbly steps.

✷ *Father God, hold us tight.*
Lift us up on to your shoulders,
so that we may rest awhile
for the going is rough
and we are very tired.

Thursday April 28   HOSEA 11.12 to 12.9

This is a difficult chapter! It is particularly confusing because past and present are intertwined: 'Ephraim' (the Israelite people) is in trouble yet again for infidelity, and is likened to Jacob when he cheated his brother Esau out of his inheritance. My own clearest picture of Jacob is when he wrestled all night with an angel and emerged, exhausted and limping, to find that it was God he had been fighting. That passage speaks to me as it does to so many others who have to do battle with their God. Doing what seems right does not always come easily and we wrestle, weeping in the small hours, eventually capitulating with a sigh or even (in my case), an expression of anger.

What an amazing insight into God we are given in this passage: Yahweh, El Shaddai, the Holy One, the all powerful Creator of the universe allows us to fight with him, struggle fist to fist and shoulder to shoulder. God, who holds our very being in existence, plays with us like a lion with its cub. The priest-poet, Gerard Manley Hopkins, cries out in awe when he realises the significance of what he has done:

'. . . That night, that year
Of now done darkness I wretch lay wrestling
with (my God!) my God!'   *from Carrion Comfort*

✷ *O wild and terrible God,*
mysterious, powerful, beyond all knowing,
we marvel at your gentle patience,
at the unbelievable tenderness of your love.
Draw us, weary and limping from our struggle,
back into the safety of your embrace.

Friday April 29   HOSEA 13.1-11

This is a chapter of amazing power and beauty, so full of colourful imagery that I long to illustrate it. In my work with the dying, I am acutely aware of the transcience of life, of the truth of Isaiah's words, 'all humanity is grass, and all its beauty like the wild flower's' (Isaiah 40.6). Oh, Lord, how we fool ourselves: we are so pleased with our intellect and inventions, our strength and beauty, that we forget that all we have is a gift, ours on trust, that it may be taken from us in a moment. Our lives are indeed like chaff, whirled from the threshing floor, like smoke escaping through the window.

What goes wrong then? As Hopkins says, 'why do men now not reck his rod'? How is it that we are so blind, that we cannot see, cannot accept our creatureliness? Could it be, perhaps, because we are no better than our ancestors, that we too worship false gods? I am not speaking now of fast cars and yachts, of power and money, but of our personal image of God. Could it be that many people reject God because the image with which they were presented as children is no longer credible? What intelligent adult could believe in a vengeful despotic old man with a long white beard, manipulating his people like a master puppeteer? Of course they don't: they reject him and rightly so. But how will they fill the vacuum? What are they to put into that aching void in the depths of their hearts?

✳ *O wondrous, amazing, lovely God,*
beautiful and loving beyond compare:
come to us now as we stand bewildered and alone,
and fill our lonely hearts to overflowing.

Saturday April 30   **HOSEA 14.1-9**

In this final reading, we are again confronted with 'fire and brimstone', men falling by the sword, children murdered and pregnant women violated. The world of the Old Testament was just as wild and wicked as ours. Our ancestors were clearly very wounded people – but then so are we today, and I suppose we always will be. Is there nothing new under the sun?

'All things are wearisome. . .
What was, will be again,
What has been done, will be done again,
and there is nothing new under the sun!' *Ecclesiastes 1.1-9*

I suppose there is a sense in which all this is true, but it should only be a cause for gloom on a cold raining afternoon, or when the searing heat goes on mercilessly drying up the already parched and hungry land. For, if that is the way our world is, it is equally true that it is full of goodness, joy and hope. Like the wheat irrevocably caught up with the tares, the good and the bad in all of us is intertwined. We are weak yet strong, generous yet greedy, kind yet cruel, for we are men and women, not God. Yet because we are finite people, we can best understand the infinite God when he is described in human terms, or at least in images that we can comprehend. God, says Hosea, is like 'an evergreen cypress', the source of all our fruitfulness, the source of life itself. He is water in the desert, the sun that makes the seed grow; he is fire and wind, light and lover. He is father and mother, spouse amd king, a babe in a stable, a man hanging dead on a cross. He is the all powerful, the unimaginable, the unknowable, transcendent one. Yet he is also 'the one in whom orphans find compassion' – for me that says it all.

✳ *Father God,*
Lord of the universe,
we are orphans adrift
in an open boat.
We are refugees,
footsore and frightened.
Open your arms
and call us home.

For personal reflection and group discussion

Make a list of those things in your life which could be described as idols because they dull your sense of God's presence and the lifestyle God requires of us all. How can you begin to resist them? How much has your understanding of God grown?

ACTION

Begin to reflect on those aspects of God's nature that shock you and which you have still to learn to accept.

LOVE CROSSES BARRIERS
(The book of RUTH)

Notes, based on the New International Version, by
Eileen Jacob

Eileen Jacob has lived in India since 1952. She has served as a missionary, taught in a city grammar school and been super-intendent of a village hostel for girls. Having retired, she lives in Hyderabad.

From time immemorial, the peoples of Israel and Moab had been enemies. Though they were all descendants of Abraham, Jews despised Moabites, saying they were the progeny of Lot's incestuous union with his daughter. Nor could they forget or forgive Moab's refusal to allow them to pass through their territory on the way to Canaan. Cruelty and war had left a harvest of hatred and mistrust. The story of Ruth, though probably ancient in origin, possibly appeared in written form only after the return of the Jews from exile. That period was marked by a resurgence of narrow nationalism and religious fundamentalism. The author reminds the people that even King David had descended from a foreigner, and that, where there is love and commitment, good relationships are possible even between traditional enemies.

Lord God, we grieve with you
over strife and conflict in your world.
Help us to understand the causes and feel the pain.
Fill us with your love
that we may become channels of your peace.

Sunday May 1   **RUTH 1.1-14**

Today the Government of India's buffer stocks of grain do much to alleviate the effects of failed harvests, but still there are areas where, as in the days of Ruth, famine conditions force the able-bodied to migrate, leaving only the old, nursing mothers and the sick to survive as best they can. No doubt Elimelech's family was not the only one to take refuge in the unfriendly land of Moab. The refugees would have had problems of orientation, but were welcomed by the locals and Ruth and Naomi reciprocated by accepting their new neighbours, even to the extent of inter-marriage – a sure sign of true integration!

Naomi's loss of her husband and later of both her sons, even before they could give her the joy of holding a grandchild in her arms, must have left her lonely and insecure. How could three widows cope? Resolving to return home, Naomi initially assumed that Orpah and Ruth would accompany her.

As they set out, did she realise the problems they might face in being accepted back by her compatriots? Laws protecting the rights of foreigners were not framed without reason!

✳ *Redeemer God,*
your harvest kingdom of caring
is meant to be enjoyed
by men and women of every race . . .
Your love makes a stranger of no-one.
                                    URC Prayer Handbook

Monday May 2   RUTH 1.15-22

Naomi was blessed with two good daughters-in-law. Ruth's commitment was total. Her words to Naomi were surely inspired and find many echoes in the Scriptures *(Hebrews 13.5 cf Deuteronomy 31.6)*.

The many jokes about mothers and daughters-in-law cover an area often full of heartbreak. In some communities, there is almost a tradition that a woman should ill-treat the wives of her son. In such situations, the example of the mutual love of Naomi and Ruth can soften hard hearts. What role models do we copy in our relationships with others? How can we find better ones? In her depressed state, Naomi could not have been easy or pleasant company for Ruth as she learned new ways and adjusted to life among strangers.

✳ *Pray for people who have committed themselves to 'stay with' those who are bereaved or depressed, that God will help them to develop Ruth's strong love and courage.*

Tuesday May 3   RUTH 2.1-16

Any fears Naomi may have had about how her foreign daughter-in-law would be received proved unfounded. The townspeople seem to have spoken only good of the stranger who came among them and the women quickly initiated her into the merciful provision made for the poor in the practice of 'the gleanings' (see Leviticus 19.9 and 10). Ruth immediately grasped that this was an opportunity to make a living for them both and went to work with a will. Notice the respect she won from Boaz: his paternal term of address, 'my daughter', his concern to protect her from sexual harrassment and generous provision for her needs. And all this was undergirded with a sense of God's loving care.

How wonderful it would be if employers still greeted each other as in Verse 4! In fact, some of the salutations we use daily have deeper meanings. The Indian greeting, 'Namaste' means 'I bow to that which is of God in you'. The English 'Good-bye' is an abbreviation of 'God be with you'.

How can we help to foster better relationships in the places where we work? And are there equivalents in the traditions of your community to recognise and meet the needs of the poor?

✳ *Lord, in all our dealings with each other,*
  give us that 'human touch'.

Wednesday May 4   RUTH 2.17-23

There was another merciful provision in the Law – that of the 'goel', 'Kinsman-redeemer' (see Leviticus 25.25). The purpose of this law was to secure a relative's property for the family if, out of poverty, he had been forced to sell it. Boaz was second-in-line to fulfil these obligations of 'goel', but, as we shall see later, he went beyond what the law prescribed.

Naomi was delighted when she realised that the man who had been so good to Ruth was Boaz, their kinsman-redeemer. She began to dream of Ruth's re-marriage, of grandchildren and her son's name honourably remembered in Israel. Her heart filled with thanksgiving as she blessed God to whom she owed this fortuitous turn of events.

In most countries, the Law provides for 'ethnic minorities'. We need more caring lawyers to inform people of these provisions and stand by them to secure their rights.

✳ *Pray for all lawyers, that they may become more aware*
  of the challenge to help the disadvantaged to under-
  stand their rights.

Thursday May 5   RUTH 3.1-18

Naomi takes the initiative in appealing to Boaz to take action on their behalf as 'goel'. She does this by sending Ruth, in all her helpless vulnerability, requesting, 'Spread the corner of your garment over me' – 'afford me your protection'.

In Syrian weddings in India, along with the 'mangala sutra' which a man ties round the woman's neck, he places a saree over her head. This saree she wears later at the wedding reception. It symbolises provision and protection.

The nocturnal encounter between Boaz and Ruth cannot have been easy for either of them. But they had their mutual respect and social norms to guide them. Naomi, Ruth and Boaz all had concern for the welfare of the whole family and acted accordingly. Such family solidarity has been much eroded in the developed world. In developing countries, it remains strong but the prevalence of nepotism and narrow loyalties remind us that this good trait also has its dangers.

✳ *Train us in our families to respect every person, recognising each one's needs and our responsibilities.*

Friday May 6 RUTH 4.1-12

The duty of the 'goel' was to buy back the deceased man's property. In Jewish eyes it was also important that a man's name should be carried on by his descendants after his death. According to the Levirite marriage custom (Deuteronomy 25.5-10), the deceased man's brother was required to marry his widow so that the first son of their union became heir to the deceased. Since Naomi had no surviving son to do this, Boaz voluntarily took this as an added responsibility. Notice the respect Boaz had for the Law and the rights of others so that he gave the next of kin his opportunity to marry Ruth.

We can imagine the joy with which he finally received the sandal symbolising the transfer of the rights of redemption. The blessing of the elders must have crowned his happiness.

Marriage concerns not only the couple or the families involved. It is a social contract and a religious sacrament. Failure to accept this fact has led to the breakdown of many marriages in the West, to loss of faith in the institution of marriage and the misery of many children born of irresponsible or temporary liaisons.

✳ *Lord God, we pray that the sanctity and permanence of marriage may be restored and guarded.*

This story has three happy endings: the wedding of Ruth and Boaz, the birth of Obed and Naomi's joy in him and, later on, Obed's grandson, the great King David.

This book reveals an astonishing broadmindedness, not only to foreigners, but also to women. Notice verse 15! One of the blocks in the family planning programme in India is that many parents continue having children until a boy is born. In their eyes any number of daughters are still not equal to one son!

In the 5th century BC, Ezra and Nehemiah saw the danger of syncretism and set themselves to restore the purity of Jewish religion by breaking off all marriages to foreigners. The authors of Ruth and Jonah saw the danger of narrow exclusiveness and set themselves to show how much people of other races had contributed to Jewish life. Reflect for a while on how these concerns together are for us the word of God.

✳ *Forgive us when neat national boundaries,*
rigid immigration laws,
or thoughtless prejudices
make aliens of anyone in your global family.
Teach us, instead, to hold out a hand . . .
forge a true internationalism,
and make friends and kinsfolk
of strangers and aliens.   *URC Prayer Handbook*

For personal reflection and group discussion

Think of occasions when have you found yourself among people of another culture. What were your feelings? Make a list of groups to which you belong, (eg. sex, race, nation, age-group . . .) Are there other groups traditionally hostile to these? Can you think of ways to 'build bridges' between them? What guidelines can we take from the book of Ruth?

ACTION

Reach out in friendship to a person you have avoided because you feel uncomfortable with him/her. 'Stay with' him/her until God's love breaks down the barrier.

THE ASCENSION
OUR EXALTED LORD

Notes, based on the Revised English Bible, by
Simon Oxley

Simon Oxley is a Baptist minister who has served churches in north west England and worked as a university chaplain. He is a former General Secretary of IBRA and is currently Ecumenical Officer for the churches of Greater Manchester.

We have reached the time of year when we celebrate the ascension of Christ. For forty days after the resurrection, Jesus appeared to his disciples. Now the time for such encounters had come to an end. From the earthly Jesus we turn to contemplate the exalted Lord. The Lordship of Christ is universal. There are no boundaries of nation, language or time. Jesus was a man of a particular place, race and time. The exalted Christ is for all people, to be worshipped in every place and in every language. Wherever and whenever we are reading this, the exalted Lord gives us hope and encouragement to show the glory of Christ in our worship and living.

Christ Jesus,
we can picture you as a man walking our earth.
Help us also to know you as the exalted Lord.

Sunday May 8   **DANIEL 7.13-14 ***

All people need hope. If you are a people suffering under a long period of oppression or find your faith under attack from other religious or agnostic influences, hope is precious. The book of Daniel was written for such people.

These verses come from a passage describing Daniel's strange visions. They were full of significance in their detail and totality. In this vision, a person is brought before God in the heavenly court. The expression used means that the person could have been standing there either as an individual or as a representative of Israel. But the message of hope, which was desperately needed, extended beyond national boundaries to universal and everlasting sovereignty. Such a vision continues to bring hope to all who feel the crushing effects of oppression or who find their faith under attack from materialism or other religious sources.

We must see the value of this powerful vision for the people for whom it was written. As Christians, we have a reality to set alongside it – that of the exalted Christ. Unlike human rulers who have their moment of power and then are succeeded, the sovereignty of the Lord for all peoples will last for all time.

✴ *When hope is dim*
may the vision of the exalted Lord light our living.

Monday May 9   MARK 8.34-9.1 *

It was not a triumphal procession with banners waving, bands playing and crowds cheering, but a slow march with each step an agony under the weight of the cross. We are reminded that the way of the exalted Lord was the way of the cross for Jesus himself . . .and it is for us his disciples.

Talk of power and glory may make us think of Christ as a magician who will wave a wand and make everything right with us and our world. Or it may give us a picture of a conquering hero who defeats the enemy in a mighty battle and rides in a magnificent show of strength at the head of his troops. If these were true, we would only stand and applaud. Instead, Mark records Jesus telling his followers to take up the cross.

This is the way God in Christ works. In our world, the powerful live comfortable lives and protect themselves from pain. In God's kingdom, the way to glory is through self-giving.

✴ *All power and glory are yours, Lord Christ.*
Yet you come to us as the servant
offering your life on a cross.
Help me, in words of praise and acts of self-giving,
to reflect your glory in my life.

Tuesday May 10   JOHN 16.16-24

The death of an author will often put books published many years before back into the list of best sellers. The death of the person does not mean the end of his or her work. Our library shelves, theatres, concert halls and art galleries are full of life in the works of individuals who lived centuries ago.

Is this how we see Jesus? Was he a man who lived long ago yet whose story in the Gospels catches our imagination, whose principles for living influence us and millions of others round the world? That would be no small achievement.

Yet John offers us more: not the influence of a man who once lived but the presence of One who is always alive; no longer the human figure limited by time and place, but the Christ who would be for all times, all places and all people. The disciples will grieve, but 'the world will be glad'.

For this to come true, the disciples had to give up their exclusive relationship with Jesus. In which ways do we also have to face the painful process of 'letting go' in order that we and others might experience Christ more fully?

✳ *You, Lord, are beyond space and time*
but we tie you down in worship at set times
in special places.
Set our imaginations free and open our eyes
to meet you always and everywhere.

Wednesday May 11   JOHN 17.1-13 *

Human leaders often disappoint us. They proclaim their commitment to our well-being and may even make changes for the good of all. Yet in the end, we find them tarnished by a desire for personal glory, wealth and power. We disappoint ourselves in the same way too. What appear to be selfless actions are often motivated by selfish desires.

The opening words of this passage come as a shock – Jesus praying to be given glory. Is Jesus no better than other leaders or ourselves? As we read on, we find that Jesus is different. He meditates on the unique personal relationship he has with the Father. Look through the passage again and note the constant emphasis on 'you', referring to God. Jesus' glory is not for himself: it is God's glory.

Jesus also prays for all humanity gathered under his sovereignty and for his disciples in particular. If the disciples present with Jesus received hope and comfort from hearing his prayer, so may we. Try reading the passage believing that Jesus is praying for you and the rest of humanity in 1994. The glory of Jesus is not for himself, it is for us.

✳ *The glory of Jesus is the glory of God and our glory too!*

Ascension Day, Thursday May 12   ACTS 1.1-11 *

Luke could have placed the story of the Ascension at the end of his Gospel. Instead he finishes with Jesus parting from his disciples in an act of blessing at Bethany (Luke 24.50-53). Would not the dramatic account of the Ascension have made a more satisfying end to the Gospel and kept the whole story of Jesus' ministry on earth in one book?

In Acts, Luke uses the Ascension not as an end but as a beginning. There would be no more encounters with a human Jesus. The story is told in such vivid images as to make this absolutely clear. The Ascension opens the way for the gift of the Holy Spirit and reveals the exalted Lord. The story told in Acts starts from this point. All that happens in the development and growth of the Christian faith bursts out of a faith in a living Christ inspired by the Holy Spirit.

✳ *Lord God, may the power of the Spirit*
   drive your church into action
   and increase our faith in our exalted Lord.

Friday May 13   ISAIAH 45.1-7 *

God breaks through all the limitations of our human understanding and imagination. God is God of all time, all places and all people. Long before the Ascension, Isaiah astounded the exiled people of God with this message from the Lord: as Israel had no leader, God was using Cyrus. Other foreign kings had been seen as instruments of God's purpose before. Cyrus, however, was proclaimed as God's 'anointed one' (verse 1), a role previously only undertaken by leaders from within Israel and Judah. The prophet's bold claim about God's activity broke away from tradition and popular expectations. The passage reminds us that God is Lord of history and Lord of creation.

The life, death and resurrection of Jesus come as a climax to God's purpose. God's rule has never been limited by race and nationhood, in spite of our efforts to do so. The activity and love of God can never be confined to 'us and ours'.

Reflecting upon our ascended Lord opens up our imaginations beyond the limits of our place, our time, our people and our words. In Christ, the God of all time, all places and all peoples works to bring everything into that unity which is God's kingdom.

✳ *When we stand gazing upwards, bring us down to earth:*
with the love of a friend
through the songs of the sorrowing
in the faces of the hungry.

When we look to you for action, demand some work
from us:
by your touch of fire
your glance of reproof
your fearful longing.

As ruler over all:
love us into action;
fire us with your zeal;
enrich us with your grace
to make us willing subjects of your rule.

Janet Nightingale
From Bread of Tomorrow (Christian Aid and SPCK)

Saturday May 14   EPHESIANS 1.15-23 *

The passage begins with a prayer for Christians in Ephesus. Among other things, Paul talks of hope and the vast resources of God. He then paints a picture (verses 20-23) of the risen, ascended Christ sitting at the right hand of the Father. The image has a double message. It is a place of supreme honour. In human terms, the person sitting there shared the glory of the king on the throne. It is also the place of executive authority. Christ has been given control, not just of the church, but of everything. We seem to be able to control only small parts of our lives. Other people's behaviour, the world economy and tragic events all affect us but often we can not do anything about them. There are no limits to Christ's majesty and power and it is beyond our words and imagination to describe them.

How do we know that we can have hope in a world where many situations in the news seem utterly hopeless? How can we act when the resources of the church are pitifully small? We know that it is the Jesus who worked in our world and died on the cross who is the Christ in glory and this vision lifts us out of hopelessness and helplessness.

✳ *Lord God, give us faith*
to draw on the vast resources of your love.

God's unchanging purpose worked out in many ways in the past, but in Christ something new and greater occurred. The writer of Hebrews sets out who Christ is in relation to the Father and what Christ has done. He does so, not by the rational argument of an academic theologian, but in words of praise and worship. The passage quotes many scripture verses, poetic images drawn mainly from the Psalms. Perhaps it is only in the language of poetry and worship that we can begin to express the wonder and mystery of God in Christ.

If we are uneasy about the idea of the Jesus of the Gospels seeking supremacy, Hebrews tells us that it is the place God has given him. Later on (Hebrews 2.17-18), the writer sets before us the humanity and divinity of Christ, the status of Jesus in relation to God's unchanging purpose – loving power used not selfishly but for the creation and redemption of everything and everyone.

✳ *Exalted Lord, you show us the Father's glory*
  because you are as inseparable from God
  as a sunbeam is from the sun.
  Light up our minds and hearts
  that we may respond to you in wonder and love.
  Renew our vision
  that we may live to your glory in the world.

For personal reflection or group discussion

What are the differences and similarities between our understanding of the exalted Lord and the sovereignty of a human ruler? What can the exalted Lord do with us which a human ruler cannot?

The writers of the biblical material we have been reading used images appropriate to their readers. What kind of images and language can we use today to express the same ideas?

ACTION

Look for images of the exalted Lord in paintings, sculpture, music, poems and meditations. What is the artist trying to convey in each image? Does it reflect or challenge the image in your mind?

WHAT IS THE GOSPEL TO THE RICH?
(Christian Aid Week)

Notes, based on the Revised Standard Version, by
Janet Morley

*Janet Morley is Adult Education Adviser at Christian Aid's London office. She is the editor of the anthology, **Bread of Tomorrow – praying with the world's poor** (Christian Aid/SPCK 1992).*

Christian Aid Week is a time when many people in the churches of Britain and Ireland are engaged in door-to-door fundraising to support projects combating poverty in countries of the South. As someone arrestingly put it, 'rich Christians get out onto the streets to beg on behalf of the world's poor.' But we often live with a continuing sense of guilt, because we are privileged at the expense of the others, and powerlessness, because it feels as if we can't do much to change things.

The gospel challenges rich and poor in different ways. These notes are most relevant to those who are not poor. It seems more helpful to develop this sharp focus than to pretend that we all hear the gospel from the same place and with identical needs which are only 'spiritual' in nature.

God of the poor,
we long to meet you
yet almost miss you;
we strive to help you
yet only discover our need.
Interrupt our comfort
with your nakedness,
touch our possessiveness
with your poverty,
and surprise our guilt
with the grace of your welcome
in Jesus Christ.

Recognise God's priorities

Moses is someone who has grown up among the wealthy and privileged, raised in the court of Pharaoh rather than experiencing the daily hardships of his people. He has tried, in an impetuous way, to intervene to prevent a particular piece of injustice (Exodus 2.11-16) but things have gone badly wrong and he has fled to Midian. It is there that God meets him – but note that it is only when Moses actually turns aside to look that God speaks to him.

What he learns is that God is a God who sees affliction and hears the cry of victims of oppression, and takes action to deliver them. This is the nature of God to which our Bible bears witness – not a God who by definition exists in some spiritual realm, but a God who is revealed to us by a profound and passionate response to the realities of this world. Moses' own intuitions and clumsy efforts about justice are given back to him in a challenging call to make the hopes and struggles of the poor his own.

✳ *O God, we long for justice in our world,*
yet we are confused about how to make a difference.
Take our best longings and make them your own.
Give us clear minds to decide what to do,
and the courage to get on and do it.

Take a hard look at economics

In the ancient world, the Jewish Law was respected as something deeply precious. In this passage of ethical instructions, with its earthy and poignant details, one can see why. Verses 10 and 15 assert the dignity and rights due even to the poorest – the indebted and those without secure employment.

But in our world, there is no such agreement that there must be limits to exploitation. The rich nations, through our funding and influence in international financial institutions, insist that Third World countries must operate in a free market system, competing with each other for a limited market in commodities like cocoa and coffee. Meanwhile, we subsidise the production of food mountains and then dump them on the world market, further depressing prices for Third World producers. We also impose tariffs on manufactured imports, so as to prevent them earning more. Had rich countries simply removed these tariffs, developing countries could have earned during the 1980s ten times what they received in aid (UN figures).

The Bible is blunt and detailed about finance. A theology which cannot address economic reality is irrelevant and unbiblical: one which supposes that the 'laws' of the market cannot be questioned by the law of God is frankly idolatrous.

✶ *Instead of praying today, read the financial pages of your newspaper and compare assumptions you find there with today's passage.*

Wednesday May 18   JOB 24.1-12

Get angry

The book of Job is an extraordinary and passionate enquiry into what we can believe about God in the face of meaningless suffering in the world. It is a simple story about a devout and well-intentioned wealthy man who has always cared about those less fortunate than himself. Suddenly he finds himself flung into the actual experience of being poor, bereft, and ill – and his perception of God is quite different.

Always this book resists the arguments of traditional religion which attempt to explain how God must have a purpose behind it all, even if we can't perceive it. This passage speaks graphically of the poverty and oppression experienced by so many – it has a chillingly modern ring to it – and then accuses God of 'paying no attention'. We have seen, in Monday's reading, how hearing the cry of the poor is basic to God's nature. So here Job is effectively accusing God of not being God. It's blasphemous.

Yet strangely, it is Job, God's angry accuser, who is commended – not his religious friends who explain suffering away and 'plead falsely on behalf of God'. Which does God really prefer, polite and careful prayers or passionate ones which arise out of our sense of outrage at the world's suffering?

✶ *O God, give me the impatience of Job.*

Thursday May 19   ISAIAH 25.1-9

Find a vision

If the persistence of injustice makes us angry, what is the vision that keeps us going? Powerful visions of the kind of world God wants for us are found in biblical writings that emerge from the bleakest times in history. This passage dates from a time of crushing defeat, after the destruction of Jerusalem – yet the God who has always been 'a stronghold to the poor' promises a great feast to be held there.

What is so moving about this passage, though, is that this vision is not only for the poor, or for those presently defeated. It is 'for all peoples', and involves the destruction of the 'covering' or the 'veil' (some translations call it a 'pall') 'that is spread over all nations'. This image suggests that the present situation, where a few prosper at the expense of the many, is one that is deathly to all, including those who apparently benefit. We in the rich nations are also damaged by the way the world is arranged, and need this vision of a common feast to lift our sense of alienation and despair.

✳ *I invite you to step out of your gloom, citizens of the old continent: you have conquered everything and all you have gained is individual isolation. Now it's your turn to discover and regain for yourselves a sense of community with all human kind.*   Tomas Borge, Nicaragua

Friday May 20   MARK 10.17-31
Make a choice

This is a passage with which comfortably-off Christians have wrestled – or wriggled out of – for generations. We can all explain why it doesn't apply to us: 'it was just this particular man's vocation'; 'Jesus didn't mean the eye of a real needle'; 'it's attachment to possessions that is problematic, and anyway, giving it all away is irresponsible'. Are you convinced? Nor am I.

The man, who has tried hard to do good all his life, is as shocked by Jesus' invitation as we would be. But Mark notes Jesus 'loved him'. His later comments then, about how hard it is for the rich to enter the Kingdom, are not so much an accusation as a sense of the man's sheer pain in trying to choose what he really wants – possessions (verse 22) or community (verse 29).

And we, too, find it desperately hard to choose. For those of us in the West, we know that our high-consumption lifestyle cannot be continued indefinitely. Indeed, in recent years, the recession has hit lives here with the sort of impact that Third World countries have felt for decades. Can we not find a way together to choose, rather than be forced into, a different use and sharing of possessions?

✻ *Is there one major way you could reduce your household's consumption – by shared ownership, recycling, etc. Explore doing it cooperatively with someone else. Don't just give something up on your own.*

Saturday May 21   LUKE 16.19-31
Unlearn not to see

This parable is like those jokes which begin with someone famous dying and turning up at the 'pearly gates'. But it has a chilling ending.

Those of us who care about injustice often cast around to see what we can do to help save the poor from their situation. The Bible, however, has an old-fashioned interest in how on earth the rich can be saved. The rich man doesn't seem to have been cruel or deliberately oppressive. He just didn't see; didn't see the great chasm between them – in life or in death; hadn't noticed anything challenging in his religion.

The story is not about wrong attitudes to wealth. It is about the self-justifying and unseeing attitudes that wealth inevitably creates. We have highly sophisticated techniques for 'not seeing' poverty: averting our eyes from beggars; choosing not to live in or walk through run-down areas; staying in ignorance of freely available statistics; regarding economics as outside the moral law. Do we want to see? Or would we rather protect ourselves for ever from life, truth and salvation?

✻ *Lord, I am blind -*
   for I do not want to see.
   You promise to heal the blind –
   and that terrifies me.   *Neill Thew, Christian Aid*

Pentecost, Sunday May 22   1 CORINTHIANS 11.17-34
Live as one community

Today is Pentecost, the day when the Church celebrates its beginnings as a subversive, powerful, inspiring new community which turned the world upside down.

But Paul's letter to the Church in Corinth, shows how easy it is for that energy to be tamed back into conformity with the

117

conventions of society – especially those that relate to wealth and poverty. What exactly was going on?

In the ancient world, where divisions of social rank were strictly observed, it was nevertheless sometimes the practice for wealthy people to demonstrate their generosity by laying on a supper for all and sundry. There would be two suppers, however – a proper spread with good wine on the high table for the host's high-ranking friends, and bread and cheap 'plonk' for all the rest. Perhaps the rich people who were opening their homes and providing the bread and wine for the eucharist, saw the occasions as similar, and behaved accordingly.

So what Paul is furious about is that the divisive conventions of society are not being challenged, but the poor are still being humiliated. The Lord's supper should demonstrate a totally different way of being community, of being the 'body' of Christ undivided by rank or wealth.

✳ *A Filipino bishop has said that in the divisions of today's world, 'we embarrass the poor outrageously'. Pray that the Church may learn to live as one community.*

For personal reflection or group discussion

Have you ever been poor? Are you poor now? Do you have real fears about poverty for the future? Read again one of this week's passages and listen for God's word in the light of what you have read. In the light of this passage, ask yourself/ves:

- – what is hard to hear?
- – what is comforting to hear?
- – what are the implications for me?
- – what are the implications for our society?

ACTION

Find out about one issue concerning global wealth and poverty. Look for connections between your society and developed or developing countries as appropriate.

THE SPIRIT LEADS US OUT

Notes, based on the Revised English Version, by
Bernard Thorogood

Bernard Thorogood served in the Pacific islands for 18 years and then in London as General Secretary of the London Missionary Society which became the Council for World Mission. From 1980 to 1992 he was General Secretary of the United Reformed Church (UK) and since retirement has been living in Australia.

If we ask any group of people to hold hands and stand in a circle, which way do they face? Try it. They will face inwards. That is what we expect when we are bound to each other; the interest and concern are within the circle.

It happens so often with religious people that it might almost be a rule of human nature. We spend most time dealing with matters within the circle. The first Church in the New Testament faced exactly that risk, for they held a wonderful mystery in their hearts and could talk of it most easily within the circle. Every circumstance led them that way. Closed doors 'for fear of the Jews' were a symbol of their inwardness.

How could the Church become a circle, still holding hands, but facing outward? It is that transformation which is described in these readings (mostly Acts 13-15). We shall gain most from the reading if we think of our own circle of faith and ask which way it is facing now.

> *Lord God,*
> *we rejoice in the spread of the good news*
> *which began at the empty tomb*
> *and has reached all nations.*
> *Help us,*
> *in the place where we live,*
> *to share your love*
> *for the whole world.*

This coming of the Holy Spirit was exceptional. There are many other references in the Bible to the activity of God the Spirit who works in human lives, both before and after Pentecost. But this event was remembered as the key turning point for the group of first disciples. They received a new kind of baptism by which their faith was given courage and they were no longer fearful of the public or the authorities. 'Wind' and 'fire' were the closest the observers could get to describing the strange inrush of the Spirit. 'Wind' was energy; 'fire' was cleansing; both renewed faith.

The immediate result was the turning towards the crowds in the streets. They were as cosmopolitan as those we find in any great capital city today. Persecution, especially in the second century BC, had led to a migration of Jews all over the world. Having fled violence at home, they had found peace in new settlements, but their children and grandchildren came back to worship, speaking many different languages. The power of the Spirit meant that none was turned away; all could hear and receive this new word of God's grace.

✳ *Dear Lord, may we hear today your word in our own lives.*

Throughout his ministry, Jesus was teaching about the Kingdom of God: God's kingly authority carried into the life of the world. All his preaching took this as the text. Most of the parables pointed to the character of God's reign. Many false ideas of the Kingdom were common then, and are still common today.

Most of those ideas are of power and glory, the kingdom of authority and command, of victory over enemies. Jesus knew that God does not rule like that, as though God is another Solomon or Herod or Caesar. The first parable (verses 26-29) tells of the quiet growth of the Kingdom which is fulfilled at harvest time. We can take that to mean human lives given to God.

The second parable (verses 30-32) is about the smallness of the beginning and the greatness of the end. One voice, a small band, a little country – a world community, a great host of believers, a home for people of every race and generation.

✳ *Into the churches*
Into our praying, into our singing
May your kingdom come.

Into our hearts
Into our hands, into our eyes
May your kingdom come. Soon!   A Czech Liturgy, WCC

Wednesday May 25   ACTS 13.1-12

The scene moves to Antioch, one of the first centres of Christian witness. Here we are reminded of how mixed the first fellowship was. There were 'prophets and teachers' instead of one solitary leader, and they came from a variety of backgrounds. At least one, it seems, was black. The powerful leading came to them that two should be set aside as travelling preachers. Barnabas and Paul were old friends. Barnabas had eased the way for Paul to make his first contact with the apostles (Acts 9.27). They remained together again until a disagreement about Mark separated them (Acts 15.39).

It was an extraordinary challenge, to set out into the Roman world with a new word of God's grace. As heralds of the King, they were insignificant: no armed guard, no power, no glory. But the very first act of witness revealed a spiritual power which was beyond human explanation. Spiritual blindness became physical; it was a word of warning, an acted parable. Paul used very strong language (verse 10). Is that right for us?

✳ *O thou great chief, light a candle in my heart, that I may see what there is therein and sweep the rubbish from thy dwelling place.*   An African schoolgirl's prayer, URC

Thursday May 26   ACTS 13.13-25

From Cyprus, Paul and Barnabas visited the country we now call Turkey, which was then a group of Roman provinces, an area of hilly country with poor roads. A major part of Paul's ministry was located here, and young churches were born in the larger towns. We meet them in some of Paul's letters and again in the book of Revelation (chapters 2 and 3).

Paul began his ministry in the synagogue. We remember how Jesus began his work in that way (Luke 4.16). Jewish people had spread all over the Roman empire, so in the major centres they had their meeting place for Sabbath school and worship. Evidently visitors were welcomed and invited to speak. Do we expect that visitors to church will bring us a message which we need to hear?

The address began with some history, linking Jesus to the story of God's acts in Jewish tradition. Paul started with what was generally agreed, before moving on to what was strange to his hearers. Missionaries in many cultures do the same. This leads us to ask how we introduce a new and challenging gospel to our neighbours. What is there in our common experience which makes a starting point?

✳ *Help us, good Lord,*
   to find the way to touch the hearts of people around us.

Friday May 27   ACTS 13.26-43

One of the surprising things about the preaching and writing of Paul is how he refers to events of the ministry of Jesus. Is this perhaps because he had not heard many stories from the apostles? All the concentration is on the death and resurrection of Jesus. For Paul, that was the vital witness to God's love and power. That was the action which draws faith and brings forgiveness. His letter to the Corinthians emphasises this: 'I resolved that while I was with you I would not claim to know anything but Jesus Christ – Christ nailed to the cross' (1 Corinthians 2.2).

In this sermon, there are echoes of Peter in Acts 2 and Stephen in Acts 7. They point to the preparation for the Messiah in the prophets and yet the blindness of their leaders to recognise him when he was before them.

It is easy to adopt a superior viewpoint and think we would recognise him. But who can see God nailed to the cross? One of the Christmas hymns says, 'Veiled in flesh the Godhead see' and for many people the veil hides the glory. We are called to see through the veils of clothing and language, politics and customs, to the presence of Christ who is with us. Then, by grace, we shall be obedient to him and discover that the will of God is wonderfully revealed to us. That was Paul's journey from the Damascus Road.

✳ *Lord God, we pray that we may recognise*
   your goodness and truth.

Saturday May 28   ACTS 13.44-52

At this point, the difference between Jew and Gentile becomes a key. In Acts 10.15, the revelation came to Peter, who was wholly surprised by the voice that told him not to call profane 'what God counts clean'. Now Paul has the same experience:

his own people violently rejecting him while Gentiles rejoiced in the message. What lay behind this division?

The answer is: two thousand years of history and tradition. From the time of the patriarchs, lost in the mist of memory, the line of God's blessing was seen to follow the genealogy. From parents to children, within the same tribal pattern, the people chosen by God were known by name. They were the people of the Law, governed by the 'jealous' God. But through the centuries and the dispersion of the Jews, their faith touched many others, so that there was an outer circle of people who looked towards the holy God but who could not be totally identified with the Jews. So in Acts 13.16, Paul addressed both Jews 'and you others who worship God'.

It was these others who heard the word and were overjoyed, for they found a route to the very heart of God, without their racial origin or tradition being a hindrance. That is where we find ourselves.

* *Lord God, we give thanks*
that your word reaches people of every generation
and every human society.

For personal reflection or group discussion

Read again Acts 2.1-11 and 13.1-5. Reflect on the outward movement of the Spirit through the apostles.

Read Acts 13.44-52. Why is it that we find it so difficult to look beyond our culture and racial origins and reach out to others? What is the value of a deep appreciation of our roots? Think of occasions when this has helped you. When are we in danger of insularity?

Sunday May 29   ACTS 14.1-7

On they went to Iconium, where the preaching of the gospel caused trouble, as it had at Pisidian Antioch (Acts 13). Preaching – resistance – division – threats – danger. It is like the gospel narrative, for the ministry of Jesus provoked a threatening response. Why is it that the good news of God's greatest gift brings violence? Surely Christ came with the word of peace and the action of love.

The deeply upsetting thing about the gospel was the challenge it presented to accepted values, accepted traditions and accepted visions of God. When people had thought everything was in order, the gospel asked radical questions:

- illness – not a punishment for sin but an opportunity for grace;
- the Sabbath – not an imprisonment of our humanity, but a day of freedom;
- the poor – no longer the underdog, but the friend of Abraham;
- the cross – not the end of a criminal, but the throne of God's love. For any traditionalist (as Paul had been) it was a threat to stability and an insult to the sacrifices of religion.

We have no reason to expect anything different, for the gospel still challenges so much current thinking. In a world where wealth is so often the aim of individuals and of whole societies, the gospel still says, 'Thou fool'. And that is hard to take. Do we sense this challenge in our own lives?

✴ *Lord, as the wind and the waves shake our island,*
may your word shake our lives
and the ocean of your love receive us all.　　　*Polynesia*

Monday May 30　　　　　　　　　　　　　　　ACTS 14.8-20

'SENSATION AT LYSTRA' – that might be the headline. The healing gift which had been present in the ministry of Jesus and with the apostles was evident again in Paul. We do not find that it was frequent, not an every day part of life, but rather a special presence of the power of God. The sight of it in Lystra quite naturally caused great excitement.

The local reaction was to hail the appearance of the gods. Barnabas must have been tall and impressive to be called Zeus, father of the Roman gods, and Paul, smaller and more talkative, was seen to be Hermes, the messenger. Just as Jesus resisted the desire to make him king, so Paul had to turn people's thoughts away from himself to 'the living God who made heaven and earth and sea and everything in them' (verse 15).

There is always a risk that preachers gather followers for themselves, a chorus line around the star. It is a temptation in religious life which we have to resist. Preachers, even the greatest, are just 'human beings' who are called to point towards the only Lord. When the riot followed, all thought of the gods had fled and the crowd stoned a very human Paul.

✴ *May the Church and its ministers*
point away from themselves to the God who saves.

Verses 21-23 tell of the nurture and strengthening of very young Christian groups, for they were tiny minorities in a pagan world. Hardships were to be expected. This is a message of the New Testament as a whole, and reminds us that our faith does not promise success, wealth and security, but the presence of God in all circumstances of life.

Here we meet elders, the leadership group in each locality. The use of this name may be a memory of Numbers 11.16, where Moses gathered elders to help him govern the Israelites during their wanderings. Whatever name we use today, all local churches need some group to exercise care for the life of the fellowship. Do we pray for them?

The return to Antioch (verses 26-28) meant a report on all that had happened. It must have been an excited gathering that heard of the groups which were now worshipping in the Christian way. The climax of the report was the phrase that God 'had thrown open the gates of faith to the Gentiles'. This brought joy but also some dismay. The questions raised had to be dealt with by the whole Church, and that points to the next chapter.

✴ *We pray for small groups of Christians*
   who feel vulnerable in a hostile society,
   that they may know the ultimate security of faith.

This chapter tells about what is often called the Council of Jerusalem, a critical turning-point in the life of the Church. As we read, we remember that the followers of Christ were seeking a way that would be faithful in a new enterprise and a hostile world. The Christian faith had outgrown its Jewish origins. There were those, (verses 1 and 5), who believed that it had to be held to those origins. If that were to be the way, then part of the Christian tradition must be the Jewish Law; the two belong together. Verse 5 suggests that there were Pharisees who would welcome that binding together.

The gathering in Jerusalem was made up of apostles and elders, perhaps quite a large group, who held a 'long debate' (verse 7). We all know church meetings like that! Then Peter stood up to give his testimony. In Galatians 2.11-14, we read of an argument between Peter and Paul about observing the

Jewish Law. That incident must have been in Peter's mind when he spoke to the Council, declaring plainly that experience had taught him the freedom of the Holy Spirit who is not bound to the way of laws.

When we hold a long debate about the way of being the church, what are the most powerful arguments – tradition, logic, the Bible, good order, personal experience . . . ?

✳ *From the cowardice that dare not face new truth,*
From the laziness that is content with half truth,
From the arrogance that thinks it knows all truth,
Good Lord, deliver me.

From Kenya – URC Prayer Handbook

Thursday June 2   ACTS 15.12-21

After Peter's speech, Paul and Barnabas spoke of their experiences, for they had a very special concern for witness among Gentiles and the decision was vital for their ministry. Then, acting as chairman, James summed up. Which James was this? There were two James among the twelve (Mark 3.17-19), but neither is referred to as leader of the apostles. So many people think this person was the brother of Jesus, referred to by Paul in Galatians 1.19.

The speech of James is puzzling and there are some different versions of it in the old manuscripts. He quotes from Amos and he supports Peter, whom he calls Simeon (in the Greek text). The key verses, 19 to 21, form his summary at the end of a long discussion. Gentile believers are to respect just the minimal elements of the Law that will enable both Jews and Gentiles alike to live in one fellowship, sharing one table. Also they are to avoid fornication and so respect the Jewish ideals of marriage. Apart from that, they are not to be bound to the Jewish laws. Verse 21 is a rather strange addition, suggesting that the preachers of the Law have to be respected.

But the heart of the decision was freedom. All who came to faith in Christ could form one community; faith and not Law would bind them together.

✳ *May the decisions we reach in our community*
be generous and fair,
open to the future
and respectful of others.
So may we walk humbly with you, our Lord and God.

As we have to write the minutes after a meeting, so the Council needed to write its decision and share it with all the local churches. We are given the text of its letter and told how it was distributed. The decision of the Council was unanimous and it was momentous. If the decision had gone the other way, then the only route into Christian faith would have been the long process of obedience to Jewish Law: to become what was called 'a proselyte'. This would have led the Church to become a sect or party within the Jewish religion. For those who gathered in Jerusalem that might have seemed the safer way. But the actual experience of witness, the actual story of the Holy Spirit among Gentiles was wholly convincing. So the Church was able to grow. So we in our turn have to come to faith. And so the Holy Spirit teaches the Church.

✳ *The new word – can we hear it?*
The new relationship – can we reach out to it?
The new face of Christ – can we recognise it?
The new risk – can we take it?

All the joy of this missionary witness, which we read about in Acts, stems from the gift of the Holy Spirit. 'You will receive power when the Holy Spirit comes upon you,' said Jesus in a final message (Acts 1.8) and Luke, the writer of Acts, shows the effects of this.

But Jesus also spoke of the Spirit in other ways. God comes not only in spectacular events, but in the steady life of discipleship. The Spirit is the teacher who leads the followers of Christ to understand his word and his judgment. These first disciples were a very mixed group, constantly misunderstanding the way of the Kingdom. So they had much to learn. It was not their brilliance that won the day. Rather, it was the gift of the Spirit, God at work in their lives, that enabled them to make decisions like that in Acts 15.

The Spirit was also at work in the hearers of the gospel. Verses 8-11 speak of the power of God to quicken our hearts, to recognise right and wrong and so to see how the kingdoms of this world are judged by the crucified Lord.

✳ *Spirit of truth, enlighten us and cast out our delusions.*
Spirit of holiness, enable us to return when we stray.
Spirit of power, grant us courage to stand for Christ.

For personal reflection or group discussion

Most churches are bad at coping with dissent. Often it remains an underground heartache, unresolved. So Acts 15 is an important indication of how divisive issues are handled. Read it again and make a list of the processes by which the circumcision debate was carried out.

Read John 16.13 – the Spirit guides us 'into all truth', and that means we are not already there. What are the difficult issues facing the Church today? How do we recognise the leading of the Holy Spirit?

ACTION

● What are the friendships, the daily contacts or the special events which provide an opportunity to share joy and the challenge of faith?

● Find out more about the way your church supports people round the world who are witnesses in tough situations.

● Where do you need a change of attitude to be able to receive the gifts of people with different ideas?

PENTECOST 2
LIFE FOR THE WORLD
(ACTS 16-21)

Notes, based on the Revised English Bible, by
Maureen Edwards (Editor)

As the story of the Acts unfolds, the challenge to the Church to become a circle facing outwards gets more demanding and makes those who follow Christ more vulnerable.

As you read, reflect on the church where you worship, but also remember that you are a member of the universal Body of Christ. Some of the issues that affect other parts of the Body may not appear to involve you, but they do. None of us can live our faith in isolation. Even attitudes expressed in private conversations influence others: young people, for example, who leave home to work in other parts of our country, or of the world, carry within them the social and religious values they have learnt from home and church. Each local church can still be centres from which a new quality of life emerges to challenge evil and proclaim the gospel of the Kingdom of God.

Holy Spirit, move within us.
Speak to us and challenge us.
Break our circle when we close it tightly,
so that we can welcome and enjoy the whole creation.

Sunday June 5   **ACTS 15.36 to 16.5**

How difficult it is for Christians, like Paul, with vision and new ideas, to move forward without causing offence to others in the Church. But the Council of Jerusalem had given Paul the support he needed to continue evangelising the Gentiles despite the reservations of the first Jewish Christian congregations. He was able to affirm the faith of those who had already experienced the living presence of Christ and then cross over into new territory. Wherever he went, Jewish Christians would respect the decisions of Jerusalem, their mother Church, and be more open to the surprising ways in which the Spirit was leading the whole Church and catapaulting them into forging new and wider relationships.

Yet Paul was sensitive to the traditions and expectations of his own people and continued to show respect when in their company. That was why he circumcised Timothy before he could work with him. How can Christians who are impatient to move ahead and face new challenges today work alongside those who resist change?

✳ *Holy Spirit, make us more open to one another.*

Monday June 6   ACTS 16.6-15

When Paul left Antioch, little did he realise where the Spirit was leading him. There was plenty more work to be done in Asia but he was led in another direction. His plans twice over-ruled by the Spirit, Paul was precipitated into a new unplanned mission to Southern Europe! Notice (in verse 10) 'they' changes to 'we', implying that the writer of the Acts (possibly 'Luke the physician') joined the expedition at this point.

The change was dramatic. Paul must have mentally recoiled. From countries of Asia, which had large well-established Jewish communities, they entered 'a Roman colony'. Was the Jewish community at Philippi so small that it had no synagogue? The text suggests it was marginalised to 'a place of prayer' outside the city, by the river. The congregation was mostly of women. The first convert was a successful business woman, a new experience for Paul and his companions coming from a male-dominated society where the woman's place was in the home! But Paul, as well as Lydia, was being converted by the Spirit, as Peter was in the encounter with Cornelius (Acts 10.25-35).

Reflect on the ongoing 'conversion' the Spirit works in you.

✳ *Come Holy Spirit,*
come renewer of life,
nourish the potential in us all.
In our work and in our leisure,
waken us to fresh possibilities.

URC Prayer Handbook

130

Tuesday June 7

Paul's next encounter in this 'day in the life of a missionary' was a direct confrontation with evil. The 'spirit of divination' in verse 16 meant literally 'spirit of Python', the serpent at the oracle of Delphi. But awareness of evil in this incident was not confined to pagan beliefs or practices. The girl had considerable psychic powers – her description of Paul and his companions was really accurate. She was mercilessly exploited by her masters for financial gain. Paul did not merely exorcise a spirit of Python but, in the power of the risen Christ, confronted the more serious cause of the girl's misery. A matter of justice for the poor and defenceless was the issue here. Political detention on a charge of practising 'illegal customs' was the result. Roman magistrates were called in to inflict the punishment.

Child labour, including child prostitution, is still an evil to be challenged by those who follow Christ.

✳ *For Jesus there was no question of neutrality in the face of evil and injustices. We must begin to understand that there is no possibility of unity or reconciliation between . . . the exploiter and the exploited, between good and evil, God and the Devil, without repentance and commitment to the truth.*

*Frank Chikane, South Africa,
from Celebrating One World
(CAFOD)*

Wednesday June 8

The drama of the deliverance of Paul and Silas from prison has as its central characters the jailer and his family. The jailer demonstrated the genuineness of his repentance by bathing the apostles' wounds and offering of hospitality, as Lydia had done. His understanding of new life in Christ was perhaps reflected in the message he brought from the city authorities, that they were 'free to go in peace', an echo of the Jewish 'Shalom' and words of Jesus.

Paul's stand against the structures of evil, however, did not mean a quiet, ignominious escape but winning his demand for a public apology. I invite you to reflect on an almost parallel situation in a town where I once lived: a black West Indian Christian was not permitted to cash a cheque over the counter at a local bank without offering proof of his identity, whereas his white wife had no such problem. A church member wrote a letter and went with him to protest to the manager until a full apology was given. To 'go in peace' does not mean that we compromise with evil.

✻ *You revealed the power of your love*
 and your victory over evil.
 Break our bonds and set us all free
 that we may know that you are the Lord.
                 From Southern Africa, Oceans of Prayer (NCEC)

Thursday June 9   ACTS 17.1-9

It was Paul's custom to begin his ministry in any new area by going first to the synagogue. His own people were best prepared through centuries of experience, prophetic insights and tradition. He could begin where they were and hoped they would help him in his mission to the rest of the world.

At Thessalonica, he preached in the synagogue for three Sabbaths before the inevitable opposition began to grow. The author of Acts reminds us of how much Paul's message was based on Scripture and how much he focused, as Christ himself had done (Luke 24.26), on suffering. Suffering and rejection were the price Jesus had to pay for proclaiming the gospel of the Kingdom and it was the same for Paul.

Like Jesus, Paul discovered that those who 'heard' what he had to share were on the periphery of institutionalised religion. Who might this mean in your community? At Thessalonica, they were women and 'God-fearers'; Gentile converts to Judaism who had not accepted circumcision or become too bound by tradition. The tragedy in the history of all religions is that traditionalists are the most vicious opponents of change. And we do not recognise our own bigotry!

✻ *Word of God, be present with us now . . .*
 forgive us as we try to imprison you
 within our traditions.
 Our itching ears listen
 only to what suits us.
 Forgive our failure to choose hope
 or to plant seeds of hopefulness.
                 URC Prayer Handbook

The response of Jews in Beroea was different. They were 'fair-minded', willing to study the Scriptures and take them seriously in the light of Christ's coming. They gave Paul a hearing.

Christians too are guilty of reading and remembering only those parts of the Scriptures that suit their own preconceived ideas. It is so easy to take texts we like and isolate them from their original context. But in so doing, we distort their meaning. St Teresa of Avila, writing for her students, said: 'I do not require you to form great and serious considerations in your thinking. I require of you only to look.'

Reflect: how do you react to new challenges?

✴ *O Heavenly Father,*
open wide the sluice gate into my heart
that I may receive your living water and be fruitful.
                                        Prayer of a Punjabi Christian
                                    from With All God's People (WCC)

Paul's arrival at Athens, the intellectual and cultural centre of Greece, was another mind-stretching experience. He may have felt intimidated by the 'secular world' but made a brave attempt to engage in dialogue with the city's leading 'gurus'.

Paul could draw on his considerable Roman education in this dialogue, yet he did not have all the answers. Clever debaters soon detected gaps in his knowledge and weaknesses in his defence. They called him a 'charlatan' (REB). The Greek 'spermologos' means literally 'seed picker'. Rather like a bird, he was picking up ideas and words from here and there and using them without a deep understanding of their meaning.

Engaging in dialogue with the secular world, and other living Faiths, makes us aware of how little we know of what others believe and evokes a deep respect for the truths they have to share with us. It also challenges us to look more deeply into our own Faith, so that we may express it with greater clarity.

✴ *Holy Spirit, you lead us into dialogue and debates*
where our knowledge is pitifully inadequate.
Let us not shrink from the challenge
but make us sensitive to the spirit of honest inquiry
and help us to bear the pain of our own vulnerability.

Paul's address in the Areopagus had striking relevance to the two major philosophies of Greek culture.

Epicureans were atheists, who scorned superstition and showed a remarkable spirit of inquiry. They believed the world was formed by chance, by ever-changing combinations of atoms. There could be no life beyond this one, so Paul's teaching about resurrection immediately challenged them.

Stoics believed that God, the universal reason, was in all things, giving equality to men and women, slave and free, educated and illiterate. Unlike the Epicureans, they believed in the immortality of the soul. But the soul did not retain its personal identity after death; it was reabsorbed into God, the universal reason. Although their outlook would resonate with Paul's, they would inevitably clash over the nature of God and life after death.

Now read the sermon again. Reflect on each sentence and see how Paul relates his faith especially to the Stoics. Notice the change of emphasis. Most sermons in the Acts develop from a strong sense of the God of history and relate specifically to Jewish tradition. Here, in the wider arena of the secular world, the emphasis is on the Creator God, but with the same strong support of Scripture.

Do Christians give sufficient witness to God as Creator? In our witness to people of other Faiths, we can begin here, on common ground. We can be one with all who believe that the world was born out of the infinite love of our creative God, whose 'offspring' we are. And we will have a more profound sense of our equality as God's children.

✴ *Creator, Parent God,*
you gave birth to all that exists.
You looked with pride upon the potential and goodness
of all you created and continue to love it all.
Give us your perfect love that crosses barriers
to bring the harmony you intended for all creation.

For personal reflection or group discussion

Reflect on times you may have been dismissive of others on account of their Faith or ideas. Did you recognise their sadness or frustration when you did not listen? Read again Acts 17.16-34 and think of how you can, with loyalty to what you believe, show respect for the beliefs and traditions of others. If possible, get to know a person of another Faith.

Monday June 13   ACTS 18.1-8

A Filipino minister told me of how he tried to encourage some British congregations to engage in mission to their own communities, but how reluctant they were. Another ministerial friend had trained as a probation officer and felt this skill could help him and his church to reach out to those most in need in their neighbourhood, but the congregation refused to cooperate. Yet another fine Christian I met in Sri Lanka has worked on the periphery of the established Churches because so few Christians share his vision. He works for reconciliation, bringing together Tamil and Sinhalese farmers to work alongside each other and learn from one another.

We are just as guilty as the synagogue at Corinth, in today's reading, when we do not enter into God's mission with those who seek, in Christ's name, to touch the world with the life of the Kingdom, or when we do not give our support.

✴ *God of love,*
increase in us an awareness of the Spirit
who leads us forward across new boundaries,
that we may share the life you have given us in Christ
with all whom we encounter.

Tuesday June 14   ACTS 18.9-17

Paul must have been aware that his deliberate stepping outside of official Judaism would incur danger. While Christians remained within the shelter of Judaism, they shared the legality afforded by Rome to their mother Faith. The decisive break in Corinth might well have led, as it did later in the century, to attempts by Rome to punish those who broke its laws. That fear may have been the reason why God came to reassure him in a night vision.

Look back at verses 1 and 2. Aquila and Priscilla were victims of an action directed against Christians in Rome. The historian Suetonius tells of disturbances there in AD49, 'at the instigation of Chrestus', involving Jews and Christians. Persecution would develop. But in today's verses, the writer assures us that the proconsul of Achaia did not regard Paul's religious allegiance as a crime.

✳ *Lord God, strengthen us when we fear*
the ostracism or scorn we may suffer,
when others hear of our loyalty to you
and, when opposition increases,
give us staying power, in the name of Jesus.

Wednesday June 15   **ACTS 18.18-28**

Paul still demonstrated his lifelong devotion to the traditions of Judaism, this time in the Nazirite vow of asceticism. This discipline, including total abstinence, was traditionally a sign of protest against the excesses of developed society and a way of showing one's respect to Moses the founder of the Jewish faith. The shaved head was an outward symbol. Ironically, his completion of the vow in the Temple, some years later, ended in his arrest by the Jewish authorities (Acts 21.23-29).

Verses 22 and 23 mark the end of Paul's second journey and the beginning of his third. The greater emphasis here is on the development of Paul's mission to the city of Ephesus. But the eloquent, well-read, Alexandrian Apollos got there first!

And we get an interesting insight into the teaching ministry of Paul's fellow workers. As a Jew, Paul had been given a thorough grounding in his faith and scriptures. Having been taught by Gamaliel, one of the best teachers of his day, he was concerned that the gift of teaching be fully used to build up the faith of individuals and the whole Christian community. How well do we use this gift of the Spirit today?

✳ *Eternal God, you have sent your Church into the world to*
be the body of Christ: his love to show, his truth to
speak, his cause to serve. May we see our work in the
light of this high calling and serve you well.
from United Church of Zambia Praise and Prayer Guide

Thursday June 16   **ACTS 19.1-10**

Paul's integration of the 'baptist's sect' into mainsteam Christianity is significant. He was deeply concerned for the unity of the Church and its mission.

His ministry in Ephesus, which lasted for three years, longer than at any other centre, focused on 'the Kingdom of God' (verse 8). The Kingdom has wider implications than the Church. Think what this meant for the people of Asia.

Paul's ministry, however, was not limited to Ephesus, but the city became the centre from which Paul and his fellow-workers were able to evangelise and establish congregations in other towns and cities of Asia, like Colossae and Laodicea.

How much do you see the church in your village, town or city as a centre from which ministry and evangelism are developed to include the whole area or, as at Ephesus, the whole province?

✳ *Welcome:*
You have come from afar
and waited long and are wearied:
let us sit side by side
sharing the same bread drawn from the same source
to quiet the same hunger that makes us weak.
Then standing together
let us share the same spirit, the same thoughts
that once again draw us together in friendship and unity
and peace.   *Prieres d'Ozawsamick,*
Canadian Indian liturgical text

Friday June 17   ACTS 19.11-22

Is there a touch of humour as Luke tells of exorcists who tried to imitate Paul? Paul's authority brooked no rivals. He had genuinely won the respect of most of the province. The motivation for healing and Church growth must always be that the name of the Lord Jesus might gain honour (verse 17).

It is tempting to look only for spectacular signs of the Spirit's activity: miracles of healing, exorcisms and numerical growth and to forget that the Christian community is formed gradually. Paul's letters to Churches of Asia and Greece show that initial, dramatic growth is often followed by misunderstandings, the misuse of gifts, even idleness and a divided fellowship. Real growth is long-term and is fostered by patient teaching, discipline, encouragement and patience. That steady growth, such as became apparent in Paul's long ministry in Ephesus, is due to the power of God's word.

There is also a process of purification. In Ephesus, this meant a complete break with evil magic. Reflect on ways in which you, your church and community have been purified.

Saturday June 18   ACTS 19.23-41

Paul's ministry, clearly outlined for us by Demetrius (verses 25-27), caused many Ephesians to conclude that Christian worship could not be reconciled with that of manufactured gods. Yet the real underlying idolatry was materialism.

Reflect: how much does the quality of your worship and witness disturb the materialism of your neighbourhood or nation? It takes courage to suggest and accept a lower standard of living so that others may be freed from poverty and oppression and live as God intended them.

Notice how the town clerk (verses 35-40) exonerated Paul. His preaching was neither sacriligious nor blasphemous of the Ephesian deity Artemis. The charges brought against him had no foundation. The new faith was not a threat to peace. Paul had said and done nothing to bring dishonour to another religion. He had preached Christ, but he had not said, 'Your religion is nothing!' Reflect on your own attitude to people of other Faiths in your community or nation.

✸ *A Christian ought to make a difference. Wherever Paul*
went there was either a revival or a riot.

Wilson Franklyn, from the URC Prayer Handbook

Sunday June 19   ACTS 20.1-16

Paul went on his way to Achaia, revisiting churches already established and accompanied by a growing number of co-workers (verse 4). At Troas, Luke invites us to see the Early Church at worship – a typical service on the first day of the week, but beginning, as in Jewish tradition, the evening before. Worship, which followed the pattern of the first Jerusalem Church, contained three elements: preaching (verses 7,11), healing (verses 8-11) and breaking bread (verses 7-11; cf 1 Corinthians 11.17-32). Time did not matter. Saturday evening's sermon extended to the small hours of Sunday morning with fellowship continuing until dawn.

The raising of Eutychus has echoes. In raising the dead, Paul was following in the tradition of Jesus and Peter. Yet, was it not through the breaking of bread that life was restored to the whole Christian community?

✳ *Come on,*
Let us celebrate the supper of the Lord.
Let us make a huge loaf of bread . . .

Let the women not forget the salt.
Let the men bring along the yeast.
Let many guests come,
the lame, the blind, the crippled, the poor.

Come quickly.
Let us follow the recipe of the Lord.
All of us, let us knead the dough together
with our hands.
Let us see with joy
how the bread grows.

Because today
we celebrate
the meeting with the Lord.
Today we renew our commitment
to the Kingdom.
Nobody will stay hungry.

Elsa Tamez, Mexico
from Bread of Tomorrow (Christian Aid)

Monday June 20   ACTS 20.17-27

Paul's active ministry was drawing to a close. The inevitability of imprisonment and death was on everyone's mind. The farewell speech augured another 'departure', from which no one could deter Paul.

Paul's understanding of ministry was never trivial: he had shared with them nothing less than 'the whole purpose of God' (verse 27). He had done what he set out to do: to bring the gospel of repentance and new life in Christ to both Jews and Gentiles, teaching in their homes and in public.

His aim was to complete the task God set him, to reach Rome (Acts 19.21). Despite the threat of yet more persecution, the Spirit led him forward and he would follow.

✳ *Lord now let your servant go in peace:*
your word has been fulfilled.
My own eyes have seen the salvation:
which you have prepared in the sight of every people;
a light to reveal you to the nations:
and the glory of your people Israel.   *Luke 2.29-32*
      Nunc Dimittis, from Hymns and Psalms (MPH)

Tuesday June 21   **ACTS 20.28-38**

Paul had been faithful to the apostolic faith from the beginning and was concerned the Church should continue to be built on truth. Later, in the second century, Gnostics undermined the Church's understanding of the person of Christ. They emphasised the 'spiritual' and denied the reality of physical things and so undermined Christian belief in the humanity of the Son of God. Even in the first century there were signs of similar heresies developing. They were dangerous and their leaders were like 'wolves'. The only protection for the Church, said Paul, was a thoroughly sound teaching ministry. This was good 'shepherding' and still is.

Verse 35 is the only written source of Jesus' saying about the blessedness of giving.

The meeting at Miletus ended with prayers and an emotional farewell. The work would continue, and they would support one another through prayer.

✳ *Let's promise to remain faithful in interceding for each other. I shall ask that you may have strength, health, patience, and protection from conflicts and temptations. You can ask for the same things for me. And if it should be decided that we are not to meet again, let us remember each other to the end in thankfulness and forgiveness, and may God grant us that one day we may stand before his throne praying for each other and joining in praise and thankfulness.*   *Dietrich Bonhoeffer,*
   from Letters and Papers from Prison (SCM 1971)

Wednesday June 22   **ACTS 21.1-20a**

Like Jesus, Paul 'set his face resolutely towards Jerusalem' (Luke 9.51). The departure from Miletus was the beginning of Paul's 'journey to the cross'. It is as though Luke is inviting us to see how much it resembled Jesus' last journey. There were those who cheered him on and many who warned him of the dangers and tried to hold him back. Paul even echoed the words of Jesus in Gethsemane (verse 14). He had to share with the mother Church 'what God had done among the Gentiles by means of his ministry' (verse 19) and with them to offer praise to God (verse 20a).

✷ *Lord God, your Spirit leads me out*
to crossroads where choices are difficult.
When I choose the easier way,
you speak through people, known and unknown,
calling for help.
Their voices haunt and disturb.

You challenge me to go with empty hands,
vulnerable and dependant upon others for support,
travelling downwards to those of least importance,
for there you wait to be welcomed and accepted.

As soon as I get used to one place,
you send me to another,
asking me to leave ways that feel safe,
situations and people I know,
to go with you:
new places to live and work,
encounters with strangers, surprises and challenges.

And so I travel with anticipation,
knowing that your Spirit leads me in the way of truth
and gives life to all.

For personal reflection or group discussion

Read again some of the prayers by people of cultures different from your own, in this section and the preceding one on Acts 13-15. How have they helped you? What fresh insights have they brought? Are there others from earlier sections that have moved you? Consider how this wider fellowship of prayer may help us to deepen our understanding of God and God's mission to the world.

ACTION

The Spirit may have challenged you do try something new through these readings. Commit yourself to put it into practice.

WHEN YOU PRAY

Notes, based on the New International Version, by

Leta Hawe

Now retired in Wanganui, New Zealand, Leta Hawe has served in parish ministry as deaconess and minister within the Presbyterian Church.

Prayer is defined in the Oxford Dictionary as 'a personal communication or petition addressed to a deity'. This would suggest a one-way conversation. 'Friendship with God' is a simpler definition which indicates a sharing or reaching out to One who has already reached out to us. In creation, humankind was fashioned to enjoy a relationship with God: a relationship fostered through the practice of prayer. Many of us find prayer difficult and few would claim to be satisfied with our praying, but the only real failure is to give up praying.

> *Great and merciful God*
> *Your life is the source of the whole World's life;*
> *Your mercy is our only hope;*
> *Your eyes watch over all your creatures;*
> *You know the secrets of our hearts.*
> *By your life-giving Spirit, draw us into your presence,*
> *That we may worship in the true life of your Spirit,*
> *With lives moved by your love,*
> *Through him who has led us to your heart of love,*
> *Even Jesus Christ our Lord.*   Church of South India

Suggestions for further reading

The Use of Praying, by Neville Ward (Epworth)
Prayer, by Richard Foster (Hodder and Stoughton)

Thursday June 23   **MARK 1.35-39**

Too busy to pray? Or too busy not to pray? The predominant impression given by Mark is of a very active Jesus, incessantly performing acts of power. Yet, throughout his ministry, there was a steady rhythm of service matched by periods of solitude.

This time alone was spent in prayer. It was from this practice that he derived the strength necessary for his demanding role.

When faced with temptation or an important decision, Jesus prayed. For an example, look at Luke 6.12 where Jesus prepared to appoint the Twelve.

On this Sabbath, Jesus was aware, not only of the physical needs of people, but of how easy it was for them to see him only as a miracle-worker. It was tempting for Jesus too (see Luke 4.9-12) – 'If you are the Christ, give these people what they want and you will be guaranteed a following.' But Jesus resisted. He had come from God to bring people back to God. When the disciples found him, Jesus resolutely refused to be persuaded to capitalise on popularity, but continued to follow God's way.

✴ *Lord Jesus, amid all my busyness,*
may prayer always be a priority
that I may know and follow your ways.

Friday June 24   **MATTHEW 6.5-8**

The Pharisees were proud of their piety. Hoping to gain admiration and respect, they paraded their religious practices openly. Jesus was not impressed: these men were play-acting. For Jesus, prayer was something other than a recital limited to set times. For him, all life was lived in the atmosphere of prayer: communion with the God he knew and trusted. Prayer did not consist of the repetition of meaningless phrases which became a monologue and allowed no space in which God could speak and be heard.

There is a great difference between 'saying our prayers' and really praying. Those who persist in repeating childish prayers learned years ago, get into a 'stuck position' in their spiritual journey. As our knowledge of God develops, so our concept of prayer changes and matures.

Consider the God to whom you pray. How do you address this holy One? There is a difference between knowing God as 'Constant Companion of our way', and addressing our prayers to some remote deity.

Before praying, take time to consider to whom your prayer is addressed. Choose an appropriate form of approach and see where it takes you.

✴ *Gracious Companion of our way, make me more aware*
of your presence throughout each day.

According to Luke's account, Jesus responded to the direct request of his followers that he should teach them to pray. In Matthew's Gospel, Jesus gave his followers a different way of praying in contrast to meaningless repetitions of the superstitious.

Our familiarity with this prayer has led to a diminishing of its effectiveness as a pattern of prayer. Because Jesus was setting out guidelines, phrases are brief and simple. In its most familiar English form (without the later addition of an ending of praise), the prayer has only 52 words. Yet, for all its brevity, there is a completeness about its petitions.

If we were to pray it slowly and thoughtfully, giving adequate consideration to each phrase, we would be led into an enriching, challenging experience of prayer. Perhaps if we followed this practice, we would not progress further than 'Our Father'!

Another important feature is the order of phrases: petitions concerning physical well-being take second place. Prayer begins with an awareness of God's presence and leads into an awareness of the world's needs, of which our personal needs are but a small part. Is this how we pray?

✳ *Pray the Lord's Prayer slowly,*
concentrating on the significance of each phrase.

We are all learners in the practice of prayer. We are often hesitant because we cannot produce the correct formula and so delay our praying or totally deny ourselves the privilege of communion with God.

We may be frustrated by the belief that at all times we have to be 'nice' to God and cannot be honest about negative feelings. The Psalms provide an effective antidote: some reveal a person so anxious to tell God how things are that words just tumble out. Questions, abuse and criticism are hurled at God as well as praise (see Psalm 44). The Psalmist found, as we also discover, that God is with us in our darkness as well as the light.

As learners we make mistakes: we are impatient and short-sighted. Yet despite our inadequacy, our pain, our lack of faith and inarticulate attempts to pray, the Spirit communicates our deepest needs for us 'with sighs too deep for words' (RSV). And we have the assurance of a wise God, who desires our well-being and answers according to what is best.

✻ *In everything, by prayer and petition, with thanksgiving, present your requests to God.* (Philippians 4.6)

For personal reflection or group discussion

Read again Matthew 6.5-18. Has familiarity robbed us of the full significance of this prayer? How can it become a guide to other prayer? Many of us are aware of failure and inadequacy in prayer. How can we be sure that 'practice makes perfect'?

Monday June 27   ACTS 4.23-31

Jesus had not promised Peter and John a trouble-free existence, so it was inevitable that, filled with new life and enthusiasm, they should encounter opposition. They were imprisoned and brought before the Sanhedrin, but refused to be silenced. Fearing the reaction of the people if the apostles were given further punishment, the authorities let them go.

When the men went back to their friends, they burst into a hymn of praise and thanksgiving to the great Creator God. They did not blame God for their situation, but saw it within the context of God's total plan. Their praise ended with the petition that they be given power to speak out with even more boldness and do greater things than before. In this context we see the Church at prayer.

God honoured their prayer, equipping the apostles for the ministry to which they had been called. This has always been God's way. Those who are called, God also equips, making them more than adequate for service. Many a person has marvelled at this gracious provision of God, changing a timid doubting follower into a fearless servant.

✻ *God, you call us to serve you in the world.*
We ask not for tasks equal to our strength,
but for strength equal to our tasks.

Solomon, having built the Temple, had fulfilled the promise made by God to his father David. The emphasis in his prayer of praise was not on his own achievements, but on God's faithfulness. This is not to suggest that the completion of the Temple brought no sense of satisfaction to Solomon, but he recognised that he owed his participation in the project to the working out of God's plan for the people of God. The praise and the glory were due to God. With the rapid advance of technology today, it is much more common to echo Shakespeare's sentiments: 'What a piece of work is man!'

Our awareness of being co-workers with God is often lacking in our attitudes and prayers. We are so anxious and impatient to present our petitions that time and thought are rarely given to praise God who makes all progress possible.

To seek God for what God is, and not for any benefits we may receive, reveals a greater maturity in our praying. Our thoughts are to be wholly of God's being and nature.

✷ *The Lord is faithful to all his promises*
   and loving toward all he has made.   *Psalm 145.13*
   To this God, bring your prayers.

Solomon was a realist. He acknowledged that his people stood under the judgment and mercy of God. He knew they were not perfect: they would sin and suffer in consequence. This sin would destroy the relationship God had intended and made possible in creation. Restoration of this relationship would require genuine repentance from the people and mercy expressed in forgiveness from God.

Using material from 1 Kings, the writer of Chronicles gives an account of Solomon's prayer and goes on to add proof that God hears and answers. God promises to a repentant people forgiveness of their sin and wholeness to their land (2 Chronicles 7.14).

Solomon sets before us the responsibility to pray for our nation. We do not readily accept or acknowledge our part in the common sin of humanity. Yet, we cannot stand aloof or simply condemn the sins of others. By our own misdeeds and by failing to oppose wrongs and injustices, we have contributed to the sin of our people.

We should not despair of any situation. There is hope for all in the grace and mercy of God who forgives and heals.

✳ *God, as I have contributed*
to the brokenness of this people,
enable me to work toward its healing.

Thursday June 30   1 KINGS 8.54-61

Solomon played many roles – king, builder, priest. Some of us might consider it strange today if a ruler invoked God's blessing upon his or her people. Apart from a brief 'God bless you all', we rarely hear a nation's leader making any specific reference to God. Nor do we hear them urging their people to live according to God's ways.

'God bless you' is a phrase that through frequent and often careless use has lost a good deal of its meaning and significance. I remember with gratitude a Christian doctor who often concluded the appointment with a sincere 'God bless you'. I valued that blessing as much as any prescription I received.

As Solomon stood before his people, he asked for the presence of God. But is not God always with us, whether we recognise that fact or not? There may be times when we feel God is silent or absent. What we need is an awareness of the unfailing divine presence.

The Psalm writers were familiar with such feelings. Usually, as they struggled with their questions and doubts, they recalled the past faithfulness of God and, in their remembering, found reason for hope and confidence.

✳ *Read Psalm 139.1-11 and affirm the presence of God*
who is with you always and everywhere.

Friday July 1   DANIEL 9.4-19

Daniel was concerned that his people's wrongdoing had brought not only suffering and destruction upon them, but dishonour to God. Every sin committed has a flow-on effect. Our lives are spoilt, other people are hurt and God's plan for the well-being of all humankind is thwarted. And, whether we recognise it or not, our lives, actions and attitudes influence the way people regard God. God is judged by what people perceive in us.

Daniel was specific in his praying, acknowledging the disobedience, wickedness and rebellion of his people. He did not blame God for the calamities that befell them or make excuses for their sin. He accepted that a righteous God must judge and punish people.

Daniel also knew God to be a God of mercy, and this gave him confidence and hope as he prayed with urgency for his people.

✳ *Lord, you placed me in the world*
to live in community.
Thus you taught me to love,
to share in life,
to struggle for bread and for justice,
your truth incarnate in my life.
So be it, Jesus.　　　　*Peggy M de Cuehlo, Uruguay © CCA*

Saturday July 2　　　　　　　　　　EPHESIANS 1.3-14

Prayer is not confined to special times and places. All that we do or say can arise out of a prayerful approach to everything that happens. These verses from Paul's letter read like that. He praises God for every blessing. From an inexhaustible reservoir of rich resources, God gives to us all that is necessary for our salvation.

● God has chosen us and given each of us a new value as children of God.

● We are chosen to be holy and blameless, recognisably different by the way we live.

● We are delivered from sin through the death of Christ. Powerless to improve ourselves, we need a power beyond ourselves to set us free from habits that enslave.

● The cross of Christ is a constant reminder of the greatness of God's unmerited love which we call grace. That such grace is costly cannot be denied.

● The life which we now experience through the mercy of God is but a foretaste of something far greater which we will share with all God's people and the earth itself.

✳ *Most generous God,*
may I treasure the gifts of your grace.
May all my living be a thank-offering.

Many a person has given up praying because of 'unanswered prayer'. While it is true that much of our praying consists of petition and intercession, there is more to prayer than this. Prayer could be described as 'sharing with a trusted friend'. But our friends would soon doubt the genuineness of our friendship if we only approached them to ask for something. Time spent in each other's company should deepen friendship and increase mutual understanding and appreciation.

Prayers of adoration and thanksgiving require no answer. Confession finds answer in the assurance of forgiveness. But why is it that when we pray for peace, people die and wars and violence continue? God grieves with us but waves no magic wand to take away pain or change human greed and lust for power. When we pray for healing for a loved one and see no signs of physical healing, we may become aware of a new spirit of acceptance, a desire to glorify God through the illness. Prayer does not prevent suffering but provides all that is necessary to triumph in the midst of trial.

✳ *Compassionate God,*
may I find your grace sufficient in my weakness
and your wisdom greater than my asking.

Here is another passage where Paul writes from his prayers for this church.

In common with most people, my life has been a mixture of joy and sadness, of good times and bad. While there were experiences that I would not have chosen, I am grateful for all they taught me and brought to me. To be assured of the prayers of others and the strengthening presence of God, brought courage and confidence and was an enriching experience. Had life been all sunshine and no shadows, I would lack understanding of the difficulties others experience and would be unable to empathise with them.

In the midst of personal suffering, some people are disappointed and hurt by the reaction of those who, because they have little experience of life's hardships, lack understanding and sensitivity.

Rather than pray only that we or others be delivered from trouble, we sould seek the spirit of positive acceptance and an awareness of the comforting presence of God. We can be sure that God will give all that is necessary for us to cope with whatever life brings. This gift of God is not ours to keep, but to share with others in similar circumstances.

✴ *God of love, you watch with all who weep or worry.*
You offer hope to those in despair
and your calming presence to the troubled.
Give us peace.

Tuesday July 5   JOHN 17.13-19

Jesus had lived life fully and been subjected to all the pressures life can bring. He had to cope with temptation, criticism, rejection, threats and danger. He knew that those to whom he was committing his work would face the same trials. It would be easy for them to seek a quiet life, away from conflict and confrontation. Jesus understood this, so his prayers were specific and practical. He did not simply pray, 'Bless them', as we tend to do.

If we are to pray for others in a meaningful way, we need to understand something of their circumstances and needs. This is not to imply that God is not mindful of them or ignorant of their situation. In our intercessions we are sharing the concerns of the Spirit and offering ourselves through Christ for the working out of God's will for the world and its peoples.

Self-offering is an integral part of our praying. While we may not be able to do more in a practical way to help the person or country for whom we pray, we may find ourselves led into a deeper trust and greater compassion. Through this fellowship of prayer, we and those for whom we pray are greatly enriched.

✴ *Assured that God's love encircles all,*
share your concerns with God.

Wednesday July 6   JOHN 17.20-26

Throughout his ministry, Jesus extended the horizons of care far beyond limits generally accepted by the religious of his day. Because his living and praying were not separate entities, there was no hint of narrowness in his praying. Jesus was not content to pray only for those known to him but included future generations who would be reached through the apostles' ministry.

If we believe that God's love reaches out to all, our praying should reflect this. This is not to suggest that every person, situation or worthy cause should feature in each of our prayers, or that we should feel guilty if we miss some. Each of us will hold certain people and causes within the scope of our love and concern and will naturally include these in our prayers. Others will be mindful of other issues and people. Together we share the wider concerns of God.

Some may find it helpful to follow a basic scheme of prayer, which will ensure remembrance of particular people, countries and issues but is flexible enough to include new crises that may arise. As our knowledge and understanding of God develops, so our praying 'edges' will be extended.

✳ *Lord God,*
we believe that your revelation comes to every nation in its real and concrete situation;
Help us to see you more clearly in our tradition and culture.
Lord God, we believe that you have called us to be your hands and feet in this land.
Help us to be living witnesses of your love and grace to all people.
Lord God, we believe you are the king of the universe. May your justice and peace reign among us.

Charles Klagba, Togo
from Oceans of Prayer (NCEC)

For personal reflection or group discussion

Read again the prayers of Solomon in 1 Kings 8. What impresses you most about them?

Are we expecting God to do something we are unwilling to do?

How can prayer become an offering of ourselves to be channels of God's love and healing to those for whom we pray?

ACTION

As a guide to praying, write a paraphrase of the Lord's Prayer.

TRUE HAPPINESS
(MATTHEW 5.1-12)

Notes, based on the Revised English Bible, by
Donald Hilton

Donald Hilton is the Moderator of the Yorkshire Province of the United Reformed Church and Moderator of the General Assembly of the URC for 1993/94. He has written several study books and compiled anthologies for Christian Education and worship, all published by the NCEC.

In Matthew 5.1-12, after a brief introduction, we are offered eight short sayings by Jesus. A ninth saying is added in a different form. Because each one begins 'Blessed . . .', they are known as 'the beatitudes'. Each saying has two parts: one describes who is blessed; the other tells us why they are blessed.

They describe an 'upside-down world' in which people who are usually ignored or scorned are honoured and valued. But they also describe the life-style Jesus followed – and he was one of the most truly happy people the world has known. The beatitudes in fact describe the world 'the right way up', – the way God intends it to be. It is our present world of self-assertion, greed and injustice that is 'upside-down'.

These notes offer material to help you reflect on the beatitudes. Follow the same pattern each day:

- read the given verse and spend a time silently reflecting on its meaning for you;

- then read the poetry or prose quotations and reflect again;

- end with the prayer given for the day.

> *Eternal God, make us more critically aware*
> *of ourselves and the society in which we live,*
> *that our deepest attitudes may reflect*
> *more of the ways of Jesus.*

Thursday July 7　　　　　　　　　　　　　**MATTHEW 5.1-3**

Jesus withdrew from the crowds and gathered a smaller group of disciples around him. The beatitudes were for the inner circle of believers. This upside-down world of Jesus will never be popular, and even committed disciples struggle to live by it.

'In spirit' probably means 'voluntarily' or 'willingly'. True happiness comes to those who put loyalty to Jesus before wealth and possessions.

'After my husband died, I offered for the ministry. I had no money. People asked, "Who is going to support you?" I said, "The God who had given me pap and water. He won't change his promise".'   *Victoria Mamane, South Africa, from*
Mission in Christs Way (Methodist Church Overseas Division)

One's value is not in what one has,
but in what one is.   *Oscar Romero*

Romero, archbishop of San Salvador, spoke against the oppressive regime in his country. He was assassinated in 1980 whilst preaching.

✳ *Journeying God,*
pitch your tent with mine
so that I may not become deterred
by hardship, strangeness, doubt.
Show me the movement I must make
 toward a wealth not dependent on possessions
 toward a wisdom not based on books
 toward a strength not bolstered by might
 toward a God not confined to heaven
but scandalously earthed, poor, unrecognized...

help me to find myself
as I walk in others' shoes.   Kate Compston
from Bread of Tomorrow (Christian Aid/SPCK)

Friday July 8   **MATTHEW 5.4**

If there is not a place where tears are understood,
  Where can I go to cry?
If there is not a place where questions can be asked,
  Where do I go to seek?
If there is not a place where my feelings can be heard,
  Where do I go to speak?
If there is not a place where I can try and learn and grow,
  Where can I just be me?   *Anon*

Thank God for tears,
the tears that flow unchecked,
that run in rivulets
down to the sea of God;
that have to merge eventually
with something larger than the self.

Thank God for tears,
the tears that bring release
for knotted nerves
twisted as sinews,
bringing a breathing out
beyond despair.

Thank God for tears,
and then beyond the tears,
beyond the hopelessness
that has to offer up the grief
till no more fall,
because no more can fall -

the tiny step that is a journey's start,
a slow step onward,
numb at first and seeming dead,
where haltingly, but gradually
one grassblade starts to grow
watered by tears;
somehow a kind of healing can begin. © *Cecily Taylor*
from Liturgy of Life (NCEC)

✳ *Lord, forbid me the luxury of selfish tears*
but let the tears I shed for others
release me for service to those cast down by life.

Saturday July 9   MATTHEW 5.5

Explorers, adventurers and governments have seized land to gain power. The strong have violently possessed the earth with money or blood. But there are gentler ways of thinking about land:

Whatever befalls the earth befalls the sons of the earth. If men spit on the ground, they spit on themselves. This we know – the earth does not belong to man, man belongs to the earth. All things are connected like the blood which unites one family. Whatever befalls the earth befalls the sons of the earth. Man did not weave the web of life; he is merely a strand in it. Whatever he does to the web he does to himself. *Chief Seathl, American Indian (1855)*

To us the land is a living thing
The land is our mother.
It is the source of our existence,
our religion, our identity.
To us land is a living thing.
We are part of it
and it is part of us.   *An Australian Aborigine*

✳ **Lord of creation, let me not so much possess the earth,**
   as live in harmony with it;
   not so much live on it, as live with it.

Sunday July 10   MATTHEW 5.6

*Fasting was thought to be like prayer. Those hungering and
thirsting for right thus longed for God's rule on earth. Hungry
prayers are answered.*

We, the people of South Africa, declare for all our country and
the world to know: that South Africa belongs to all who live in it,
black and white, and that no government can justly claim
authority unless it is based on the will of all the people . . .
All shall be equal before the law!
All shall enjoy equal human rights!
There shall be work and security!
The doors of learning and of culture shall be opened! . . .
There shall be peace and friendship!
                    From the Freedom Charter, South Africa

The kingdom of God
   is justice and joy,
for Jesus restores
   what sin would destroy;
God's power and glory
   in Jesus we know,
and here and hereafter
   the kingdom shall grow.

God's kingdom is come
   the gift and the goal,
in Jesus begun
   in heaven made whole;
the heirs of the kingdom
   shall answer his call,
and all things cry 'Glory!'
   to God all in all.
                    Bryn Rees © Mrs A Rees

✻ *Satisfy my hunger, Lord.*
  Let your kingdom come with its joy of renewal
  and pain of its sacrifice.

Monday July 11   MATTHEW 5.7

The gift of mercy to those who show mercy is not a reward. The fact is that only the merciful understand mercy when they receive it.

The quality of mercy is not strain'd.
It droppeth as the gentle rain from heaven
Upon the place beneath: it is twice bless'd;
It blesseth him that gives and him that takes.
                William Shakespeare, from The Merchant of Venice

O Lord, remember not only the men and women of goodwill but also those of ill will, but do not only remember all the suffering they have inflicted upon us. Remember the fruits we bought, thanks to the suffering: our comradeship, our loyalty, our courage, our generosity, the greatness of heart which has grown out of all this. And when they come to judgment, let all the fruits that we have borne be their forgiveness.
                A condemned Jew in Belsen Concentration Camp

God is rich in mercy, and because of his great love for us, he brought us to life in Christ when we were dead because of our sins; it is by grace you are saved.   *Ephesians 2.4-5*

✻ *Father, give me the double gift:*
  first to offer forgiving mercy when others wrong me,
  and then the ability to welcome
  those who forgive my faults.

Tuesday July 12   MATTHEW 5.8

In ancient thought, the heart was the centre of the will rather than the emotions. This beatitude proclaims the happiness of those with a pure intention to serve God: they will see and know God now and in the age to come.

It is the special function of prayer to turn the self away from the time-series and towards the eternal order; away from the apparent and towards the significant; away from succession and towards adoration and adherence. Prayer opens the door of the psyche to the invasion of another order, which shall at its full term transform the very quality of our existence.   *Evelyn Underhill*

It is good to renew ourselves from time to time by closely examining the state of our souls, as if we had never done it before. For nothing tends more to the full assurance of faith than to keep ourselves by this means in humility, and the exercise of all good works. *John Wesley*

My friends, all that is true, all that is noble, all that is just and pure, all that is lovable and attractive, whatever is excellent and admirable – fill your thoughts with these things. *Philippians 4.8*

✳ *Lord, lead me to purity of heart*
so that my aim is towards goodness.
Lead me to purity of thought
so that your Spirit can form my mind.
Lead me to purity of action
so that I may be your true servant.

Wednesday July 13   MATTHEW 5.9

If you come at me with your fists doubled,
    I think I can promise you
that mine will double as fast as yours;
    but if you come to me and say,
'Let us sit down and take counsel together,
and, if we differ from one another,
understand just what the points at issue are,'
    we will presently find that we are not
so far apart after all,
    that the points on which we differ are few
and the points on which we agree are many. *Woodrow Wilson*

Peace is my parting gift to you, my own peace, such as the world cannot give. Set your troubled hearts at rest, and banish your fears. *John 14.27*

✳ *Set free, O Lord, the souls of thy servants from all rest-*
lessness and anxiety. Give us that peace and power
which flow from thee. Keep us in all perplexity and
distress, that upheld by thy strength and stayed on the
rock of thy faithfulness we may abide in thee now and for
evermore. *Francis Paget*

Thursday July 14   MATTHEW 5.10

When the Pro-consul pressed him and said: 'Take oath and I let you go, revile Christ,' Polycarp said: Eighty and six years have I served him, and he has done me no wrong: how then can I blaspheme my King who saved me?

Polycarp, before his martyrdom, first century

There is a freedom that man fears:
The freedom of his fellow-man
In the eye of the tyrant
In the eye of the oppressed
In the eye of the neighbour
Who makes his fence too high – or low;
In the eye of the traveller in the tube
Who, like him, eyes the seat he makes for.
There is a freedom that threatens,
That disturbs the freedom he has carved out for himself.
So we live
Shut in by fences, regulations, gates.
Apartheid in a thousand forms
Secures us from the freedom of the world
To invade and to destroy.
Our liberty of isolation.

Jim Bates, from Liturgy of Life (NCEC)

✳ *Lord, though times are easier for us and dangers small,
still we seek your help lest we fail before the lie,
or hide behind the half-truth.
If we are scorned or pushed to the side,
criticised or neglected,
still help us to hold to the eternal truths.*

Friday July 15   **MATTHEW 5.11-12**

True happiness Offers of happiness come from all sides.
Advertisers and a consumer society parade their wares before
us. In developed countries, football pools and 'free' offers
shower through our letter boxes. Their picture of happiness
cannot be casually dismissed. Money, decent clothes, holidays
and labour saving devices do add to happiness. The Christian
gospel however, asks deeper questions. Why did Francis of
Assisi, devoted to poverty, find such deep peace? Why did
people marvel at the inner calm of Oscar Romero who lived in
daily fear of his life? What was Jesus' secret?

There is a happiness that derives from deep confidence in
God and shows itself in gentleness, mercy and forgiveness.
Sorrow can lead to God's consolation. Perhaps those who find
such happiness are the grand exceptions: the rest of us living
half way between the advertisers' dream and the beatitudes.

The truth remains: our present 'upside-down' world is flawed. True happiness lies in these simple statements Jesus made on a mountainside.

✳ *Lord, let me seek you in my desire,*
  Let me desire you in my seeking
  Let me find you by loving you,
  Let me love you when I find you. *Anslem*

For personal reflection or group discussion

Examine the implications of the beatitudes as they relate to

- private spirituality
- relationships
- community issues
- political issues.

ACTION

Examine the advertisements in one week's newspapers or one night's television. Analyse what is truly valuable and what is false in 'the good life' they offer.

AS MEMBERS OF ONE FAMILY

Notes, based on the Revised English Bible, by

S Andrew Morton

Andrew Morton is Director for Communication with the Council for World Mission. He was responsible for education and training at the Church Missionary Society until 1991 before becoming Publicity Director for the Mothers' Union (UK).

1994 is the United Nations' **International Year of the Family**, devoted to raising awareness about the needs and rights of the family unit. Most churches will be celebrating it too, rethinking how family-friendly their worship really is. But what are the prospects for the family in the closing years of the millenium? With patterns of Christian marriage under question, reports of child abuse and juvenile crime increasing, and high birthrates putting scarce natural resources under strain, what should Christians be doing? Do Christian values need updating to meet our changing societies?

Biblically, the family is a rich source of analogies for describing God's care for us. In the next two weeks, we will explore three main themes:

● Describing God – God's relationships with people;
● The loving family – God's expectations of the family;
● The responsible family – living in God's world today.

All this day, O Lord, let me touch as many lives as possible for thee; and every life I touch do thou by thy Spirit quicken, whether through the words I speak, the prayer I breathe or the life I live.

> *Mary Sumner, founder of the Mothers' Union,*
> *a worldwide Christian organisation for*
> *marriage and Christian family life.*

July 16-20 Describing God

Saturday July 16   **ISAIAH 54.1-8 ***

God's relationship with us

After two centuries of political turmoil and war, the people of
Judah find themselves captives 500 miles from home in
Babylon. You could forgive them for wondering if their ancestors
meant anything more. So what's new? The Christian bedrock of
our society – which honoured parents and frowned on divorce,
cohabitation, homosexuality and abortion – has been eaten
away and family values, as with so many things, are a tangled,
confused mess.

It is to language about the family that Isaiah turns as he tries
to describe what God is like. How many different aspects does
he mention? Verses 6-8 remind the exiles and us of our worst
nightmare, abandonment, which we have all experienced at
some time or other. But they also describe how God wants to
relate to us: like a husband reconciled to a divorced wife (verse
6) or as a lover (verse 7). God's values are like those of the
Middle Eastern extended family, which literally extends its tent
(verse 2) to make room for more relatives.

Yet, however lovely the vision is, one cannot ignore the pain
of past and present. What difficult experiences underlie the
relationships mentioned here? One can only say that
humankind and God have still a long way to go together.

✳ *Christ is my refuge,*
   he is my calm.
   And when I am in his hands,
   I revel like a child in its mother's arms.   M A Thomas,
                              an Indian Christian quoted in Another Day,
                                                  John Carden (SPCK)

Sunday July 17   **EPHESIANS 5.21-33 ***

The marriage contract

The sexual stereotypes of New Testament times are increasingly difficult to accept today. The marriage contract
described here is guaranteed to produce heated debate
between Christians. But is the writer's intention really to dish up
a bunch of social commandments for his readers? This passage
abounds in analogies – 'as A is to B, then C is to D' (verses

161

22-25). The writer is trying to describe God's relationship to us (verse 32).

As far as we know, Christians of Asia Minor were apt to mix Christian worship with other practices. Just as their everyday morality was confused, so were their loyalty and obedience in matters of faith. They knew the custom of sealing the marriage contract with a bath (verse 26); in the same way, Christ has made a binding contract ('word') with the Church which makes her exclusively his. As in a human marriage, we have been made one flesh, indissolubly, with Christ.

What responsibilities does that impose on our behaviour as the Church? One can and should turn the analogy back on itself as the writer of this letter does: our own family lives (verse 33) should also reflect the standard of love which Christ showed the Church (verse 25).

✳ *Lord, we thank you that our churches*
are like large families,
that we have sisters and brothers in all the world.
Be with them that make peace.

From a West African prayer

Monday July 18   PROVERBS 3.1-17

Like father and son?

We have just eavesdropped on the correspondence between a wise old man and a young son starting out in life. He is warned that setbacks are for his own good, like an occasional strapping (verses 11-12). What an optimistic view of life! Later on, the book of Job takes the stuffing out of that explanation of the problem of evil.

At the heart of the question 'Why evil?' is another religious one – 'What is God up to?' If only we could understand! It is how to gain this knowledge with which Proverbs, Job and the other Old Testament 'Wisdom' literature struggle.

What is the old man's basic advice? His 'commandments' (Hebrew 'torah', verse 1) are the accumulated experience of many generations. 'Trust in the Lord' (verse 5) can only be gained through 'wisdom' (verse 13ff). The fact that wisdom (note the Greek, 'Sophia') is a 'she' is not accidental: wisdom is an intimate relationship or 'understanding' (verse 13). Is your knowledge of God from the heart or the head? Do your prayers really say, 'Thy will be done'? To know God is the only way to understand the world around you.

✳ *May we become of one will, one knowledge, one dis-
position, one understanding, that relies upon Jesus
Christ our Lord*　　　　　*From a prayer by Martin Luther*

Tuesday July 19　　　　　　　　**DEUTERONOMY 6.1-9**

The family tree

Deuteronomy carries on the idea of intimacy – and then takes it
much further. How was Israel expected to demonstrate its
relationship to God (verses 7-9)? God is involved in everything
we are! To realise that is the goal of wisdom. What can we do to
remind us of God's intimate concern for us?

As far as Jewish – and this passage's – thinking is
concerned, the Protestant insistence on personal conversion
and individual salvation misses something important about God.
Can you say what? Look at how much of the community and,
specifically, one's family tree is involved in verses 2, 3, and 7. In
Northern Kenya, it is not unusual to have baptisms and
confirmations for upwards of 300 people who have committed
themselves as families and villages. Evangelists took this
passage and deliberately applied it. Among people in Britain,
who increasingly experience social fragmentation, does the
ideas of nurturing families-of-faith have a value?

Similarly, while Christians in Africa and Asia have a strong
emotional concept of themselves in relation to their forefathers,
Western Christians have tended to lose it. Could older people in
congregations be encouraged to have specific roles – perhaps
prayer and pastoral ministries – so that we do not lose sight of
their value?

✳ *Our Lord Jesus Christ, send you forth in the power and
strength of the Holy Spirit to be his faithful witnesses to
your family, to your own country and to the ends of the
earth.*　　　　　*From the Persian Confirmation Service,
quoted in Morning Noon and Night, John Carden
(Church Missionary Society)*

Wednesday July 20　　　　　　　**EPHESIANS 6.1-4 ***

Children and parents

The author of Ephesians turns his attention to children and his
style is an uncanny echo of Proverbs. Children should behave

in a way that pleases God (verse 1; cf Colossians 3.20). Fathers pass on the 'torah' knowledge of God which they had once learned (verse 4). And it is living in God's way that will bring success and long-life (verse 3; cf Proverbs 3.16-17). In keeping too with much of Proverbs is the practical, even secular, advice with which Ephesians 5 and 6 are peppered.

Of course, there is more than a hint here that parenthood is a two-way contract! What must fathers do? I remember as a child grumbling resentfully when Dad told me off with 'Honour your father and mother'. It wasn't fair that he had the last word! Now doesn't verse 4 excuse your children's tantrums when you caused the upset?

Whatever respect a parent receives isn't his by right, but by what s/he embodies. Biblical use of family language to describe God has given the family an almost sacramental status. Our families and relationships are where God lives and breathes. What of God do we find in our children – or our parents?

✳ *May parents and children together be learners in the school of Christ.*   Timothy Dudley-Smith
             quoted in Anthology of Public Prayers (Mothers' Union)

For personal reflection or group discussion
Read again Deuteronomy 6.1-9. Reflect, with the help of family photographs, on those who taught you your faith and how to live. Is it possible to understand ourselves without talking about our family history? This passage reminds us that God loves families. But do our churches?

July 21-24 The loving family

Thursday July 21   MARK 9.33-41*

The most vulnerable

Can you see what links the two halves of this passage? Both episodes are about the quest for power, but Jesus turns conventional power on its head. The first is last, a child or a servant greater than any power-broker. Look how Jesus reinforces his point (verse 36). Jesus' hug identifies him – the Master – with the littlest.

These verses, written some 40 years after Jesus' death, betray the experience of the early Christian community: its internal wranglings, its struggles against fringe sects also using Jesus' name, and its persecution. By then, Christians attached a great deal to a simple but dangerous act of kindness (verse 41).

Faced with these huge problems, the Early Church was searching for something to guide its action. Verses 37-39 and 41 provide the answer. Jesus – his 'name' – is not to be found in posturing or jealousy but in compassion for the weak.

So why is it that we allow a third of all Christians worldwide today to live on or below the poverty line?

✳ *There he crouched,*
Back and arms scarred like a hunted thing . . .
Then, a change.
Through his eyes I saw Thy glorious face.
  Adapted from a poem by C F Andrews, missionary in India

Friday July 22   MARK 6.30-44

Everything in common

The writer of John's Gospel (John 6.5-13) saw an immediate connection between this miraculous picnic and the Eucharist as a fellowship meal. Indeed, we see the ideas of 'togetherness' and 'sharing' throughout the story. Where?

The crowd was leaderless but expectant: Jesus could fill the need for direction, a theology for living (verse 34). But, although he recognised their physical need, Jesus declined. Why? The powerful, national Saviour was not Jesus' kind of Messiah: the grand gesture was one of Satan's temptations (Matthew 4.3). So how did Jesus get round the problem?

It would be handy (and less expensive) if God intervened and wiped out world poverty. It would also remove the mind-twisting problems of international debt, trade tariffs and, underlying them all, the huge responsibility we have for each other globally: for whatever we do, as a rule, always has an effect on someone else.

The disciples took responsibility (verses 37-38). Jesus blessed it. One wonders if all the bankers and industrialists in the crowd (who said they were all poor?) didn't take the point and share their sandwiches too. If ours did, there would be many more than twelve baskets left over.

✱ Help us to build with you the kind of family which welcomes the stranger, the lonely and the needy. Teach us through our small family to love the family of all nations and to realise our part in it.

From a prayer by Brother Charles SSF
quoted from Into the Hand of God (Mothers' Union)

Saturday July 23   MARK 7.24-30

The battle of the sexes

Compare this passage with Matthew 15.21-28. Most interpretations of this story forget that the main character is a woman. They are missing something quite shocking.

Her attitude is arrogant, by Orthodox Jewish standards: she refuses to be patronised as a social inferior – 'dog' – and so challenges the social norm which binds her into a sexual stereotype. She asserts her intellectual worth in debating Jesus' point, Rabbi-to-Rabbi. Matthew's Gospel reports it with flair: the woman is enjoying flirting with Jesus.

Jesus, after his initial annoyance (verse 27), actually rewards her for her action and thereby tacitly approves her claim to intellectual and social equality. Matthew's account (verse 24, 28) even infers that as a woman she has an added spiritual insight which the men of the 'House of Israel' lack and he praises her for her faith.

One's experience as a man or a woman undoubtedly affects one's spirituality, how one finds God. Do you react best to God as 'Father' or 'Mother' or neither? How do you describe God's 'love'? There is of course something much more mundane about sexuality and worship: does your church still leave the tea and flowers to the women?

✱ Thou art enough, for in thee we sinners find sonship and daughterhood again – the one thing that we most need.
From a prayer by D T Niles in The World at One in Prayer

Sunday July 24   DEUTERONOMY 10.12 to 11.1 *

Outside the family circle

Verses 12 and 13 are already familiar to us – and to the people Moses is addressing here. One can almost hear Moses mutter to himself, 'So, what's the point?' His answer (verses 14ff) blows the lid off the Israelites' idea of God.

Who is he (verse 14)? What do you think their experience of having been chosen (verse 15) has led them to believe? Sectarianism is the biggest threat to religion because it is one-eyed and self-defeating. It puts value into routine and ritual, but true faith is more than an outward sign (verse 16). The chosen believe they are the only ones to be chosen (verse 17). They are concerned with themselves and their own organisational needs: they lose compassion for those they were sent to serve (verse 18). Moses is not condemning any fringe sect, but mainline Judaism! Do you see this tendency in your own church? What is the cure?

The Swiss theologian Emil Brunner said, 'The Church exists by mission as a fire exists by burning.' So what vision of God will motivate a missionary Church (verses 14, 16, 17)? What are the three marks of a missionary, rather than a sectarian, Church (verses 18-21)?

✳ *Lord, even before we were born, You had your plan for us. You engaged us to be Your witnesses to others. Help us to go where you send us and to speak what You command.* From All God's People (CLS Madras 1978)

July 25-29 The responsible family

Monday July 25   **LEVITICUS 19.1-4 and 9-18**

Everyday holiness

What do you think is meant by being 'holy'? We think of holy people as being very special. The early Jews thought the same: a holy God meant someone very distant from human affairs who was both placated and invited to help through sacrifices. The prophets though, among them the writer of today's passage, disagreed. God was concerned with our daily lives. Being holy meant doing what that compassionate God wanted. Can you list what God expects (verses 9ff)?

A priest made 'holy' to God would have lived and ate apart from other people. How does verse 2 change all that? The people of God are the very opposite of 'distant'. We are to revere others because they too belong to God (verse 3). The poor and the foreigners on the fringes of society are to be provided for from our surplus (verses 9-10). Lying, mistreating the disabled and hating one's neighbours are all equivalent to denying God's Lordship. To be holy is to bring God into the ordinary things of our community life.

These ideas again challenge Protestant ideas about salvation. Can an individual be 'saved' who then rejects the community from which he came? What should his task be?

✳ *Father, do not let our prayers excuse us from paying the price of compassion. Make us generous.*

> From a prayer by Caryl Micklem,
> in Anthology of Public Prayers

Tuesday July 26   1 CORINTHIANS 12.14-26 *
Working together

God's view of people stands in judgment against the individualism of western society. How might the Christian see him / herself (verse 13)?

I once visited Christians in a refugee camp in Sudan. The contrasts between us made me feel very self-conscious. There was I with cameras and tape recorder: they worshipped under a dead tree and lived in Oxfam tents. So I was astounded by their final prayer before I left: 'We thank you God that one day we and these people will be together in heaven.' They had caught sight of that 'familyhood' we shared as Christians, whatever the differences between us. How would God have us experience it (verse 26)?

The Aid response to refugees is to develop their self-reliance, but Paul would have us recognise ourselves as one among them (verse 21). In other words, caring isn't the same as feeling sorry for people worse off than us: it is about recognising family when we see them (verse 25).

✳ *Blessed be your name that, in a world where men and women are driven apart, your love unites them.*

> Michael Walker From Everyday Prayers (IBRA)

Wednesday July 27   GENESIS 2.4b-17
Partners in creation

'In the world', or 'of the world'? It is another familiar Protestant conversation stopper and John 1.10 and Luther are to blame. They drew a sharp line between the 'Word' and the 'world' which was hostile and ignorant, and between the realms of government and the Spirit. Forever afterwards, we have been suspicious of getting involved. Small wonder that non-Christians have led the way in 'green' issues. How might today's passage change our attitudes to the world? And what has it to do with our family theme?

The writer sees us as sons and daughters of the soil (verse 7). Man the gardener is rewarded by food from the earth (verses 15-16). It is in very simple language, of course, but it echoes our modern understanding of food chains and responsible management of the earth's resources.

In Japan, a Christian community – the Asian Rural Institute (ARI) – teaches that food production is at the root of all that is good and destructive about human community. It is a source of greed, the cause of desertification, but, properly managed, it forces cooperation and guarantees health. ARI's motto sums up today's reading: 'That we may all live together'.

✳ *God our Creator, you have made us one with this earth, to tend it and bring forth fruit.*

From a prayer by Janet Morley All Desires Known (SPCK)

Thursday July 28   **GENESIS 2.18-25**

A duty to love

All our readings have taught us not to see people just as individuals. Today's passage sees humankind as what (verse 18)? We are reminded that even the basic family unit – man and woman – is not a thing unto itself, but part of a wider family with our environment and Creator.

Woman was 'a close run thing', though. Man's partner might have had a long tail and big ears (verse 20) – a throw-away mention to remind us of our family obligations to the animal kingdom. But now we are turned to that age-old question: Why do men and women fall in love? Verse 24 explains that we become one flesh because we are one flesh! (Does that explain why married couples so often look alike? Or why dogs look like their owners?)

However you take the story of Adam's rib, it is true that we 'click' with those people who are like us in some way. But what affinity do we have with the natural world, our other partners? Hard to say, isn't it? The tragedy is that most of us don't 'click' with the natural world and we even say, 'It is nothing to do with me', even though it is. But unless we fall in love with it soon, it will die and so will we.

✳ *We believe that there is a rhythm to God's creation, like a drum beat. When we lose the beat, or the drum is damaged, the music is out of tune.*

From a Pacific Women's Creed

Going beyond love

We end this section really at our beginning. Just how do you describe God adequately? Does verse 14 give you a clue? (You can't!)

The truth is that God is above and beyond anything we know (verse 11). The metaphor of the family is good as far as it goes: God is like the best of fathers (verse 13), but he is better than any of us. Can we match the family ideals in verses 8-10? God would take us beyond love to experience his 'steadfast love'.

I once met someone who believed that God told him what colour to paint his yacht. Apart from the fact that a yacht is not an ordinary thing to own, his perspective was seriously wrong. His prayers were exclusively for himself: but God's steadfast love is for each person plus. God's love embraces you-in-community, you-and-your-calling, you-and-your-world. This God is waiting to take us far beyond our tiny preoccupations to share a love that is higher than heaven (verse 11).

Can you let go of your worries and wants? Are you willing to look for God with new eyes, to experience him again in new and familiar places like your partner, family or even your back garden? And are you willing to help God pour his love into those places?

✳ *Renew our bodies as fresh*
as the morning flowers.
We thank you for the gift of this morning,
and a new day to work with you.
       From a prayer by a Japanese Christian, Masao Takenaka

For personal reflection or group discussion

This section has asked many questions already. Read it again and reflect on the new insights you have received. Mark those questions you would like to discuss with others.

ACTION

What ONE task does God want you to do in his family?

THE KINGDOM IN OUR MIDST

Notes, based on the Good News Bible, by

John Atkinson

John Atkinson is a Methodist minister in Leicester. He has been a circuit minister, a college tutor (in the Caribbean), a District Chairman and General Secretary of the Methodist Division of Social Responsibility (UK).

Jesus often spoke of **the Kingdom of God,** a phrase with many facets of meaning. It is, for example, the reign of God's love in the heart of each follower of Christ. That is why Luke 17.21 is sometimes translated, 'The Kingdom of God is within you' (eg. GNB and NIV). But others translate it, 'The kingdom of God is in the midst of you' (eg. RSV). They remind us that we live in a world in which God's Kingdom is always growing, both in the Church and in others who do God's will in the wider community. It is important to hold together all these meanings of the Kingdom and we shall explore them in these readings.

> *Lord, open my eyes to read your truth,*
> *that your kingdom may grow within me,*
> *as it is already growing in your world.*

Saturday July 30   **MARK 4.1-9**

● The sower – Jesus, sows the seed of the Kingdom. Wherever it grows, God rules and God's purposes are worked out. It takes root in the lives of individuals who accept God as King and do God's will. It may take root in a church, producing not only deep devotion and close fellowship, but also more effective service in and far beyond its neighbourhood. It may take root in the community – wherever goodness is found, God is there.

● Much depends on the soil – the seed of a flower, vegetable or cereal has immense potential for growth. The 'Kingdom seed' has the power of God within it. But its growth is frustrated by individuals and communities whose minds are closed with prejudice, whose commitment is shallow, or whose thoughts are choked by materialism. How can we become more receptive to God's planting?

171

● Jesus assures us of a harvest of unimaginable proportions. Reflect on the wonder of this. How much does the coming of the Kingdom depend on the reponse of individuals? Where can we see signs of its coming for the peoples of the world? Where do you see signs of the activity of God?

✴ *Pray for good harvests.*
Think how you can help to bring them about.

Sunday July 31   MARK 4.21-23

We should not be afraid to lift high the light of loving service and witness in the name of Christ. We should also look for places where this light is most needed.

✴ *Lord, you placed me in the world*
to be its light.
I was afraid of the shadows,
afraid of the poverty.
I did not want to know other people.
And my light slowly faded away.
Forgive me, Jesus.   Peggy M de Cuehlo, Uruguay,
© *Christian Conference of Asia*

In ones and twos, several people entered a series of dark caves. Each had a torch, but on its own it did not show them the spectacular beauty of the stalactites. Then, by accident, all the visitors entered the same cave. When they shone their torches together, they were astonished by the beauty they saw. To make the light of the Kingdom visible, we need to join together with other Christians in mission and service.

✴ *Grant us, O Lord, a love big enough to reach the world*
and small enough to make us one with you.

Mother Teresa

Monday August 1   MARK 4.26-29

Imagine that you are holding in your hand a tiny seed, so small that you can hardly see it. Now think of its potential. In a few months time, you may have a host of colourful flowers or a vegetable large enough to feed you and your family. Although we help the seed to grow by watering, feeding and caring for it, we can never fully understand the power within the seed that gives it life. We do not know how it happens (verse 27). Neither can we analyse the growth of the Kingdom within our hearts nor the ways it transforms the world. Often we are slow to recognise its presence.

✳ *Lord,*
isn't your creation
wasteful?
Fruits never equal
the seedlings' abundance.
Springs scatter water.
The sun gives out
enormous light.
May your bounty teach me
greatness of heart.
May your magnificence
stop me being mean.
Seeing you a prodigal
and open-handed giver,
let me give unstintingly . . .
like God's own.

Helder Camara, Brasil
from The Desert is Fertile © Sheed and Ward

Tuesday August 2   MATTHEW 13.24-30

There is more goodness in the world than newspapers suggest, but evil is never far away. Good and evil are so intertwined that it seems that no country, no government, no race, no organisation, no community and no individual are exempt.

In this parable, Jesus reminds us that in God's time, evil will be overcome. In the meantime, he warns us not to act like farmhands trampling down the corn as they try to pull out a few weeds. We can and must, however, encourage all that is good, resisting evil and helping its victims.

We can also begin with ourselves and tackle the mixture of good and evil in our own lives. We can ask God to forgive us for all that is wrong and seek God's strength to grow in grace as we seek the good of others.

✳ *Lord, help me to encourage what is good in the world,*
to challenge evil and in humility to recognise my own sin.

Wednesday August 3   MATTHEW 13.33

Yeast is a remarkable substance. It consists of tiny single-cell organisms, far too small to be seen by the unaided eye. Each cell creates other cells, living and giving life. It is this process fermenting within the dough which makes our bread light and good to eat.

Like the yeast, the Kingdom is at work, disturbing, creating within us a state of ferment which is always necessary before we can begin to change. There is nothing static about the love of Jesus when we let him take possession of our lives.

But the Kingdom is not only within us. It is in the world challenging nations and their values. We should praise God that injustice and evil are being overthrown. Have we the eyes of faith to recognise where this is happening?

✳ *Pray that Christ's love may transform your life.*
Give thanks for the way in which it is changing the world
and pray that we may be challenged by
and respond to its ferment.

Thursday August 4   MATTHEW 13.44-46

Finding the Kingdom is like finding a priceless treasure, whether we find it by accident like the farm labourer or by searching like the pearl merchant. The question is whether we are willing to pay the price.

✳ *The great love of God*
  Is revealed in the Son,
Who came to this earth
  To redeem everyone . . .

It binds the whole world,
  Every barrier it breaks,
The hills it lays low,
  And the mountains it shakes.

It's yours, it is ours,
  O how lavishly given!
The pearl of great price,
  And the treasure of heaven.   *Daniel T Niles, Sri Lanka*
                                      © Methodist Publishing House

Friday August 5   MATTHEW 13.47-52

The first of today's parables makes a similar point to that of verses 24-30: good and evil continue to co-exist in the world and even the Church, but eventually God will destroy evil. If we are wise, we will deal with the evil in our own lives now.

The second mini-parable (verse 52) points to our accumulation of treasures: our culture, experiences of Jesus and discoveries about the gospel of the Kingdom. All have a value, though as time goes by, this spiritual wealth may make us less eager to discover new treasures.

There are some who think that old customs, buildings and books are so precious that nothing modern is worth a moment's consideration. Others are so excited by new trends that they are blind to the glories of the past.

In our pilgrimage, we need to hold all these in balance and be open to what God is seeking to reveal to us now.

✳ *Thank Jesus for his many blessings to you in the past. Pray that you will also be open to the ways of the Spirit who leads us on to new truths.*

Saturday August 6   MATTHEW 7.13-14

'Believe not those who say
The upward path is smooth . . .'

So wrote Anne Bronte, an English novelist of the nineteenth century. Anne and her sisters Charlotte and Emily, who were also novelists, were daughters of an impoverished clergyman. Anne, the youngest who died before she was thirty, could speak with great faith. The next verse of her hymn begins:

'It is the only road
unto the realms of joy . . .

It is never easy to follow Christ. It involves discipline, a struggle against the evil around and within us and with hardships and sorrows we may have to face. But it is 'the gate to life' (verse 14) and brings real and lasting joy.

✳ *Light is stronger than darkness;
Life is stronger than death,
Victory is ours through Him who loved us.*   Desmond Tutu

For personal reflection or group discussion

How would you describe to someone who is not a Christian why the Kingdom is for you like finding treasure? or like a harvest?

Write your own prayers on some of the key-words of this week's reading: seeds, soil, growth, light, yeast, treasure, road . . .

ACTION

List five ways in which you could enable the love of Jesus to grow in your heart. Keep the list in your Bible and check it regularly.

AS GOD SEES US

Notes, based on the Good News Bible, by

Mary Cotes

Associate minister of South Street Baptist Church, Exeter, with Brampford Speke, Mary Cotes is chaplain to the Palace Gate Centre, a Christian Community project in the heart of the city.

'Seeing is believing,' folk often say. Yet in matters of faith, perhaps we might want to suggest that 'believing is seeing'. Having faith in God through Jesus Christ means that we are called to see ourselves as God sees us. This is what the passages in this section help us to do. They present us with the pain and injustice of the world and remind us that we are party to them. They present us with the demands of a holy God and convict us of our sin. But although this message is painful, we are not left condemned. We are offered a new start. We are challenged to walk with Jesus on the way to the Cross, trusting that, as we do so, we will begin to see the world as through the eyes of his suffering love.

Lord, you promise to heal the blind,
but I fear what I might see.
By the power of your disturbing Spirit,
help me to claim the miracle
that I may see as you see,
face the fear of your judgment
and, accepting your forgiveness,
be your servant in the world

Sunday August 7   **MICAH 6.1-8 ***

In a nearby town, there are two churches. The first is growing rapidly. Worship is lively and highly enjoyable. Members have just refurbished the premises and bought sophisticated sound equipment. There are fellowship meetings most nights of the week. Worship at the second church seems less enjoyable. Members concentrate their resources on running a help-centre for the unemployed, and on organising events to raise public awareness of the issue. Many people are aided by their contact with the centre, but very few of them ever come to the church. If you were to move to the town, to which church would you go?

In the eyes of God, true worship does not consist in offering extravagant sacrifices. Rather, it means learning to act with the same justice and constant love which God showed in delivering the people out of slavery in Egypt. The message is a hard one, undoubtedly. But until we heed the warning, God's case against us will continue to stand.

✳ *O God, teach us what true worship is.*

Monday August 8   ISAIAH 5.1-7 *

Ours is a society which makes a moral virtue out of greed. If we say someone 'has done well', we probably do not mean that he or she has lived for others, or prayed faithfully. More likely, we are referring to a successful career and a high salary. 'Goods' are not acts of justice, but purchases or belongings. Those for whom the system has worked are known as enterprising. The poor, meanwhile, are blamed for their poverty.

God sees through the sham of our life and language. By playing on the Hebrew words, Isaiah exposes the false values upon which his society is built. God looks for goodness (mishpat) but sees murder (mispach); for righteousness (zethaqah) but hears crying (ze'aqah). Until the vine bears fruit worthy of the gardener, he says, the nation will fall under God's judgment. It is a message to terrify us all.

✳ *Almighty God, bestow upon us the meaning of words and the light of understanding . . .*
Grant that what we believe, we may also speak.

St Hilary

Tuesday August 9   ISAIAH 6.9-13

Jonathan is homeless. Until he has accommodation, he has no hope of work. Rooms to let are available in the city. But the deposit required to secure one is far more than he can afford. It is a vicious circle. Besides, all his time is taken in the tasks of survival – looking for somewhere safe to leave his few possessions while he goes for a wash, queuing in the Social Security office, searching in dustbins for food. He is exhausted, depressed and ill from eating badly and sleeping in the wet. Citizens find young men like Jonathan a disgrace to the city. 'They are criminals and spongers,' they say. 'They should be moved on or locked up. Their presence lowers the value of property and threatens the tourist trade.'

Isaiah brings a message of devastating judgment to those who see without understanding. The nation may look prosperous, but it is only an impression. In reality, disaster is near. Healing can only come if the people turn to God, and, forsaking hard-heartedness, start to look with God's eyes.

✴ *Do not bring us to the time of trial,*
but deliver us from evil.

Wednesday August 10 MARK 4.10-12

Commentators argue continually over this passage. Is Jesus really suggesting that his parables are meant to keep people from being forgiven? Is this what Mark intended to write, or did the scribes, who made copies of the Gospel, make a mistake? Perhaps the clue is here: Jesus is quoting the words of Isaiah. Jesus implies that his disciples must be different from the closed-minded nation of Isaiah's time. As disciples, they have a special calling to be true to God's way of seeing.

Just as the passage requires us to have 'inside' knowledge of Isaiah's prophecy, to make sense of it, so the church needs 'inside' knowledge of Christ's teaching in order to grasp the secret of the Kingdom of God. According to Mark, Jesus' disciples never really understood the message of servanthood. In the end, they deserted him (see 14.50). The challenge to us is to be different. We must understand that in God's sight, it is not the rich and important who are the winners, but those who take the servant's place – as Jesus himself demonstrated.

✴ *Brothers and sisters, in the presence of the God of glory,*
As members of a people called to follow Christ
and live in his new righteousness,
We need to repent for the evil in the Church's life.
Church of South India

Thursday August 11 MARK 12.1-12 *

My God, my God, why have you abandoned me? . . .
Tanks surround me,
machine guns take aim at me,
barbed wire, loaded with electricity, imprisons me . . .

My bones can be counted like on an X-ray sheet,
Naked they pushed me into the gas chamber
and my shoes and clothes they have shared among
themselves . . .
I am contagious with radio-activity
and people avoid me for fear of infection.

Translated from Ernesto Cardenal, Salmos, Universitad Antioquia, Columbia, n.d., Ps 22, from Hans-Ruedi Weber – On A Friday Noon: Meditations Under the Cross 1979, WCC.

It is tempting to button up the parable Jesus told, and understand Jesus' rejection only as a historical event. Yet the powerful words of the Latin American poet Cardenal remind us that the image of Christ, who took upon himself the suffering of humankind, is still to be seen today. Let us pray that God will open our eyes to his rejection: as the Pharisees and scribes of our story show, it is often the religious establishment who are blind to God's Christ.

✶ **Open our eyes, Lord:**
  we want to see Jesus.

Friday August 12   **REVELATION 2.1-7**

The hero rides into town, seeking revenge on the two men who murdered his brother. The first he avenges when he beats him up in the saloon bar, humiliating him in public. The second he shoots dead in a thrilling mountain battle. The sherriff's daughter, young, attractive and marriageable, falls instantly in love with him, and the whole town acclaims him the victor.

Cowboy films represent in caricature the images upon which western society is built. Male aggression, competitiveness and individualism are seen as seductive virtues, and there is little room for mercy or forgiveness. These values are even reflected in the Church, where 'good' leaders are often thought to be the men who appear the most invincible.

In God's sight, the 'one who conquers' is not the one who shows the greatest lust for power, nor even the one who shows the greatest zeal for truth. It is the one who loves. This is what the church at Ephesus needs to learn. Perhaps we should learn it too. It might turn our cowboy mentality upside down.

✶ **Reflect: If I have no love,**
  I am nothing.   *1 Corinthians 13.2*

'Like anybody, I would like to live a long life . . . But I'm not concerned with that now. I just want to do God's will. And he's allowed me to go up to the mountain. And I've looked over. And I've seen the promised land. I may not get there with you. But I want you to know tonight that we, as a people, will get to the promised land . . .'

These well-known words of Martin Luther King, the night before he died, contain the two basic ingredients. First there is a refusal to compromise. Second, there is the belief that there will be new life. Death, therefore, is nothing to fear.

Christ's message to the church at Smyrna is both realistic and hopeful. Holding fast to God's values will inevitably mean hardship and conflict with the powers that be. Yet the believers will be redeemed from death. Following the murder of Martin Luther King, the battle for black rights was strengthened and finally won. It is not persecution which threatens the Church's life. Rather, it is the danger of refusing to see what is wrong, and failing to stand against it.

* *Reflect: In what ways does your church endanger itself by standing against the false values of society?*

For personal reflection or group discussion

Reflecting on your own life and that of your local church, write letters from the Spirit to yourself and to your church.

Keep them in your Bible and use them in your prayers.

On my local hoarding, there is an advertisement for a soft bottled drink. It shows the upper half of a young, attractive woman. She is naked apart from two bottle-tops which cover each of her nipples. A larger-than-life bottle-opener is pictured to the side, and the caption reads, 'Come on, boys!' In western society, whose influence is only too obvious throughout the world, the female body, understood as the object of male desire and power, is sacrificed to the idols of lust and boosted sales.

Pergamum, the first city of the cult of Rome and its Emperor, was a centre of Roman power. The values of this pagan culture found expression in sexual licence and in the banquets (probably of the trade-guilds), where food served had first been sacrificed to idols. Those who wanted success in business would need to attend such events. For John, however, lust and materialism form a Satanic combination. A Christian's allegiance must be not to the values of society, but to the values of the crucified Christ. He, not Rome, is the one with the 'two-edged sword'. Ultimately, the power belongs to him.

✳ *Lead us not into imitation.*
East Asia Christian Youth Consultation Council

Monday August 15   REVELATION 2.18-29

In the Old Testament, the idea of sexual infidelity is frequently used as an image for religious unfaithfulness and the worship of idols. One figure particularly associated with this 'adultery' is Jezebel (see Kings 16.13ff). These ideas play an important part in the letter to Thyatira. God's complaint against the church there is the religious infidelity of those who follow false teaching.

In other parts of the Old Testament, the close relationship which God desires with us is seen in terms of faithfulness in marriage. The New Testament takes this up in describing the Church as the 'bride of Christ'. For all this, the Church over the centuries has been reluctant to speak of its relationship with God in sexual terms. More often it has thought of sex as a sin, relating women's sexuality in particular, with evil and temptation. Yet if, as John asks, we are to repent of our 'adulteries', perhaps it is time that, in picturing God, we rediscovered images of sexual fidelity. At the same time, we might be saved from our negative sensibilities.

✳ *Tender God ,*
  love-maker,
  pain-bearer,
  life-giver,
  touch us,
  that we may in turn touch others with your love.

Tuesday August 16   REVELATION 3.1-6

'I'm on the slab.' The phrase is a familiar one amongst the homeless men of my city. The slab to which they refer is a large concrete ledge, tucked away behind the city-centre shops, where they sleep rough. To the unknowing visitor, the evening lights of the city present an illusion of vitality and well-being. Yet,

181

in the shadows, lies a group of people who are ready to describe themselves as if they were corpses in the morgue, or dead meat at the butcher's.

The letter to Christians at Sardis implies a parallel between the city and the church. Sardis' great acropolis presented an image of invincibility and watchfulness. Yet this was a false impression. Twice in the past, it had fallen to surprise attack. If the Church is to be seen as truly alive to the Spirit of God, writes John, it must not fall prey to the same shortcomings as the city. It must wake out of its sleep and penetrate the illusions to see the reality beneath.

✳ *Lord! Give us weak eyes for things which are of no account and clear eyes for all Thy truth.*

Soren Kierkegaard

Wednesday August 17   REVELATION 3.7-13

A city centre church, seeking to be relevant to the busy community around it, decided to open its premises every weekday, and offer tea, coffee and a welcome to whoever came in. At first, most of the comers were elderly shoppers wanting a rest. Gradually, however, young unemployed people started coming. Many arrived dirty, drunk or drugged. The church silver went missing. Terrified of what they had taken on, the church called a meeting to decide what to do.

While Christians are often tempted to keep themselves well-protected from the world, God presents them with an open door. As the letter to Philadelphia shows, God sees and understands their weakness and their fear. But nonetheless, the dare is to be faithful to God's values. If only they will hold fast, they will no longer be just a church with rambling premises. In the midst of a bustling, worldly city, they will be signs of the City of God.

✳ *Reflect: Your idol is shattered in the dust to prove that God's dust is greater than your idol.*

Rabindranath Tagore, Bengal

Thursday August 18   REVELATION 3.14-22

In Roman times, Laodicea was the wealthiest city in Phrygia. It was known for its banks, its linen and wool-industry, and for its medical school, which produced a famous eye-ointment. Six miles away, in Hieropolis, there were hot springs. The water cooled as it travelled across the plain, and was luke-warm by the time it poured over the cliff opposite Laodicea. Anyone drinking this water was violently sick.

Taking these aspects of the city's life as metaphors, God condemns the church for its lack of commitment. It has absorbed the false values of its context. The church must shake off the apathy and complacency which arise out of a worldly sense of success, and, using God's eye-salve, must begin to see itself as God sees it. Although the letter is one of biting condemnation, it closes with words of grace. To those who are willing to be open to the ways of God, Christ's loving presence is assured.

✳ *God be in my eyes and in my looking.*

Friday August 19   PSALM 51.1-19

I have had a bad day. I learn this morning that a young man with whom we have been working has been found tragically dead. His death is all the more painful because yesterday, fearing that he was in danger, we spent hours on the telephone trying, in vain, to persuade the powers-that-be to take up his case.

Then we are worried about the future of our soup-kitchen which feeds the hungry. As I write, the days are getting colder, and still we have found no suitable building. There are many empty premises in the city. There are thousands of folk in the city who support our work . . . but no one wants to have a soup-kitchen in the road where they live. Why do I do this job? I ask myself. Just sometimes it seems that the structures and prejudices of the city are hewn in stone, and that nothing will ever change them, no matter how loudly we cry.

Failure is a draining business. It feels like reaching a dead end. This is the psalmist's experience. Suddenly he sees himself as God sees him: all he has to offer is brokenness. Yet this allows him to glimpse something also of God. It is this God of mercy and love who provides the grace to continue, creating a new and steadfast spirit, lifting exhaustion to joy and hope . . . Maybe that's why I do this job!

✳ *My sacrifice is a humble spirit, O God;*
You will not reject a humble and repentant heart. Verse 17

Saturday August 20   MARK 10.46-52

When Oscar Romero was appointed Archbishop of El Salvador, he thought that the Church should avoid political involvement, and concentrate on revitalising spirituality. But his eyes were opened when a friend, a priest who worked with the poor, was brutally murdered alongside a man and a boy by government violence. Thereafter, the more aware he became of the oppression of the people, the more he found himself speaking out on their behalf. 'We can see clearly,' he once said, 'that neutrality is impossible here. Either we put ourselves at the service of the people ... or we are accomplices in their death.' A month later, he was murdered.

The road on which Bartimaus follows Jesus is not just any old road. It is the road that leads to the cross. We are not all gifted with the leadership of Romero. Yet our prayer might be that Christ would touch our eyes and help us to see as God sees. Then we might be enabled to walk as Christ does, with all those who suffer. For only the way of the Cross will lead to God's new life for us all.

✳ *You asked for my eyes*
to see the pain of poverty.
I closed them for I did not want to see.

Father, forgive me,
renew me
send me out
as a usable instrument
that I might take seriously
the meaning of your cross.   *Joe Seremane, South Africa*
                              from Lifelines (Christian Aid)

For personal reflection and group discussion

Which people in your area are most in need? and of what? Read again Revelation 3.20-22 and reflect prayerfully on its meaning for your community. Discuss together how you can respond in Christ's way.

ACTION

Try to raise awareness of the need you have identified in your local church or group. Invite a local social worker, or someone who is already involved, to come and help you to understand the problems.

THE POWER OF GOD

Notes, based on the New Jerusalem Bible, by
Brian Hearne

*Brian Hearne is a Roman Catholic priest in Ireland, a member of
the Missionary Society of the Holy Spirit, who teaches mission
theology in various institutes and is a staff member at the Irish
School of Ecumenics. From 1968 to 1991, in East and Central
Africa, he was involved in ecumenical work including six years
at the Mindolo Ecumenical Foundation in Zambia. He edited the
African Ecclesial Review, and was consultant to the Catholic
Bishops of eleven African countries.*

'Power tends to corrupt and absolute power corrupts absolutely'
– these are famous words of Lord Acton, in a letter to an
Anglican Bishop. A Buddhist monk told an inter-faith gathering in
North America, some years ago, that the greatest obstacle
Buddhists found in attempting dialogue with Christians was the
way Christians use power. In the Gospels, we find Jesus worried
about how his followers will exercise authority, or use their
power. Peter is called 'Satan' because he protests against the
foretold weakness and failure of Jesus; the apostles are pilloried
by Jesus because they argue about who is the greatest.

These problems are still with us. In this week's readings,
various aspects of God's power come to light. The main one is
that we are created in God's image and likeness to share in
God's power. Our creative God uses power to let people be, to
let people go, to give people room to grow, to live life to the full.
This power often looks like weakness to those who judge by
greed, pride and lust. But God's power is the triumphant force in
life, in history and in creation. God's Kingdom of love, peace
and fellowship will come. Our glory is that we are called to share
in the coming-to-be – often painful and even heartbreaking – of
this Kingdom where God reigns. 'Our God reigns.'

O Wisdom, I give myself to you;
for you are wiser than I.
Emmanuel, I give myself to you,
for you are more loving than I.
O Light, I give myself to you,
for you can see better than I.

John Henry Newman, 1801-1890

Read the verses and then reflect on the immensity of God. You can think of better prayers than I can! Be creative, and use your God-given power!

A lot of the way we think and talk about God is just ignorance and folly. Are we too sure about God? Do we jabber about God aimlessly, instead of keeping a great silence before the awesome majesty of the Love that moves the sun and the other stars? The immeasurable grandeur of God can never be grasped by us. Can we give more time and space in our lives to contemplate God's glory?

✴ *O God our Father, Creator of the universe,*
whose majesty is unfathomed,
and whose greatness knows no bounds.
You are the Lord of glory,
whose love is unending and absolute
and whose grace is all-embracing.
You are the Supreme Matai (family chief) *of all nations,*
big and small,
of all people and all races.

　　　　　　　　　　　Samoa, from Oceans of Prayer (NCEC)

Read the verses, take a moment of quiet reflection and then draw a symbol or picture of some aspect of what you have read.

Idols are easy to deal with when we feel we understand them. I have an interest in African masks, and I often discuss pictures of masks with my students. Their immediate reaction is: these are 'primitive', 'pagan', 'idolatrous' – although some may come up with words like 'celebratory', 'mysterious' and 'solemn'. Leopold Senghor wrote about the way he encountered the mysteries of eternity as he looked at the masks of the ancestors, so solemn, so profound, so beautiful. These masks are not idolatrous, for they lead beyond themselves 'to the mysteries of eternity'. So perhaps we need to ask, 'Where are the idols of our world, where are my idols? Where are the things that draw me away from the one true God, who alone is to be worshipped?' Remember Paul's condemnation of those whose god is their belly. But the idols of the mind are even more dangerous.

✴ *The dangers of life are infinite, and safety is among them.*

　　　　　　　　　　　　　　　　　　　　　Goethe

Tuesday August 23   ISAIAH 40.25-31

This time, after reading the text, think of a moment when you have felt empowered to do something, to take a new step, to learn a new language, to make a new friendship.

There is a very moving moment in the Video film of the Vancouver Assembly of the World Council of Churches in 1983. Special attention was paid to the handicapped people at that Assembly. In one of the worship events, the text we are now looking at was read by a man confined to a wheelchair. Just look at the words of the text and see the poignancy in that moment, for the reader and for all those who heard his proud and joyful proclamation. God gives power to the powerless and new heart to the discouraged – not just in a vague spiritual sense, but in the to-ing and fro-ing of daily affairs. So what are we doing to empower those who are disabled, or who are 'differently abled' in our communities? Are we sensitive to their needs – getting onto a bus or going to the cinema?

＊ *.. . . In our world*
the poor and the weak
are always insecure,
at the mercy of human political powers,
at the mercy even of their own brokenness
and inner violence.
We who are called by Jesus
to walk with them
and to enter a covenant with them,
are called too
to discover this road of insecurity,
where the power and wisdom of our gentle God
are revealed. *Jean Vanier, from The Broken Body (DLT)*

Wednesday August 24   PSALM 113.1-9

Why not try to make a song about this text: it calls for celebration and for joy. In Africa, people celebrate all the great moments of life; here we are told about some great moments:

so let's make a song and dance about them! But read the verses first!

God's power is for the poor. God's justice is not impartial; it is to defend the helpless, the widows and orphans. The name of the Lord, 'I am he who is' – made known in the call of Moses and the liberation of Israel – is God's being. The name is not just a handy label but the expression of the innermost being of the One who bears the name. God's name is the name of a liberating God, who gives hope even in the darkest moments of life, who makes the desert bloom, who makes the barren fertile. God casts down the mighty from their thrones and fills the hungry with good things. Praise God; but work with God too.

✳ *Give us the patience of those who understand,*
and the impatience of those who love;
that the might of your gentleness may work through us,
and the mercy of your wrath may speak through us.

Tonga, from Oceans of Prayer (NCEC)

Thursday August 25   JOHN 14.8-14

John's Gospel is at once the most personal and sacramental of the Gospels. So read this passage, and then think of a deep personal experience you have had, or of a symbol that means a lot in your life. Then pray about it.

Jesus, in his human life, in his words, dealings and relations with people, makes the mystery of God known to us. He called God 'Abba', 'my Dad', a term of loving intimacy. The goal of his life was to make the Father known, as a presence of overwhelming love, compassion and forgiveness for all God's children. The invisible is made visible to us in Jesus. The love of God – motherly and fatherly – shines out to us in the caring and friendliness of Jesus. The power of God manifest in the life of Jesus is the power of love and kindness. The works of Jesus are works of healing, forgiveness and encouragement. We too can perform these works and so carry on the mission of the One who came so that we all may enjoy fullness of life.

✳ *God our Father and our Mother, be with us your children*
that we may see one another with new eyes,
hear one another with new hearts
and treat one another in a new way.

Corrymeela Community, Ireland

Can you think of a time when you made a fool of yourself, and perhaps learned something from it? Make a prayer about it.

Paul was worried about the divisions and sectarianism of the Church at Corinth, where people had got involved in all kinds of arguments about who was the most powerful among their leaders: Peter, Apollos, Paul, or even Christ. Party factions grow up so easily, when everyone claims to know better than the others. Paul attacks the false 'wisdom' that uses reason to justify power struggles. The language of the cross is illogical, but it is God's language. God's weakness is stronger than human strength. This is an amazing claim. Looking at our world, what does it mean?

✳ *For Mercy has a human heart,*
 Pity a human face,
 And Love, the human form divine,
 And Peace, the human dress.   *William Blake*

This is an amazing picture of the manifestation of the eternal mystery to and in creation. George Bernard Shaw, in an irreverent moment, said that the Book of Revelation was obviously written by a drug addict! But can you think of a moment of glory in your own life, a moment when the Mystery we call God became real to you? Reflect and pray about this for a few moments.

Hope in the future, wonder and praise in the present: the God who moves the sun and other stars, in Dante's great line, the God who is reconciling and reuniting all things in heaven and earth in Jesus – symbolised in the four animals who bring together the wonder and diversity of creation – this is the God we adore. A poem of Rilke describes the wonders and horrors of our world, but the response of the poet, as of the Christian, is always: 'I praise'. But there is also the Christian response of anger: anger against the evil and greed that obstruct God's purpose for all people, an anger that leads to courageous action for the transformation of the world, believing in the One who affirms: 'I make all things new' (Revelation 21.5).

✳ *Today you offer us your Power,*
 So that we can help change the world,
 Announce your Kingdom,

And acknowledge you,
The source of all power.
'For thine is the Kingdom,
and the power,
and the glory,
for ever and ever.'

Diego Frisch, Uruguay
from Oceans of Prayer (NCEC)

For personal reflection or group discussion

Recall experiences in your life, and the life of your community, when the power of God has been made real to you. How did you feel? What images of God helped you? Read again and reflect on the meaning of Isaiah 40.31 in the light of other readings this week.

ACTION

Think of a case of injustice in your local community. First, make sure of the facts and then write a letter of protest to those who are responsible, or choose another more appropriate way to express your convictions.

THE POWER OF LOVE

Notes, based on the Good News Bible, by
Sybil Phoenix

Sybil Phoenix left her country Guyana in 1956 to settle in Britain, where her outstanding work in the community and struggle for racial justice led to her being awarded the MBE in 1973. In 1987 she received the Medal of Service from Guyana for her caring of nationals in both Britain and the Caribbean. She writes this section from a background of personal suffering, tragedy and achievement.

Our Father God, Creator of all your different children
all that has come to be has come through you,
lives in your energy,
takes breath because you willed it,
is clothed in your beauty and dignity,
valued by you, Father,
and is part of your world.

Our Father, God, Creator of all your different children,
teach us to love what you have created.
Help us to shed the arrogance that cocoons us
and restricts our growth.
Help us to split the binding threads of self
that we may crawl out into the warmth of your light,
borne on the wings of understanding.

Teach us to see people one by one
and to acknowledge them as our Father's children,
our brothers and sisters:
not to pigeonhole them;
not to hammer them into unnatural moulds
of our own making,
but to rejoice in our differences,

Accepting people as they are
- different but of equal worth -
each one a part of God's creation,
showing something of his love and glory.
From With All My Love, Sybil Phoenix (1992)

The greatest commandment

As in every century, this commandment to love our neighbour needs to be lived. For each of us, the way to a life of service to our neighbour is the way of love that identifies with the love of Christ. This happens, not with actual nails in our hands and feet, but with a bliss that knows anguish, as we love others 'heart to heart', feeling as our very own, their hurt and pain.

Sybil's home has always been full of children. Her friend Constantia Pennie writes of her, 'A foster mother of which Lewisham is rightly proud, Sybil has cared for hundreds of children, giving them the home and family which they needed. She is Mum to lots and Community Auntie to many.'

We serve Christ in bringing hope and healing. By lovingly embracing the pain and suffering of others, we characterise every time the renewal of life in the risen Lord. For the greatest power in the universe is the joy of Christ-like love. Jesus' words to his disciples in their last hour together before his agony, told this awesome truth. Love is indeed the first and last requirement for life.

✳ *It is love that prevents God from ever letting go of us. God's forgiveness has no limits.*

Monday August 29   **1 John 2.7-13**

The new command – friendship grounded in love

These verses remind me of John 1.29-51 where Jesus drew together a group of friends and called them to discipleship. By the river Jordan, the hermit John and his friends were enjoying one another's company, when John saw Jesus coming and pointed to him as the Lamb of God, God's chosen leader. They asked where he was staying. 'Come and see,' said Jesus.

Andrew brought his brother Simon. Jesus welcomed him and gave him a new name 'Peter'.

Then in Galilee came Philip who found Nathaniel: 'What? you can't accept anything from a place like Nazareth,' he said.

'You had better come and see for yourself,' said Philip.

Jesus saw him coming, a man in whom there was nothing false. 'I saw you under the shadow of the fig tree,' said Jesus.

We too are drawn together by Jesus as members of God's family. Dear friends, let us really care for each other, for such love is God's gift to us to enable us to live in the light and defeat evil.

✳ *What is it I feel so deep*
that makes me go on
fighting for equality
Why, brothers and sisters
there is only one race
We are all members of that human race
Instinctively I feel without being told
that the injustice of South Africa
deeply pains my soul
will the struggle go on forever
as I work to bring about change
to bring about a more just society
I pray for the day South Africa and me
Are set free
Oh God when will you
let us Africans be free?   *From With All My Love*

Tuesday August 30   **ROMANS 12.17-21**

Practise forgiveness

In the 1950s, Sybil was still in Guyana helping those who were applying to work in Britain. The news of rejection and poor living conditions they sent back prompted Sybil and her husband to come and see what they could do. Sybil opened youth clubs in churches and community centres in various parts of London and began adopting and fostering children. But all this happened against the background of her non-acceptance in British life because she was black. When one of her clubs was destroyed by fire, she rebuilt it and invited Prince Charles to be its patron. She knows what it is to forgive and make new beginnings:

We are each one members of God's family and inheritors of God's love. I ask you therefore to remember that you cannot be free to say the family prayer Jesus taught you unless you forgive each other the small wrong, as God constantly forgives you. I have learnt something about God's love and want to share this thought.

Don't go about with high and mighty ideas of your own self-importance: 'try to be humble'. As friends of Jesus, we are all different, but of equal worth to our Father. God has given each of us a different gift to use for one another. As far as you can, be friends with everyone. Never try 'to get your own back'. Leave that in God's hands. And greet every sunrise with new gladness and grateful thanks. Give yourselves to God's service. Keep the doors of your homes open to those who need it. Be warm-hearted in your service and never forget to pray.

✷ *Lord, grant me I pray thee,*
  a loving and understanding heart.

Wednesday August 31   1 JOHN 4.7-21
How to love God

Sybil has also worked to change attitudes and since 1975 has been well-known for her Racism Awareness workshops in both church and society. Community workers and policemen have been sent to learn from her. Her only regret is that 'these courses are still needed as much now as ever they were.' Yet she harbours no bitterness and is respected for her honesty and love:

John assures us that 'God is love'. Love is the greatest gift we have been given along with life itself. It is also the greatest gift we can offer to one another. For in loving and caring, we are practising the one new law our brother Jesus left with us.

✷ *Love is joy;*
  love is happiness;
  love is life;
  love is hope:
  it is the energy of life.
  For where love is, God is.
  For it is in each other's shadow
  that we live our lives
  through God's love for us all.

✷ *God of love, help us to celebrate*
  the beauty of life
  and make us good stewards we pray.

Thursday September 1   1 CORINTHIANS 12.27-13.3
God's presence is in our hearts

Each of us is given God's Spirit in our hearts for the good of one another. We have all been given different gifts, but the one Spirit who works through each gift. For when you were baptised and became friends of Jesus, you began with his help to live in the Father's way. Living in God's way means that we do not talk of one another as being 'white', or 'black', or 'working class', or 'male' or 'female' as though that was the only thing about us that matters. What matters is that, as sons and daughters of God, we are a company of friends who boast only of our love of God and one another.

Using our different gifts to God's honour and glory, all together, and with love, we make up the body of Christ.

✳ *You, only Father God*
are worthy of our worship and prayers.

Friday September 2　　　　1 CORINTHIANS 13.4-7 *

Is it possible?

In 1992, Sybil was asked by the Methodist Recorder whether she was ever disheartened by all the disappointments and frustrations in her work. She replied that she had often echoed the words of Jesus, 'My God, my God, why have you forsaken me?' and wanted to give up and run away. But then she has remembered that the gospel is about being despised and rejected. And so she writes for us:

Through Jesus Christ, we are made friends of God who wants us to take this message of friendship to others. It is possible to flood our world with 'love'. We associate the word 'flood' with devastation and destruction, but look at it today in a positive light. For love is patient and kind; it never gives up. When an area is flooded it is completely saturated, covered all over. We have the God-given power to cover our world with love. It is possible! through the goodness of God whose 'will be done'. We must be willing to look beyond the outer appearance and focus on the inner truth that we want to come true.

Flood your surroundings with love, starting with yourself. Be forbearing, show kindness, encourage patience, see yourself lovingly, feel the harmonising power of love moving through you and all your relationships.

Our attitudes can open the floodgates of love.

✳ *May our prayers be an expression*
of our love and gratitude.

Love is eternal

✳ *Love is the tide*
and God the eternal sea.
When we are tired as we sail that sea,
faith and the prayers of our friends
keep us going
for we live in one another's shadow.

It is the hope of our Father's forgiving love
that keeps us sinners struggling after goodness.
For God's grace changes our despair
into hope –
not a mere wistful hoping for the best
but a lively confident anticipation of heaven
which rests on the God who raised Jesus from the dead
and gave him glory,
so that our faith and hope might be in him.
And so we are assured of God's never failing,
everlasting love.

✳ *Forgive us Lord our sins*
and give us courage to be faithful.

For personal reflection or group discussion

How is God's love nurtured within us? Think of situations where
it is not easy to cooperate with God in loving words and action.
How can we help one another to overcome our difficulties in this
respect?

ACTION

Resolve to think on all around you with love and work to change
the attitudes of those who discriminate against others because
of their sex, class or race.

DARE TO STAND ALONE

Notes, based on the Revised Standard Version, by

Lesley G Anderson

Lesley Anderson is a former Chairman of the Panama/Costa Rica District of the Methodist Church in the Caribbean and Americas. He now serves the British Methodist Church Overseas Division in London as Area Secretary for the Caribbean, Americas and Europe.

There comes a time when we must confront challenges. This might mean facing death, firmly holding on to the faith, boldly confronting iniquity, proclaiming with conviction the power of the gospel, wrestling with awesome problems of our own making, or reaching out to help someone. Sometimes the help we offer makes a radical difference to our lives as well as others.

Jesus is our supreme example on whom we must rely for direction and encouragement. He bore the burden of our sins and it cost him his precious life on Calvary's cross. Through him we are forgiven and reconciled to God and have the assurance of the gift of eternal life. Jesus dared to face the cross and through the power of the living God was resurrected. From him comes the power to be, to become, to live, to love, to serve and dare to take up our cross and follow him.

O God, how wonderful is your love!
We draw near to you in praise and thanksgiving,
in recognition that in our weakness,
you can make us strong
and in our fear courageous,
that we will dare to stand alone. So be it.

Sunday September 4   **1 KINGS 21.1-16 ***

In the face of death

Naboth, whose name means 'to grow', 'to sprout', was the proprietor of an ancestral vineyard near to the royal palace. King Ahaz offered Naboth the equivalent in money or a better vineyard in exchange. The proposal was just, but he dared to refuse it (verse 3). His title 'the Jezreelite' suggests he was a person of some importance and influence and his attitude shows a strong family bond. It was inconceivable that he and his family should become royal dependants.

Ahab was stunned by his reply, but Jezebel, roused to anger, conspired to have Naboth stoned to death on a false charge of blasphemy. Why was the community prepared to accept the flimsy evidence of two reprobates (literally 'sons of worthlessness')? Why did the stoning of Naboth take place outside the city? What reasons can you give as to why his family suffered death with him?

Chico' Mendes, like Naboth, dared to stand for justice. His historic struggle to defend the rubber tappers' way of life in Xapuri, Acre, in North West Brazil, was in fact a fight in defence of an ecological inheritance – the Amazon Forest, which is vital to the survival of his people and all humanity. On Thursday 22 December 1988, he was assassinated by hired gunmen.

✳ *O Lord, our God, we pray that all forms of violence for properties, personal gain and profit, may cease.*

Monday September 5   EZEKIEL 4.1-17

Actions speak louder than words

Like the prophet's words, symbolic actions were thought to carry power.

Ezekiel's first act (verses 1-3) was to place an iron plate, commonly used for baking, between himself and the city. Iron was used to symbolise the overwhelming power of the Babylonians and the prophet represented God whose decisive judgment faced Jerusalem.

In the second act (verses 4-8), the prophet lay for 190 days upon his left side, bearing the punishment of Israel whose people were exiled to Assyria in 722 BC, never to return. Then for 40 days he lay on his right side on behalf of Judah's 40 years of exile from 586BC.

His third act (verses 9-17) portrayed the hardships the continuing siege would bring. Why was Ezekiel commanded to perform symbolic acts? How helpful is this way of delivering God's message?

The majority of Bolivian women in the districts of La Paz wear the 'pollera' or skirt. It is an outstanding symbol of 500 years of resistance which is woven into the fabric. It is spun in the colours of the rainbow and the Andean mountains, with pleats and geometric designs – refusing to follow western styles. It is the national symbol within and outside the native community. Reflect on this symbol and those of Ezekiel. How are they related?

✴ *The cross, O Lord, which once signified death,*
through your power, now symbolises life,
hope, triumph and victory for us all.

Tuesday September 6   DANIEL 3.13-30
Relying completely upon God

Life often presents us with trials and tears, but God offers power to cope. What experiences of God's power have you had in times of trouble?

Daniel's three companions, Shadrach, Meshach and Abednego, courageously chose death rather than compromise their faith in God before King Nebuchadnezzar and were saved by a miracle.

Miracles, however, like the one in this story, do not often happen. The Archbishop of San Salvador, Oscar Romero, despite many death threats, became the fearless voice of the voiceless poor against the repressive government of his country. He died a martyr while celebrating Mass on 24 March, 1980. But the truth for which he stood is still alive in his people's determined struggle for justice. Reflect on the difference between these two experiences.

✴ *Lord, you are the great Liberator.*
Help us to work fearlessly for a new lease of life
for the poor who suffer in their millions
throughout the world.

Wednesday September 7   MARK 6.14-29
A firm stance for righteousness

Herod Antipas, Tetrarch of Galilee and Peraea, was a sly, cruel, superstitious man – a lover of luxury and utterly destitute of principle. John the Baptist, who dared to reprove his immorality, was put in prison and later beheaded. The 'voice of one crying in the wilderness' was silenced but the crime was to haunt Herod for the rest of his life: Jesus' mighty works in Galilee made him afraid John had come to life again! Some described

Jesus as Elias (or Elijah) or as one of the prophets, recognising that he spoke words given to him by God. The mark of the genuine prophet is that he fearlessly declares the message God has put into his mouth. Why do you think Herod was troubled? How was his attitude a serious threat to Jesus?

Aung San Suu Kyi of Myanmar (formerly known as Burma) is valiant in her struggle for human rights and justice. In the first free elections held in over 30 years, her party won but the military government has refused to hand over power. The famous Nobel Peace Prize winner was humiliated and placed under house arrest. She may have her freedom only if she leaves the country and gives up the struggle. But she will not be silenced.

> ✳ *Lord of justice,*
> *enable us to stand and fight*
> *injustices and oppression,*
> *that righteousness and peace may reign.*

Thursday September 8   MARK 12.35-40 *
Making a definite choice

Jesus silenced his critics and raised a question. 'Son of David' was a popular title: the Messiah was to be a second and greater than David. The quotation from Psalm 110.1 in verse 36 shows that David thought of the Messiah as his Lord, a being higher than himself. If David called him Lord how can the Messiah be David's son? Messianic hopes must rise above an earthly and human level.

This messianic hope was foremost in the mind of the people, but there was no one definition of this figure and his work. He was never actually called 'the Messiah' in the Old Testament, but described as 'a branch', 'a ruler', 'Immanuel', 'Prince of Peace', or 'King'. As prince of the royal house of David, he would receive superhuman powers and be judge of humankind. In Zechariah 9.9, the Davidic prince is meek.

Jesus, who fulfilled these expectations, was given all power in heaven and on earth. Yet he chose the lonely way of the Servant, suffering and accepting the death of the cross.

Why did Jesus warn against attention seeking, greed and hypocrisy? Why did he expose the faults of the scribes when all scribes were not like that?

* *Lord Jesus, teach us humility and help us never to neglect those precious moments when we can speak and walk with you.*

Friday September 9   **GALATIANS 1.1-10 ***

Assert your right to be and to become

Paul asserts his right to be an apostle, though his enemies argued he was not. The Greek word 'apostolos' means 'sent forth with a commission' from Jesus Christ. Paul presents his credentials: he is an ambassador of the Lord Jesus Christ. No less a person than the Risen Son of God had been revealed to him and commissioned him. Proof of this was the blessing of God upon his work (2 Corinthians 12.12).

In verse 1 what is especially significant is that the names Jesus and God are linked together by the words 'who raised him from the dead'. Why were these words added? Why does Paul break forth into a doxology in verse 5?

Paul's opening word in verse 6 is one of great surprise and astonishment. He cannot understand how anyone, who has once experienced the magnitude of Christ's grace, should lightly turn away from it. He dares to tell the Galatians that, in seeking to come under the Law, they are actually deserting God. There is only one gospel. If people can be saved by obedience to the Law, then they need neither the divine grace nor Christ's sacrifice. For Paul, both his life and his gospel are based on a rock foundation – Jesus Christ.

When certain men wanted to stone the woman taken in adultery, Jesus confronted them and spoke words of kindness to her. She needed a friend, one who would dare to help her change her life. Jesus offered her love and forgiveness.

* *Lord, teach us not to be afraid to reach out to others in love and concern.*

Saturday September 10   **REVELATION 1.9-19**

Dare to uphold God's justice

John presents an undeviating self-affirmation of God's justice and its implications for us. The expected signs have already been set in motion by the Lamb's victory and so the coming of the 'son of man' is at hand. The exodus and the cross, powerful symbols of the liberation of the poor and despised from exile and oppression, are dominant.

John looks forward to Christ's final coming, the consummation of his death and resurrection. He shares the Old Testament hope that God will gather in all nations – through the death of God's Son and the witness of God's people.

The vision of the 'son of man' refers back to the days of Daniel, to persecution, vindication and judgment. Daniel saw the vindication in heaven of a human figure, representing Israel suffering on earth for its faith over against a series of beasts symbolising oppressing empires (Daniel 7.13). In John, the 'son of man' is the living one who died and is alive for ever. It is this living one who calls us to stand firmly at the side of those who suffer injustices. It may be a loved one, a friend or an enemy. He challenges us to share a word of hope and offer love and care.

Rigoberta Menchu, human rights activist, indigenous campesina leader, survivor of army massacres in the highlands of Guatemala and 1992 Nobel Peace Prize winner, speaks of a day when Guatemala will never again see a mother tortured, a father burned alive, or brothers executed – all of which she has experienced.

✳ *O God of love, power and justice,*
give us strength to witness thoroughly
in and through your name.

For personal reflection or group discussion

Think of situations, similar to those of this week's readings, in your own community or nation. Are there also prophetic personalities like Rigoberta Menchu? How do ordinary Christians support those within whom the Spirit moves to change the world?

Think of other biblical passages which might encourage us.

ACTION

Dare to commit yourself to healing the broken parts of society and work systematically for justice, peace and civil rights, that black and white, rich and poor, women and men, young and mature may live together in peace and love.

RICH ENOUGH TO BE GENEROUS

Notes, based on the New Jerusalem Bible, by
Rosemary Wass

Rosemary Wass, a farmer's wife in North Yorkshire, is a lay preacher and former Vice President of the British Methodist Church. In recent years, she has visited partner Churches in many parts of the world on behalf of the Church in Britain.

How rich do we have to be to be generous? What is it that motivates generosity? Does it ever come naturally? I heard a story recently of a man who was drawn to one of the poorest vendors in a market in an African town. The man purchased a box of matches. He gave the vendor 10 dollars and told him to keep the change, feeling pleased that he had been able to help. But then his feelings changed. He began to feel ashamed that he felt pleased – and then he was pleased that he felt ashamed. Think about it and explore your own feelings.

Come near us, God, giver of life in all its bounty.
Come near us, God who became poor,
giving your Son to a hurt world.
Come near and show us the richness
that reduced you to poverty and gives us life.

Sunday September 11   **2 CORINTHIANS 9.6-15 ***

God loves a cheerful giver

What does this well-worn phrase (verse 8) strike in our minds? Is it an immediate association with finance and our weekly commitment to supporting the life of the church? Money is only one resource. Using all our resources for God often has consequences reaching far beyond what we can imagine. Paul was encouraging Corinthian Christians to make a 'lovegift' for Christians in Macedonia – one of the first appeals for a Church grant. He assured them that 'giving' was not an end in itself, but the beginning of a shared experience, an attitude which generates a spirit of thanks to God whose greatest 'lovegift' to us is Jesus.

When did you last make a gift of love? Was it genuinely from your heart? Was it a liberating experience? Are you conscious of having received a 'lovegift'? What difference has it made to your life?

٭ *Exemplary God, your giving to us is beyond comparison. Your reflection in Christ is clear.*
Help us with your grace to encourage others to receive your gifts and share them with your world today.

Monday September 12   MARK 12.41-44 *

Sacrificial giving

The Temple in Jerusalem had several collection boxes for its upkeep and other freewill offerings. Jesus stressed that the true value of the gift is defined not by its size but by the spirit in which it is given. The widow 'in her poverty has put in everything she possessed.' What does this say to us about the way we act towards offerings for the Church?

Do you remember the widow of Zarephath (1 Kings 17.7-16) and her response to Elijah in the famine, sharing with him all she had for herself and her son? She could never have imagined the consequences of her act of giving.

٭ *Lord you know*
what we earn and how we earn it;
what we give and how we give it;
what we own and how we own it.
Make us open to offer, glad to respond,
honest in our giving and faithful in our calling.
Make us mindful of those who 'give their all',
trusting that you will honour their faith.

Tuesday September 13   MARK 14.1-9 *

A significant gift

Here, in a crowded room, a woman made an expensive response to Jesus and attracted criticism from those who neither understood the action nor performed the common courtesies of hospitality. The only one to defend her was Jesus who made his own feelings clear. Simon had, perhaps, been anxious to impress his friends. After all, he had managed to persuade the controversial Jesus to come for a meal, but he had neglected to give him the proper care required of a host.

The woman had performed an unselfish act of worship which gained importance in the light of the events which followed.

How quick are we to judge an event and then, in retrospect, learn the real significance? How easy is it to seek forgiveness and learn from our mistakes? Pause for a few moments to think of mistaken judgments you have made, of criticisms you have heard of yourself and of people from whom you may feel estranged as a result.

✳ *Loving God, take our thoughts today.*
Anoint them with your precious ointment of forgiveness,
so that our actions may reflect your care for your world.

Wednesday September 14   DEUTERONOMY 15.1-11 *

Lending and cancelling

One phrase links yesterday's reading with today's, though there are many centuries between! Compare verse 11 with Mark 14.7. In a world context, the gap between rich and poor countries, in terms of world trade, increases every year. The poor are often paying more to the donor country in interest than they receive in Aid, so they have little or no bargaining power to improve their lot. If only there could be a Remission Day, debts could be cancelled and the exploited freed.

In our towns and cities, those who are literally rich enough to be generous often use their wealth to build up barriers and security to protect their possessions against the poor. A lack of trust, a closed hand, a desire to be private and judgmental leads to frustration and fear on both sides.

✳ *Take time today*
TO THINK of the most recent newscast you have heard –
of the powerful and the powerless, of good news and
bad news.
TO PRAY for the rich and the poor, for people who work
to bridge 'gaps' in society – social workers, counsellors
and chaplains.
TO REMEMBER those who seek to work alongside the
poor, the broken and the outcast, whose only reward is
their commitment to justice and peace.
TO ASK YOURSELF What am I doing about it? Who can I
encourage to think about cancelling a debt?

Thursday September 15 — MATTHEW 6.19-21

Time treasures

A creeping infestation of woodworm leads to an inevitable collapse of a structure. A moth gnawing into a beautifully created garment spoils the whole. The idolatry of earthly treasure corrupts and distorts life.

Examine our own lifestyle and how that affects our feelings towards other people and to God. Do you have something that is your pride and joy – your car, your house, a piece of jewellery, or the latest piece of technology? Do you think your treasure should be protected and admired at all costs? Have you built yourself 'a tower of Babel' (Genesis 11.1-8)?

What priorities are you going to make in your life to keep your focus on God, your life-giver and greatest treasure?

✳ *Lord God, forgive us the distraction of materialism.*
From the powers of persuasion, protect us.
Generous God who continually watches over us,
may the power of your love draw us and keep us always.

Friday September 16 — PHILIPPIANS 4.10-20

Thanks for help received

In this letter of thanks for a gift which supported him in a time of unjust imprisonment, Paul shows that learning to be content is one of the treasures of a fulfilled life. You might like to read the whole of this chapter to appreciate the depth and spontaneity of Paul's response to his Philippian friends. Although letter-writing is a dying art, it is a gift worth cultivating to encourage others and express your convictions.

Today, I encourage you to write at least one letter – being generous in giving your time to do so, to encourage or to thank someone for something. It is easy to entertain the thought but how often the practice is squeezed out by 'modern' living. Sometimes, enforced circumstances change our lifestyle – hospitalisation, holiday or injury. In Paul's case, prison gave him time to reflect on messages he wanted to pass on. Read these verses again and reflect on Paul writing from prison.

✳ *We pray for all who are unjustly isolated or detained,*
whose faith has cost their freedom,
whose calling to Christ
has proved the victory over suffering.

The richness of generosity

Paul, writing from Macedonia on his third missionary journey, was organising a collection from his congregations for needy believers in Jerusalem. None of the Christian communities were materially rich, but Paul worked hard to engender a spirit of co-operation and care for others, broadening each congregation's horizons, encouraging them to feel part of something bigger. Giving is a natural response of love.

I have two vivid memories of West Africa and my visits to churches there. In one, a 'blessing box' was placed near the communion rail and, as individuals felt the Holy Spirit inspire them through the various facets of worship, they danced their way down to the box, giving cheerfully to God.

The other memory is of a hungry, foodless community where a minister's wife was bidding me farewell. She pressed into my hands a loosely wrapped newspaper parcel revealing bread – a miracle in itself – given with a generous hand, expressing the love and joy of being part of a world family.

✳ *To give and give, and give again,*
  What God has given thee;
To spend thyself nor count the cost,
  To serve right gloriously
The God who gave all worlds that are,
  And all that are to be.

Geoffrey Anketell Studdert-Kennedy

For personal reflection or group discussion

If you were given a large sum of money, would you choose to buy basic necessities, invest it or buy some luxuries? How much would you share with others? Read again and reflect on 1 Corinthians 8.1-9.

ACTION

Over the next week, make a note every time you are at the receiving end of a generous gesture and when you think you have practised generosity. Reflect on your attitudes and think again of God's generosity.

INTERNATIONAL APPEAL

IN OVER 80 COUNTRIES YOU WILL FIND CHRISTIANS USING IBRA MATERIAL

Some Christians will be using books and Bible reading cards translated into their local languages whilst others use English books. Some of the books are printed in this country but more and more of the books and cards are printed in their own countries. This is done by the IBRA International Fund working through churches and Christian groups and Christian Publishing houses overseas.

Each year we receive more requests for help from the IBRA International Fund, with greater emphasis on helping our overseas friends to produce their own versions of IBRA material.

THE ONLY MONEY WE HAVE TO SEND, IS THE MONEY YOU GIVE

SO PLEASE HELP US AGAIN BY GIVING GENEROUSLY

Place your gift in the envelope provided and give it to your IBRA representative,

or send it direct to
The IBRA International Appeal,
Robert Denholm House,
Nutfield, Redhill, Surrey RH1 4HW, UK

THANK YOU FOR YOUR HELP

DREAMS AND VISIONS

Notes, based on the Good News Bible, by
David Cowling and
Magali do Nascimento Cunha

David Cowling (who has written for September 18-24) worked in East Africa for 20 years on various development programmes. He has visited Latin America and works at present with Magali in the Grassroots programme in the UK.

Magali do Nascimento Cunha (who has written for September 25 - November 1) is a journalist working with an ecumenical agency in Rio de Janeiro, Brazil. She is in the UK for one year as a Partner in Mission with the Grassroots Programme.

Dreams are very important in the life of the Latin American Church. They are the means of sustaining hope in the face of poverty, oppression and suffering, and of energising people to struggle for change. Ruben Alves, a Brazilian Professor of Philosophy, says, 'If you are interested in communicating with ordinary people, you have to encourage them to dream. A person is an incarnated dream and the purpose of education is to enable those dreams to be realised.'

The people of Latin America can also help the secular world of the West to rediscover the power of dreams and visions.

Hidden God, we praise you for your presence
in the deepest parts of our being.
Mysterious God, we rejoice
in our ability to discover and discern your truth.
Hopeful God, give us minds and hearts that are free
to dream of your Kingdom.

Sunday September 18   **JOEL 2.28-32**

It was a bad time for the people of God. Their land had been over-run, the Temple destroyed and they were exiled in Babylon. As if that was not enough, there was a serious drought (1.12) and a devastating invasion of locusts (1.4). Were their dreams an escape from painful realities or the vision of a new world?

Today in Latin America, people who are oppressed and suffering dare to dream. Jean-Bertrand Aristide, deposed President of Haiti, wrote, 'Here in the waste land where you had not thought to find life you will suddenly find signs of God's renewal, blooming and flowering and bursting forth from the dry earth with great energy. In the driest month, you will find on the branches' tips new shoots of life. Under the rock in the desert will sprout a flower, a delicate bud of the new life.' *(Quoted with permission from Continent of Hope, CAFOD)*

There is nothing like a drought to make one appreciate water. Those who have faced crisis or their own personal spiritual drought affirm that it can be a time of new awareness. This awareness is not limited to those who have special theological training. The gift is available to all, but the clarity of dreams, visions and prophecy is perhaps greatest where people are passing through some form of crisis.

✳ *Lord, help me to rediscover a sense of vision through the dreams of those who suffer.*

Monday September 19   GENESIS 32.22-32 *

Jacob was running away from the consequences of his deception of Isaac, the anger of Esau and an argument with Laban. He had become very prosperous and yet lived in fear. He thought he could buy good relationships through gifts (Genesis 32.20).

1992 was celebrated as the 500th anniversary of the arrival of Columbus in Latin America. For many in Europe, it was the painful opportunity to reflect on past deception, present anger, and contemporary arguments. Whilst we are awake, we can persuade ourselves that history was different. We can try to buy better relationships with Latin America through aid. We are careful to protect ourselves from the consequences of that history for the majority of people in Latin America today. Until in the silence, in our sleep, we catch a glimpse of the eyes of the suffering; we struggle with our conscience and we are filled with guilt and shame.

There is no escape: we have the choice of living in fear, or we can come to terms with the ways in which we benefit at others' expense. It is a painful struggle. We are forced to recognise our own limitations and disability, but even though we limp, we move ahead, liberated from our fear.

Tuesday September 20   1 KINGS 3.4-15

What would you like me to give you? In many countries, people
are bombarded by offers of free gifts if they will purchase an
insurance, a book, a holiday apartment . . . It is an attempt to
dull our critical faculties, to break down our reluctance to spend.
God does not offer such cheap and empty gestures that
devalue our potential. We are challenged to dream. When two
disciples first followed Jesus, he asked them, 'What are you
looking for?' (John 1.38)

Are we so preoccupied with surviving tomorrow that we are
not able to discern future needs? To listen to the promises of
politicians, one would assume that people only hope for more
money, more pleasure or indeed 'long life, riches and the death
of our enemies'. In Latin America, there is of course the need for
money and jobs, but the demand is for justice and more lasting
benefits. Oscar Romero wrote, 'The hope we preach to the poor
is hope for the restoration of their dignity. The hope we preach
to the poor is the courage to become authors of their own
destiny' *(From Continent of Hope – CAFOD).*

✳ *Forgive me Lord, if I have allowed*
  my narrow personal interests and concerns
  to prevent me becoming an agent of change in your
  world.

Wednesday September 21   ISAIAH 40.1-11

Fear dominates much of Western society in the same way as it
did the people of Judah. For Judah, their fears were being
realised. All the security, which apparently came from having
God on their side, was shattered as they saw their enemies
triumph. Gone was their privilege and wealth as they became
refugees in a foreign land. In the midst of this pain and trauma,
Isaiah offered a message of hope.

Ignacio Ellacuria, a Jesuit priest murdered in El Salvador
wrote, 'All this blood of martyrs shed in El Salvador and

throughout Latin America – far from moving them into despondency and despair – infuses a new spirit of struggle and new hope in our people. In this way, even if we are not a "new world" or a "new continent", we are clearly and verifiably – and not necessarily by those from outside – a continent of hope. And this is something of utmost importance for future development in the face of other continents which have no hope and have only fear.' *(Quoted in Continent of Hope, CAFOD)*

Since the Second World War, the economies and policies of the West have been dominated by fear. We need to rediscover the gospel of love which will enable us to speak out and not be afraid.

✳ *Lord, help us to overcome the fear which stifles love and kills all hope.*

Thursday September 22   Isaiah 35.1-10

In a world dominated by technology and the products of human creativity, it is easy to forget our relationship with the wider, divinely created world. Judah was threatened by the Assyrians and the dominant concern must have been that very real and immediate threat: 'Protect us day by day and save us in times of trouble' (Isaiah 33.2). But Judah was still depending on its traditional power to defeat the threat.

Isaiah's vision is of a different world where the unproductive becomes fertile, the disabled discover new talents, and the weak are given new strength. The deepest need of the human spirit is for that peace and harmony which comes when we are ready to encourage and affirm rather than dominate and destroy; when we are in tune with the created world.

Land is a very important issue for many people in Latin America. Biblical images of the Promised Land speak to those who see vast areas unused. For the majority of the world's population, this passage immediately comes to life because they have known the agony of toiling on the land when the rains have failed. And in the West, with the need to create jobs and increase production, we need to be reminded of living in harmony with the whole creation.

✳ *Creator God, enlarge our minds with a vision of the world beyond our control and manipulation.*

For a people whose life centred on the Temple where God was present, the destruction of Jerusalem and its Temple must have been devastating. Ezekiel was with his people in exile and must have faced their questioning: Why has this happened? National tragedy provides an opportunity for reflection and evaluation.

It is necessary, first of all, to recognise that there is a crisis. Ezekiel and other prophets often had a hard time making people realise this. It required defeat and exile for the message to get through and to make it possible to plan for renewal. Ezekiel suggests that the Temple had been domesticated, used for the benefit of a few, and its real message and promise ignored (Ezekiel 8).

In the new Jerusalem, the living water that flows from the presence of God will be so deep and powerful that it will carry a person away. It will replace the dead water that destroys life, and bring freshness and renewal. It is difficult to retain the purity of spring water as it flows on to become a large river. In the same way, much of the energy and vigour has been lost from church life in the West. It needs to be renewed by water from the source.

✳ *Father, we confess:*
our church life has become stale and lifeless.
Renew us with the living water of your Kingdom.

In Latin America, the Church was allied with the powerful for nearly 500 years. It became a symbol of oppression for many. Since the 1950s, there has been an awakening within the Church which has led to a willingness to challenge the corruption and oppression of governments, a rediscovery of the value and significance of indigenous spirituality, and a renewal of worship and liturgy. Over the same period, there has been a move away from military governments towards democratic systems. The Church is emerging in a new role, able to provide a vision of a just and democratic society which inspires and mobilises support from those who previously thought they had no voice.

In the 1992 elections in Britain and America, no political leader really caught the imagination of the electorate. There was even debate about the 'vision' thing. 'Where there is no vision the people perish', and throughout the world there is hunger for prophetic leadership which can act as salt and light for the whole of society. It is not just individuals who need dreams and visions, but all people, the 'whole world'.

✳ *Lord, help us not to be content*
with a gospel that is only personal and private.

For personal reflection or group discussion

Think back to a time when you had dreams for your future. How did those dreams influence choices you made? How far have they become a reality?

Look at Luke 4.18-19. Is this a realistic dream? What is your church doing to make this dream a reality?

Sunday September 25   **PSALM 65**

The people of Israel were under pressure in all their history. First, they had no land to live on or work. Then, when their land, which they had conquered with great effort, was coveted by others, they lived in fear and uncertainty of war, death, and oppressive leaders. They had feelings of helplessness and powerlessness. How could they overcome this situation?

The psalmist gave a clue. There was Someone in whom they could trust: God. With a psalm of praise and thanksgiving, people were invited to see the great things God had done among them, the beauty of nature, calming the uproar of peoples, rich harvests . . . By experiencing the signs of God's presence in the world, there would be the possibility of dreaming of a better future. Trust in God. This is the clue for us today who continue suffering pain and uncertainty. God is still doing good things among us. We have just to be opened to see and dream.

✳ *Lord, I trust in you.*
Forgive me
when I find it difficult to see
what you have done today.

The story of Paul's conversion is full of symbols. He had been a persecutor of Christians and sent many of them to prison. Paul was against Jesus Christ. When Jesus revealed himself on the road to Damascus, Paul's eyes were closed and he became blind. It was the outward evidence of an inner reality: Paul was blind. He was refusing to accept the truth of the gospel preached by Jesus and the renewal proclaimed by his presence in the world. Paul had closed his eyes to all that.

On the road to Damascus, Jesus used Paul's blindness as a symbol of Paul's attitude to the Christians' faith and gave him the possibility to open his eyes and the eyes of others, turning from darkness to light.

For a long time in Latin America, Churches had the same experience. Their eyes were closed to people's struggles and search for liberation. In their 'journey to Damascus', however, there was a vision. Movements that came from the grassroots were used by God to show the Churches that their place was among those who seek for life and justice.

Do you have your eyes opened to see and support God's renewal in the world?

✳ *Father, show me your light*
and give me the vision of your will.

Paul gives thanks to God for the Christians in Rome. They were under pressure and suffering some persecution, but their spiritual blessing made them strong to preach and spread the good news. Their testimony was an inspiration to Paul.

Today, we can give thanks to God for Christians in places like Latin America. Their testimony can be an inspiration to other Churches in the world. For 500 years, Latin American people have received bad news: colonisation, slavery, death, exploitation, dependency. Although, for a time, the Church was part of the oppressive system, from the beginning many Christian men and women have put their faith into practice and the 500 years of oppression have been also 500 years of resistance. Celebrating their faith, studying the Bible and sharing their lives and struggles in communities, those Christians have had a vision of the Kingdom of God: that it will be fulfilled, not only in heaven, but on earth, today.

* **God, I would like to have the vision of your Kingdom
  and be a builder of hope and peace.**

Wednesday September 28   COLOSSIANS 1.15–20

God dreams! All the time that we come across the stories told in
the Bible, we perceive that God is dreaming and inviting
everyone to dream as well. God dreams of a world in harmony,
with justice, peace and solidarity among its people. God dreams
of a world where the last can be first and the powerless can
have the best places.

Dreaming, God decided to be revealed as a human being –
Jesus Christ. Through Jesus, God is sharing with all the people
a great dream: the Kingdom of Heaven. Indians in Latin
America have talked about the 'Land without Evil' – their vision
of the Kingdom. 500 years of oppression were not strong
enough to stop people's dreams in that continent, which is the
reason for resistance and survival. When we dream, we renew
hope and when there is hope, we have strength to continue our
daily life and help others, and, in solidarity with them, to live in
harmony, justice and peace.

* **Lord, our life is in your hands.
  Show us the best way to follow your will.**

Thursday September 29   REVELATION 5.1-14

Some people think about the Book of Revelation as a strange
book that inspires fear. Some never open it. But Revelation is a
book full of beauty and hope. John wrote to all Christians who
were suffering persecution and facing torture and death. Many
of them were disheartened, distressed and without hope. John
himself was in prison for his faith and from there he shared his
visions and dreams.

One of them has many symbols: a scroll, angels, elders,
living creatures and a Lamb, to express that Jesus Christ, the
Lamb of God, has power over heaven and earth. He was the
last sacrifice for all the world and his death brought victory for
every people on earth. The blood of the Lamb is a sign of relief
for all who suffer and put their confidence in him. The study of
the book of Revelation has brought support to Christians in
Latin America. It is a key to unlock and liberate those who are
prisoners of fear and despair. Revelation is saying to them and

to all of us, in every part of the world, 'Courage! Do not be afraid. God is with you and we can have the victory.'

✽ *Thank you, God,*
because through Jesus Christ
we can be released
from all chains of fear.

Friday September 30   REVELATION 21.1-7

The book of Revelation encouraged people to get rid of fear by sharing a vision of 'a new heaven and a new earth'. It was a dream about the Kingdom: God's home with humankind, no more death, grief, crying or pain. New life, new things. How good it is to dream! It is not difficult to imagine the relief felt for all those who were in Roman prisons, ready to be burnt or sent to be eaten by lions, when they had a letter like that.

Do we believe in it, or has secularised society influenced us in such a way that we are only rational and extremely realistic? How often do we dream of the way we would like to see 'a new heaven and a new earth'? How often do we share our dreams with others who suffer pain and grief, encouraging them to dream as well. This should be the beauty of the mission of the Church: the Church being able to dream and encourage others to do the same, believing that this new world is possible, the Kingdom is possible and the good news can be made concrete through our attitudes of love and fellowship.

✽ *Lord, help me to help others*
to feel the possibility of your Kingdom.

Saturday October 1   REVELATION 22.1-5

Nations in our world have not had a good time. From east to west and from north to south, there are problems. Rich countries have faced recession, violence, internal divisions; poor countries have become poorer, facing famine, illnesses and more violence. The environment has been affected by the destruction of forests, pollution of rivers and seas, and the ozone layer is being reduced. Some people are very pessimistic and say we are walking in the direction of disaster, chaos and darkness.

But a word comes from the past and speaks today because it is a living word. The word is spoken by someone in prison, sharing hope with his own people who were facing disaster, chaos and darkness. He shares his vision of a future under God's hands when there will be 'a river' and 'a tree of life' – nature alive for the healing of the nations – life brought into darkness.

For Christians, there is no pessimism, no conformity with the standards of our world. Starting with ourselves, in our family, in our neighbourhood, we shall believe that the Word of God is alive and speaking today, sharing visions and dreams to restore life on earth and bring integrity to God's creation.

✳ *Lord, we want to be your instruments*
   for the healing of your creation.

For personal reflection or group discussion

Make a list of your dreams for your church and community for the year 2000. Then think of a person in your community who is unemployed, homeless, or in some way excluded. Try to imagine what his or her dreams would be. How do the two lists compare?

How do young people catch a vision which will inspire and sustain?

ACTION

Ask some young people to share their dreams with you. Consider how they relate to the life of your church.

IN SUFFERING STAND FIRM
(1 PETER)

Notes, based on the Revised Standard Version, by

David Dunn Wilson

After thirty years as a minister in British churches, David Dunn Wilson served in Panama City, and then in the Valiente Indian Mission as Principal of the Instituto Biblico Metodista. He is now tutor in Pastoral Theology at Hartley Victoria College, Manchester.

---

1 Peter was probably written in Rome (called 'Babylon' in 5.13) and, according to tradition, may have been written by the apostle Peter with the help of Silas (5.12 cf Acts 15.22). It was written to encourage Christians in Asia Minor who were facing persecution and is truly a call to stand firm in suffering. But it is more than that. It is a celebration of the new Christian life upon which Peter's readers have embarked and it may even include advice for those recently baptised.

Peter reminds us that we have been born again into a new kind of living, and shows how we can live our new life in Christ even in the darkest days. The letter sparkles with glorious ideas which are linked with many other passages in the Bible. References to some of these passages are included.

Almighty God, who has called me to new life in Christ, open my heart and mind to hear and understand what you have to say to me through your servant.

Sunday October 2   **1 PETER 1.1-7**

Journey into a new life

How apt is the idea that Christians are spiritual refugees, scattered throughout the world like exiles, travelling towards a heavenly home (see Philippians 3.20). Peter says that, like all refugees, Christians will suffer on their journey, but he gives four reasons why they should travel joyfully (verse 6).

● God has given them a positive approach to suffering: God stands with them, enabling them to look beyond their suffering.

● God has paid them a compliment: they are God's new Chosen People (cf Ephesians 1.4) and have been brought into a wonderful new relationship with God through Christ's sacrificial death (verse 2 – contrast with Exodus 24.4-8).

● God has given them a life filled with God's peace, in which the Holy Spirit's power is refining them (verses 2-3).

● God has given them a vigorous new hope: for life here and beyond (verse 4). Contrast this with the 'perishable inheritance' of Israel (Deuteronomy 15.4; 19.10).

Perhaps Peter has in mind his readers' baptism. Symbolically, they have 'died' to their old life (being 'buried' by immersion in the water, like Jesus going into the tomb), and 'risen' to begin their new life with him.

✷ *Lord, if I have to suffer today, hold me steady.*

Monday October 3   1 PETER 1.8-12

Faith – the foundation

'Seeing is believing', is a popular saying, but the author says that, sometimes, it is necessary to believe without seeing. In the New Testament, the link between 'faith' and 'sight' is important, (John 20.29; Romans 8.24f; 2 Corinthians 5.7; Hebrews 11), and here, Peter points to three examples of noble faith:

● **Christians** themselves (verses 8-9), who have loved and trusted Jesus, although they have never physically met him;

● **the prophets,** who continued to trust God even though they did not see their prophecies fulfilled (verses 10-12);

● **the angels,** who, without fully understanding God's plan, accept it completely and strain their eyes to watch it unfolding (verse 12; cf Luke 15.10).

Each is rewarded. Christians who trust Jesus so completely, are given a foretaste of greater blessings in store for them (verse 9). The prophets, who were faithful, were used to prepare for Christ's earthly ministry, revealing his forthcoming suffering and victory (verse 11). Angels who believe that God has further truth to show them, are given greater understanding (verse 12; cf Ephesians 3.10).

The principle holds true: faith without sight is still noble. When we trust God, even in darkness, God can bless and use us.

✷   *I do not ask to see*
. . . The distant scene; one step enough for me.
                                              John Henry Newman

Tuesday October 4 1 PETER 1.13-25

Beginning the new life

We have begun to live a totally new kind of life (verse 23). Conversion marks its beginning and embraces, not only our emotions, but also all our powers of mind and will.

● **True conversion includes acceptance** – acknowledging that we cannot save ourselves – and allowing Christ to rescue us from sin's mastery, not as slaves once bought their freedom by money or animal sacrifices, but by his own sacrificial death (verses 18f).

● **True conversion includes rejection** – deliberately turning away from our old lifestyle, which was clouded by spiritual ignorance (verse 14; cf Acts 17.30; Ephesians 4.18), controlled by selfish impulses (verse 14; cf Ephesians 2.1-3), and limited by lack of purpose (verse 18) and lack of permanence (verses 23f; cf Isaiah 40.6-8).

● **True conversion includes obedience** (verses 14,22) – embracing our new lifestyle with total determination (verse 13). Our new lifestyle contrasts with the old way at every point. It shines with understanding of spiritual truth (verse 22). It is controlled by a desire to be holy (verse 15; cf Leviticus 11.44f; 19.2; 20.7), showing itself in reverence towards God (verse 17) and love for fellow-Christians (verse 22). It is caught up in the eternal purposes of God (verses 21, 25).

Verse 17 reminds us that we cannot claim to be children of a just God if we live unjust lives. Conversion is not simply a private emotion; it is a public testimony to our new lifestyle.

✳ *Lord, let me do nothing today*
which will damage your reputation.

Wednesday October 5 1 PETER 2.1-10

Sustaining the new life

How is the new lifestyle of Christians to be sustained?

● **Jesus the food** – Stripping off their old pagan ways (verse 1; cf Mark 7. 21ff; Romans 1.29-31), and having already 'tasted the joys of being a Christian (verse 3; cf Psalm 34.8), they are to feast on spiritual food for 'born again people', lest they die of spiritual starvation (cf Hebrews 6.4-6).

● **Jesus the stone** – Jesus is the living stone which exposes the dead idols of paganism (verse 4). Jesus is the rejected stone, now exalted by God (verse 4; cf Psalm 118.22). Jesus is the stumbling stone, which is the downfall of unbelievers (verse 8; cf Isaiah 8.14). He is the cornerstone of a new spiritual temple, the Church (cf Isaiah 28.16; Ephesians 2.20).

Christians are the living stones of which the Church is made (verse 5; cf Acts 7.48; 1 Corinthians 3.16f; 2 Corinthians 6.16), supporting and maintaining it. Unimportant though they were (verse 10; cf Hosea 1.8-10), they have now inherited Israel's privilege of being God's people in the world (verse 9; cf Exodus 19.5f; Isaiah 43.10ff; 20f; 44.8), offering God true worship (verse 5) and testifying to God's glory (verse 9; cf Psalm 43.4).

Although personal devotion and public worship are vital for keeping faith healthy, they are not enough. Faith grows when it is exposed to scrutiny by others and its insights are shared.

✳ *Lord, give me an opportunity to share my faith today and save me from ignoring it!*

Thursday October 6   1 PETER 2.11-17

Christian realism

Christians may have changed, but the world has not! The author gives practical advice about living the new lifestyle in old, difficult circumstances. He calls for realism on the part of Christian 'refugees' (verse 11).

● **Be realistic about the stress which Christians can experience** (verse 11). The world is a hostile environment which is constantly trying to reabsorb the Christian into itself (cf Romans 7.22ff; Galatians 5.16ff; James 4.1ff).

● **Be realistic about the difficulty of living among non-Christians** (verse 12). People often look for opportunities to expose you as hypocrites, so obey Jesus (Matthew 5.16) and be above reproach. Who knows? On Judgment Day, you may discover some of your critics have been converted (cf 4.7; Isaiah 10.3)!

● **Be realistic about non-Christian authorities** (verse 13-15). Becoming a Christian brings a wonderful sense of freedom (verse 16; cf John 8.32), but that does not mean that we can do whatever we like (cf Romans 6.15; Galatians 5.13)! We must live as responsible, law-abiding members of society.

● **Be realistic about your relationships** (verse 17). Christians cannot please everybody! Although we must respect everyone, we will always have a special relationship with fellow-Christians.

Although we will respect human authority, we will stand in awe only of God.

Christians were accused of undermining Roman society (eg Acts 16.16ff; 19.23ff) and the author urges them to disarm criticism by their obedience. Is not the Church greatest, however, when it is most disobedient to unjust authority?

✳ *Lord, help me to know when I ought to be disobedient.*

Friday October 7   1 PETER 2.18-25
Acceptance and the new life

The treatment of Roman slaves varied enormously. Some were beaten to death. Others received respect. Peter, believing the End is near, sees no need to attack slavery itself, but seeks to help Christian slaves to live in Christ's way, especially in situations of cruelty and injustice.

He stresses that the new life is not controlled by the treatment they receive from others, but by their obedience to God (verses 18ff). They are to follow Christ's 'example', just as a child copies the letters of the alphabet drawn by his teacher ('example' is the word used of a child's copy-alphabet). Jesus often bore criticism but, although he suffered unjustly, he did not retaliate (Isaiah 53.7). It was only because he was ready to die an unjust death that he was able to save humanity (verse 24; cf Galatians 3.13; Colossians 1.22). Now that Christians are under his care, he will help them to remain faithful (verse 15; cf Isaiah 53.6; Hebrews 13.20). Sometimes life is unfair, but must be accepted as it is, just as Jesus accepted and used it. Because Jesus has faced the worst possible situations, he is qualified and able to sustain us.

✳ *Jesus, you faced suffering and death with great courage. When life seems unfair, give me your strength.*

Saturday October 8   1 PETER 3.1-7
New life – old partners

How should Christians relate to non-believing partners? Peter concentrates on Christian wives, whose rejection of their husbands' religion would have been regarded as infidelity.

● Following Sarah's example (Genesis 18), they should 'submit' to their husbands (verse 6; cf Ephesians 5.22;

Colossians 3.18; 1 Timothy 2.9-15), using patient tact so that their husbands do not become opposed to their new faith.

● They are to influence their husbands by radiating attractive faith and rejecting the extravagant lifestyle so often condemned by pagan writers (verse 2-4). By showing the same kind of winsomeness, Christian husbands may also influence unbelieving wives (verse 7).

The idea of 'submissive wives' may disturb us, but Peter is describing conditions under which many Christian women in the world still live out their faith. His realism reminds us that we live in a cultural context and are not given easy, ideal conditions in which to be Christians. Whilst seeking to transform society, we may have to be faithful in the world as it is – not as we should like it to be. The passage poses another question. What does it mean for Christians to 'submit' (cf 2.13, 18), and how can true Christian submission be reconciled with our modern emphasis upon self-awareness, self-expression and self-assertion?

✴ *Lord Jesus Christ,*
   save me from waiting until I have ideal circumstances
   before I begin to obey you.
   help me to obey you here and now.

For personal reflection or group discussion
Many of the instructions of New Testament writers about marriage and family life are rooted in the culture of their people and time in history. How does this affect the way we interpret their words? What are the timeless values? and how can we continue to preserve them?

Sunday October 9   **1 PETER 3.8-12**

The new life decribed

Peter sums up the characteristics of the new life, detailing first its effect upon the Church (verse 8). Each characteristic fits into the others like pieces of a jig-saw puzzle. The 'harmony' which excludes divisions (cf Romans 12.16; 1 Corinthians 1.10; Philippians 1.27) fits into the 'sympathy' so necessary for Christians facing hard times (cf Romans 12.15; 1 Corinthians 12.26). 'Brotherly love', which integrates Christians into a spiritual family (cf 1 Thessalonians 4.9f), has, as its essential ingredients, the 'compassion' and 'humility' of Jesus (Matthew 11.29; Philippians 2.3ff).

Peter turns to consider the new life in a hostile world (verse 9). It is not enough for Christians simply not to retaliate when attacked: they must actively 'bless their enemies' (Cf Matthew 5.44; Romans 12.17). 'Blessing' (which occurs over 400 times in the Greek Old Testament) includes active prayer on behalf of others (cf Acts 7.60; 1 Corinthians 4.12).

To explain how Christians sustain such a lifestyle, the author uses Psalm 34.12-16, which originally implied that good people live long lives. He expands that idea to mean that Christians desire life in all its fullness – both here and in eternity. This makes them very determined to turn away from their old life, to turn towards the new, and to march along the road of peace with God, under God's protection. Determination is important. The Christian life is not lived by absent-mindedness; it requires constant discipline and vigilance.

✳ *Lord, I know the way,*
but often I forget to walk in it.
Give me your Spirit
to keep me walking straight.

Monday October 10   1 Peter 3.13-22
Testifying to the new life
When Christians tell others about their new life, they often meet opposition, so Peter urges his readers to testify tactfully and bravely (verse 14f; cf Proverbs 15.1; Isaiah 8.12f).

He points to the perfect example of Christ, the **Suffering Witness.** The exact meaning of verses 18-22 is unclear. Peter may be saying that, in order to bring us to new life with God, Jesus came, lived and died as a human being (cf Romans 5.2; Ephesians 2.14ff). He also went to preach to those who had been drowned in the flood – reputedly the worst sinners of all time (verses 19ff; cf Genesis 6.5ff).

Peter suggests that, as Noah's family was saved from death by the ark, so Christians have been saved through baptism which unites them with Christ's saving work. Their triumphant Lord will care for them as they continue his work of witness.

The implications are clear. With gratitude for Christ's sacrifice, and trust in his power, we must witness to him through our new lifestyle, even if it means being misunderstood and attacked.

✳ *Lord Jesus, you died to give me new life.*
Make me brave to share the good news with others.

Tuesday October 11   1 PETER 4.1-6
Dangers to the new life

When life gets hard, Christians may be tempted to go back to their old ways. Instead, they should allow their sufferings to purify them by following Christ's example. Then they will be 'armed with his mind' (cf Ephesians 6.11-17; Philippians 3.10) and see themselves as 'dead' to the demands of this present, temporary existence, just as he did. The old way of life must be dead and their new life completely controlled by God's will (cf Jesus himself John 4.34; 5.30). They cannot relive mispent years but can ensure that no more time is wasted on old worldly priorities and sins (verse 3).

Peter raises another point. If fear of persecution does not make a Christian fall, love of popularity may! Because non-Christians often do not understand the new lifestyle, they begin to hate it and reject those who live in it (cf John 3.19ff). However difficult it may be, Christians must not surrender and rejoin their critics in the old, mad, worldly race (literally to 'run with them'; cf 1 Corinthians 9.24; Galatians 5.7; Hebrews 12.1ff). They must remember that both the end of life's race and the end of time are imminent: all who have heard the gospel will be judged by it.

✳ *I have entered the Christian race, Lord.*
Help me not to drop out.

Wednesday October 12   1 PETER 4.7-11
The marks of new life

Peter and his readers are convinced that Christ will soon return and must find them living in a way appropriate for his followers (cf Luke 12.35ff; 17.26ff). Christ will expect to find these marks of the new life:

● **discipline** (verse 7) – the nearness of the End must lead them neither into apathy nor into mindless, religious frenzy. Thoughts and feelings must be properly controlled;

● **devotion** (verse 7) – new life with God depends on prayer;

● **love** (verse 8) – an old tradition attributes to Jesus the saying 'love covers a multitude of sins'. It refers to frequent, loving forgiveness both by God and by Christians (Matthew 18.21ff; Mark 11.25; John 13.35);

● **hospitality** (verse 9) – an expression of love, especially for Christian travellers. Notice that it is to be 'ungrudging', even if it is abused;

● **stewardship** (verse 10; cf Luke 12.42ff; 1 Corinthians 4.1f) - the gifts God has given to individuals, are intended to be used for the benefit of the whole Church.

The new way is a **corporate** life for all Christians. The Church is to be God's 'shop window' to display the new lifestyle which God longs to give to **every** community.

✳ *Lord Jesus, make my church fit and ready for your inspection.*

Thursday October 13   **1 PETER 4.12-19**

Hard times

It is suggested that, at this point in the letter, the persecution hinted at in 4.1-6 has become a terrible reality. It has stunned the church, so the author gives his readers a positive attitude to their frightening experience. He tells them that, incredibly, they can embrace authentic Christian suffering with joy (verse 13; cf Acts 5.41; James 1.2). Notice the warning in verses 15-19.

Christian suffering is:

● **natural** – part of what it means to follow Christ (verse 12);

● **strengthening** – testing the reality of faith (verse 12), 'firing' faith like a pot in a kiln. Peter even suggests (verse 17) that it is a sign that the End is near, purifying Christians and preparing them for judgment;

● **a privilege** – it shares Christ's own sufferings, 'taking up the cross and following him' (verse 13; cf Matthew 16.24; Romans 8.17; Philippians 3.10; Colossians 1.24);

● **a blessing** – it brings the Holy Spirit's glory upon the persecuted (verse 14: some versions add 'and power');

● **an act of worship** – it gives glory to God (verse 16);

● **an opportunity for trust** – suffering Christians can entrust themselves to God, as Christ did on the cross (Luke 23.46).

What a challenge we are given! So often we complain as

soon as our commitment to Christ causes us even minor inconvenience.

✳ *O Christ, who did not run away from suffering,*
  help me today to set my suffering in the light of eternity.

Friday October 14   **1 PETER 5.1-7**

Leaders and followers

As one who knows the responsibility of pastoral care, the author addresses leaders of local congregations (cf Acts 21.18), setting out qualities of leadership the Church needs:

● **a caring leadership** – accepting responsibility for each member of the flock (verse 2);

● **a humble leadership** – which acknowledges the privilege of being entrusted with the care of Christ's people (verse 2);

● **a willing leadership** – not toiling with a sense of resentment;

● **a selfless leadership** – not exploiting its authority for personal gain (verse 2);

● **an enthusiastic leadership** – providing the drive necessary to encourage dispirited followers (verse 2);

● **an enabling leadership** – releasing members' gifts instead of crushing them in an authoritarian way (verse 3; cf Mark 10.42ff).

The Church also needs **good followers**. They must be:

● **respectful,** giving proper support to those who bear the burden of leadership (verse 5);

● **humble**, not seeking prestige or power (verse 5; cf Proverbs 3.34; James 4.6);

● **active** – the rare word for 'clothe yourselves' (verse 5) was used of a slave putting on his apron ready for work!

● **disciplined** – accepting God's control (verse 6), God's 'hand of discipline' (cf Exodus 3.19; Job 30.21; Psalm 32.4);

● **confident** – trusting in God for everything (verse 7; cf Matthew 6.25ff, also God's 'hand of deliverance' cf Deuteronomy 9.26, Ezekiel 20.34).

In practice, we often fulfil both roles in the Church, sometimes leading, sometimes following. How do we measure up in the light of Peter's analysis?

✳ *Lord, help me know when to lead and when to follow,*
  and to do both equally well.

Just as it is

Peter concludes with a call for clear thinking.

● **Never underestimate the power of evil** (verse 8). He personifies all forces opposed to God and says that the devil is like a ferocious, starving lion (cf Psalm 22.13; Job 1.7). Let no one be in any doubt that he is 'prowling', looking patiently for the right opportunity to destroy the Christian.

● **Never underestimate the will-power needed to defeat evil**. If the apostle Peter was the author, the warning to 'watch' (verse 8) would come with special force from his lips (cf Mark 13.35ff; 14.34,38). Christians all over the world have discovered that evil does not go away simply because it is ignored; it has to be effectively resisted and attacked (Ephesians 6.11ff).

● **Never underestimate the power of Christ.** The Christian's strength lies in Christ's personal care (verse 10; cf Philippians 1.6; 1 Thessalonians 5.23f). He 'restores' (a word used of repairing boats) when we are damaged by disappointments. He 'strengthens' us against temporary failures, and he 'establishes' us when the very foundations of life tremble.

● **Never underestimate the reward for faithfulness.** God, who has always been gracious, will bring those who follow Christ through their sufferings to share God's eternal glory (verse 10; cf Psalm 73.23f; John 17.22ff).

Amid the confusions of modern living, here are four certainties which can hold us steady. New life in Christ is not easy but it is the only life which can satisfy us eternally.

✳ *Lord, give me your new life in all its fullness.*

For personal reflection or group discussion

What is the Christian lifestyle you would hope your neighbours would recognise in you? When is it costly for you? Which of the ways of Christ do you find most difficult to follow? How does strength come?

ACTION

Live the new life Peter has described and find true happiness.

THE EARTH IS THE LORD'S

Notes, based on the Revised English Bible, by
Jan S Pickard

*Jan Sutch Pickard is the Editor of **Connect**, a Christian magazine linking faith and action, and also a yearly Prayer Handbook used by Methodists in many places. A poet and lay preacher, she has lived and worked in Ibadan, Nigeria and in Notting Hill, an inner city area of London.*

Although the readings for this theme are taken from some very ancient writings and oral traditions (stories passed down from generation to generation), they are still 'words for today'. They speak to our society, as they raise issues of how we live in this world as good stewards of God's creation and in just and caring relationships with each other. They also speak to us as individuals, each of us a precious part of creation, gifted with senses and imagination, the ability to use language and the capacity to care. So the readings start, 'in the beginning', by inviting us to use our imaginations and reflect on the mystery of God at work in creation.

These notes encourage us to ask: How do these words from the past relate to our experience today? How can they bring us closer to God? How can we become part of the 'New Creation' of which Christ's birth was the beginning, and which the Second Coming will bring to fulfilment?

God of beginnings
you were there at our birth,
you were there when the first light
broke upon the world,
you begin each day alongside us.
Be with us as we begin each journey,
and bring us home.

Sunday October 16   **GENESIS 1.1-5**

Maybe you are reading this first thing in the morning, while it is still dark. But is it? Look outside. Are shapes of buildings and trees becoming visible? Is there a faint light in the sky? Are the first birds singing? How do you know that dawn is coming? Those who told this ancient creation story probably drew on their daily experience of light returning to the earth – and with it hope and warmth and life. But here we are imagining the very first light ever, the creation of light: 'And God saw that it was good'. This passage does not say that the darkness is bad. Day and night are separate but complementary. We need both – times of rest and reflection as well as activity and everyday awareness.

In some versions, God's Spirit is described like a bird 'hovering' or 'brooding' over the waters of chaos, or else like the wind that springs up before dawn: it both nurtures new life, like a bird hatching an egg, and disturbs our old life, bringing change. Are we open to God's Spirit working in different ways in our lives? Are we willing to be cared for, stirred up, challenged and changed?

✳ *Pray for openness to the Holy Spirit.*

Monday October 17   GENESIS 1.6-13

Two stages in the story of creation are described here. On the 'third day' we are on familiar ground – dry land as it emerges from the sea. But the second day is much harder to imagine. We glimpse an ancient middle-eastern way of understanding the universe. God is described as dividing the waters of chaos, on which the first light dawned. A space is created in between – where the known world takes shape. Those who told the story believed that the 'waters above' were prevented from falling on the world by the sky, like a great vault. This may seem strange to us, but it spoke to the Hebrew people of God's over-arching care for the world.

The plants which begin to colonise the dry land, on the third day, are signs of God's generosity in creation. Does your church celebrate a harvest festival? If so, think of the beauty of shape, colour, smell and taste of all the fruits and vegetables gathered there. Think of your local market, week after week. Think of a wild flower meadow, or the variety of trees and plants in a tropical rain forest.

✳ *God who brings all things to birth,*
God of all-embracing love,
we praise you for the beauty and variety of creation.

Tuesday October 18   **GENESIS 1.14-25**

Our diaries mark significant dates. We know the day and date
when Christmas Day will be celebrated. For people of the
ancient world, and Jewish and Muslim believers today, festivals
are signalled not by fixed dates, but by prayerful observation of
the moon's changes, the movement of stars. The sky, by night
and day, not only gives light to the earth, but the heavenly
bodies provide 'signs for festivals', for people to worship God
their Creator.

In the Church calendar, there are many different occasions to
praise God, remembering the fullness of creation and salvation,
from All Saints in a few days time, to Easter and Pentecost. Do
we make the most of every opportunity for worship?

Today we also read about the creation of all living things, in
the air, the water and on land. Think of a creature which you
have never seen in its natural free state – a whale or a dolphin,
a humming bird or a gazelle . . . Now think of one you know well
– a cat or dog, or a bird which comes to your window-sill for
crumbs. Think of the ways in which, by their very being, they
praise God.

✴ *O God, may we, daily and yearly,*
   each in our own way,
   join all your creatures in a festival of praise.

Wednesday October 19   **GENESIS 1.26-31**

Look at yourself in a mirror. Thank God for the person you see.
You are made 'in the image of God'. Male or female, you carry
God's imprint in your body and soul. By being the person God
made you to be, you can help others to know and love God.

We need to be careful not to 'make God in our image' – not to
worship and teach others about a God who shares only our skin
colour, gender, culture, prejudices. God is greater than any
single human experience. But all human beings, in all their
diversity, have 'that of God in them'.

The reading reminds us of several ways that human beings
reflect facets of God's image. 'Be fruitful and increase' – we are
gifted by our Creator with many kinds of creativity: not just
having children, but being able to make useful and beautiful
things, use language and our imaginations. 'Have dominion' – in
the story, God gives people power over all other living things.
We know we have that power, to tame and farm, mine, hunt and

fish, plant, build and destroy, and change the face of the earth. Do you think we are using that power wisely?

✳ *Creator God, may we reflect your image,*
as we live in your world, creatively, responsibly.

Thursday October 20   PSALM 8.1-9

For those of us who live in cities, the glow of lights can make it difficult to see the full glory of the night sky. Imagine the Psalmist, on a rocky hillside, gazing with awe out into the unknown – deep darkness in which every point of light was 'the work of God's fingers'. Modern scientific knowledge and theory about the universe – its immensity of space and time – can only increase our wonder.

The sequence of ideas in the psalm is helpful:

● God is glorified 'throughout the world' – people of every culture feel awe before God's creation, though the names we give to the Creator are different (verses 1-2).

● Where are human beings, small, weak and limited in understanding, in the scheme of things (verses 3-4)?

● Amazingly we are given a share in God's glory and power – with responsibility – over other living things (verses 5-9).

● How can we respond? First, by glorifying God (verse 10).

In verses 1-2 we are reminded that children have a gift of wonder, which adults have sometimes lost.

✳ *Lord of the universe,*
maker of the starry sky,
restore in us, your children,
small and frail as we are,
the gift of wonder
so that we may glorify your name
through all the world.

Friday October 21   GENESIS 2.1-4a

We return to the 'seventh day'. In this account, God completes creation in a week – which bears more relation to geological time recorded in the rocks than to the calendar on our wall. Yet one way we can try to understand this tremendous process of creation is through thinking about our daily work – paid or unpaid.

As each stage of creation was completed – as the earth produced growing things, for instance – we read 'and God saw that it was good'. Do we feel the same pleasure in a job well done, in the completion of something which fully uses our gifts, which will benefit others?

✳ *Thank God for the last time you did something*
'and saw that it was good'.

Then, at last, 'God saw all that he had made and it was very good'. The day that follows is a day of rest and it is blessed. For the Jewish people this day, the Sabbath, is Saturday. It is a day of rest and refreshment, as well as worship. While some hedge it round with laws which prevent any activity which could be interpreted as 'work', it is, for the whole Jewish community, a time of joy and recreation in family celebration. Christians have transferred the idea of the 'day of rest' to Sunday (linked to our celebration of the resurrection). But has it become for us either a day of dutiful observance or a day of work and worry like any other day? How can we rediscover the blessing of rest and re-creation? How can holy days be holidays – and vice versa?

✳ *Pray for fulfilment in our daily work*
and blessing in our times of rest.

Saturday October 22   **LEVITICUS 25.23-28**

It would be easy to dismiss these laws as relics of a vanished way of life. Yet they embody a wisdom we need today.

Land rights and property prices are often in the news now. These ancient laws came from a society where land belonged, not to individuals, but to the community which held it in trust from God. The Israelites saw themselves as God's tenants. So land could not be sold outright. A 'holding', surrendered when the family who farmed it became poor, could be redeemed if their fortunes changed, and would in any case return to their care in the seventh year.

That year was called a 'sabbatical rest'. The land, lying fallow, would regain its fertility. As we see land around us, and in other parts of the world, being over-farmed, or stripped of the trees and plants which put nourishment back into the soil, or overdosed with chemical fertilisers, we see sense in the farming practices of these 'primitive' people.

There is also wisdom in a society not permanently divided into rich and poor; without landowners who can drive others from their homes and farms, as happened when Highlanders in Scotland were evicted in the last century, or still does to Palestinians in Israel or peasants in many countries of Latin America.

✳ *Pray for justice in this world we share,*
  for good use of God's land, everywhere.

Sunday October 23　　　　　**DEUTERONOMY 28.1-8, 15-20**

Today is the beginning of **One World Week** in the British Isles. Churches and development agencies, local congregations and action groups are working together to bring world issues to the attention of the whole community. Why? Because we believe that God calls us to be responsible citizens, to act in love for our neighbours – all over the world.

The books of the Law, from which this reading and yesterday's were taken, spelled out in great detail how this might be done. Rules specifying oxen and boundary stones and kneading troughs might seem irrelevant to us now. But the spirit of the Law makes plenty of sense. Respect and love for God and others need to govern all that we do. In these verses, the rewards for acting in that spirit, and the results of neglecting it, are spelled out.

Cursing, to many people today, merely means using insults or bad language. We come nearer to the meaning with the words used in verse 20 (REB): 'confusion and rebuke'. Our lives will be a mess, we will know we are in the wrong, if we neglect the essentials.

In the tradition of Hebrew poetry, the curses of verses 16-19 are a mirror image to the blessings of verses 3-6. These may remind us of another tradition: that of Celtic spirituality, with its beautiful prayers still used by Christians today.

✳ *The blessing of the God of life be ours,*
  The blessing of the loving Christ be ours,
  The blessing of the Holy Spirit be ours,
  To cherish us, to help us, to make us holy.

© *Iona Community*

United Nations Day, Monday October 24　　　**1 KINGS 8.35-40**

'You alone know the hearts of all.' This passage is a prayer, attributed to King Solomon, praying in the Temple on behalf of his people.

In the city of Beijing is a beautiful temple, constructed with great skill of wood intricately carved and painted. It stands alone in a park and here, once a year in the old days, the Emperor would come to pray for a good harvest. Remembering the millions of people in China who have died over the centuries because of drought, or flood, or political misjudgments, or wars, and the famines that followed, we can imagine why that temple was such an important symbol.

Today is **United Nations** Day. The UN is also a symbol of our hope for peace in the world. We have a dream that one day the nations might be able to co-exist and co-operate, so that no-one starves or feels the need to go to war. Yet in the last few years, we have been painfully aware of famine in Africa, besieged cities in the former Yugoslavia.

Solomon's prayer is not a political statement. He is pleading with God to hear the prayer of people who know that they have done wrong, who want to live in God's way, praying for forgiveness and a new beginning.

✳ *God of the nations*
you alone know the hearts of all;
we know that we have failed
to live in your way, in unity;
help us to change ourselves
and so to change the world.

Tuesday October 25   ISAIAH 65.17-25

In Genesis we read that, looking at creation, 'God saw that it was good'. Then human beings were given a unique responsibility for the world in which they lived. Here we are reminded of the 'hurt and harm' experienced by people in the world as they – and we – have made it:

- the exhausting, unrewarding toil of the poor;
- the unnecessary death of a child;
- refugees uprooted from homes and farms;
- 'the sound of weeping, the cry of distress'.

If we have not experienced these at first hand, we know that they still exist in many places in the world.

But God is still at work. 'New heavens and a new earth' are coming into being, where joy and blessing and holiness belong. The lion eating straw like an ox is a word picture that may make us smile with surprise. But the prophecy says that God will take a delight in changed people. God will rejoice over us as we become as we were created to be – caring for each other, whole and holy.

✳ *God of surprises*
make us new,
make us whole,
make us loving,
make us part of an earth renewed in your love.

For personal reflection or group discussion

Many questions have been asked throughout this section. Look back and reflect again on some of them.

At the beginning of this theme, you were asked to pray for openness to the Spirit. Why not write down such a prayer, summing up some of the ideas of this theme, and share it with others.

ACTION

Find out more about the work of the United Nations and its related bodies, for example: UNICEF, or the United Nations High Commissioner for Refugees. Pray for the work of these agencies and others which seek to bring peace and justice among the nations and to share the earth's resources more fairly.

USEFUL ADDRESSES

Amnesty International – The address is different for each country. Ask at your local Library.

World Council of Churches – 150 Route de Ferney, 1221 Geneva 2, Switzerland.

World Federation of UNA – The Pavilion du Petite, Caconnex, 16 Avenue Jean Trembley, Geneva, Switzerland.

United Nations House – No 3 United Nations Plaza, New York 10017.

ACT IN FAITH

Notes, based on the Revised Standard Version, by

Nihar Chhatriya

Nihar Chhatriya and her husband are ministers of the Church of North India. Nihar is Director of the Christian Education Department of the Diocese of Sambalpur.

We talk of 'having faith', but we are never quite sure what we mean. To talk of faith in God, whom we cannot see, presents more problems. When things go well, the way we want them to be, we say that we trust God. But as soon as things go wrong, our immediate reaction is to ask the question, 'Why?'

We tend to confuse faith with emotion. Faith is not just a feeling and does not depend on feeling. We exercise faith and experience it every day. Only when we are confronted with problems and difficulties do we wonder how much faith we really have. Faith becomes a reality when we know God (not about God) as a Friend who dwells within us, whose life is shared with us. Our relationship with God can then grow in the bond of perfect love and help us to surrender ourselves completely to God's sovereign will.

> *Lord, help me to trust you wholly*
> *for you yourself are the answer to all my need:*
> *My help in trouble,*
> *My refuge in danger,*
> *My strength in temptation,*
> *My comfort in sorrow,*
> *My guide in uncertainty.*
> *My God, now and for evermore.*   *Author unknown*

Wednesday October 26   **EXODUS 2.11-22 ***

The mystery of faith

God reveals, reverses and restores. This is God's mysterious way of dealing with us. God was preparing Moses through many reverse experiences before revealing his purpose.

Moses was hidden as a baby; then, when he had grown up, he had to flee into hiding and God came to him in his hiding place, Mount Sinai. Finally he was buried in an unknown grave (Deuteronomy 34.6) and God testifies to him as 'more meek than any men that were on the face of the earth' (Numbers 12.3).

Many times, we have within us a combination of godly concerns and human perspectives. We are eager, alert and full of natural enthusiasm. But God has to 'change gear' for us and put things into reverse, as God did with Moses. God brought him to the point of realisation that it was not in his own strength but in God's power that he needed to trust.

God intervenes in human affairs to restore his purpose, because he knows what he is doing.

✶ *Lord, help me to trust you*
when I cannot understand,
for you are my stronghold.

Thursday October 27   **HEBREWS 11.23-28 ***

The secret of faith

Faith is the ability to lay hold on the strength and sufficiency of the power of God in times of weakness and impossibilities. When God called Moses out of the burning bush to go and deliver the people from their bondage, Moses knew for sure that he could not do it, for he knew his limitations.

But 'man's extremity is God's opportunity.' It is where human strength ends that God's power begins to work. The secret of Moses' faith was 'not by might, nor by power but by my spirit, says the Lord' (Zechariah 4.6). God was preparing Moses as a child and all the way through. The different experiences he went through were not a waste of time, but God's way of preparing him for the task.

Many times we wonder what is happening, when things are not the way we want them to be. Remember, it is God's way, not yours. Wait patiently for the full revelation.

✶ *Father, thank you for knowing me*
more than I know myself.
Help me to know,
to love,
to trust you more,
and to grow stronger in you.

239

The role and reward of faith

Lot, the man of this world with its fleeting rewards, took advantage of the opportunity to get the best for himself. In contrast, Abram was a man of faith and so was blessed by God with an eternal reward: the gift of land for Abram and his descendants to possess.

Abram did not argue, did not regret, did not fight back or make a demand. He accepted the least as an act of self-surrender to the will of God. Those who honour God will themselves receive honour. Abram reflected God's image in his life and action and was rewarded for his faith and all generations of his descendants.

What are we reflecting in our lives?

✳ *Lord, help me to put others first*
and serve those in need,
without expecting anything in return,
for you are my greatest reward.

The challenge of faith

The theme of the book of Job is the problem of suffering. 'My God, where are you?' is a question that springs from the suffering of the innocent, but it also has its source in faith. The apparent silence of God is hard to bear for those who believe that the God of our faith is a living God. Job's faith was challenged, but God knew Job and Job knew God. Although he did not find an answer, suffering brought him face to face with God. It made him look away from himself to the all-sufficiency of God. Job stands here as a spokesman of his own personal experience as well as the experience of all humankind. Can a person continue to assert his or her faith in God in the midst of unjust suffering without experiencing the strength of God's presence?

No matter what your present circumstances are, never lose hope. God is still in control. God has the final word.

✳ *Help me Lord, to trust you*
when life is in struggle
and faith is challenged.
Give me eyes of faith
to look beyond what is perishable.

Sunday October 30 — 2 Samuel 16.1-13 *

The honesty of faith

King David was in dire trouble. His own son Absalom had won over thousands of David's subjects and incited them to rebel against him. It looked as though God had given David's kingdom to Absalom. Even Mephibosheth, the only surviving, lame heir to Saul's brief dynasty and whose life David had spared, began to think he might be crowned King.

David was utterly humiliated, insulted, scorned and attacked by men like Shimei (verses 5-8). Angry though he was, David exercised restraint. He knew that he was not entirely blameless. His adultery and lack of sensitivity to the different needs and expectations of each of his children had divided his family and fuelled his present troubles. Shimei was only voicing what doubtless many others were saying in private.

Despite the grave mistakes of David's personal life, his unique greatness lay here. Instead of ordering Shimei's death or political detention, as many political leaders might do, he admitted that, although Shimei's action was wrong, Shimei might, in God's sight, be right.

Only faith in God's unfailing presence can help us to be as honest with ourselves: to recognise the evil we have done and the good we have failed to do.

✳ *Brothers and sisters, in the presence of the God of glory,*
We need to confess our true human condition.
In the light of Christ's self-giving life,
his way of the Cross,
We see the darkness in our lives.   *Church of South India*

Monday October 31 — ACTS 7.54 to 8.1 *

The cost of faith

Stephen is remembered as the first Christian martyr. His preaching had made it clear that Christianity was not tied to the Temple or to the Jewish legal system.

'The blood of the martyrs is the seed of the Church.' In Christian history, and in some countries today where Christians are not free to profess their faith, the Church has grown. The seed has to die before the plant can bear fruit. Stephen's death was a consequence of faith, and his forgiveness of his enemies (verse 60) was a sign of the wholeness of his faith.

What is the value of your faith? What has it cost you? Can it stand the test?

✳ *... In all these things we have complete victory through him who loved us! For I am certain that nothing can separate us from his love: neither death nor life, neither angels nor other heavenly rulers or powers, neither the present nor the future, neither the world above nor the world below – there is nothing in all creation that will ever be able to separate us from the love of God which is ours through Christ Jesus our Lord.*

Romans 8.37-39 (GNB)

✳ *Lord, teach me day by day*
to know what it means to follow you
and make me a true follower.

Tuesday November 1　　　　　　　　MARK 13.3-13

The test of faith

This was a private discourse, but one through which Jesus speaks to the whole Church. From the Mount of Olives, Jesus looked down across the valley to a doomed city and its Temple. His people were oppressed: they suffered and longed for freedom. Those who followed him, like these four disciples, would know loss of freedom and suffer for their faith. There would be religious distress, external dangers and political upheavals. God has not promised us an easy journey, but a safe landing.

✳ *Nailed to a cross because you would not*
compromise on your convictions.
Nailed to a cross because you would not
bow down before insolent might.
My Saviour, you were laughed at,
derided, bullied, and spat upon
but with unbroken spirit,
Liberator God, you died.

Many young lives are sacrificed
because they will not bend;
many young people in prison
for following your lead.
Daily you are crucified
my Saviour, you are sacrificed
in prison cells and torture rooms
of cruel and ruthless powers.

The promise of resurrection,
the power of hope it holds,
and the vision of a just new order
you proclaimed that first Easter morning.
Therefore, dear Saviour, we can affirm
that although bodies are mutilated and broken,
the spirit refuses submission.
Your voice will never be silenced,
Great Liberating God.

Aruna Gnanadason © Christian Conference of Asia

Wednesday November 2   2 Corinthians 4.1-18

The triumph of faith

God always chooses ordinary people to do extraordinary things, so that there will be no reason for boasting. God loves to put valuable treasures inside ordinary people. Hardships and difficulties are stepping stones and opportunities for growth. Even though life surrounds us with infirmity, Christ surrounds us with glory. As followers of Christ, we may have to learn the hardest lesson that Jesus learnt in Gethsemane, to accept what we cannot understand. Although we may be at our wits' end, we have hope in the presence of the risen Christ.

✳ *If we fight or wrestle,*
we shall not be destroyed;
fear and poverty may rise against us,
we shall not be overwhelmed.
For all the powers of earth and heaven
Are beside us – the Messiah has risen.

The flesh may die,
but the Spirit will live;
The kingdoms of the world will end,
but God will reign in his kingdom.
Its inhabitants shall live forever
As children of God – the Messiah has risen.

The joy of God's children
can never be measured . . .

Ikoli Harcourt Whyte,
translated by Ebere Nze, Nigeria

Thursday November 3   **2 CORINTHIANS 5.1-10**

The eye of faith

The eye of faith looks beyond life into the life beyond. That is the Christian hope. We have a glorious home. Paul sees eternity, not as an escape into nothingness, but as entry into life. Christians are citizens of two worlds: we have one foot in time and one in eternity. Jesus said, 'In this world, ye shall have tribulations but be of good cheer, I have overcome the world' (John 16.33). Christ, our pathfinder has gone ahead and knows the way. All we need to do is to follow him.

✳ *My body is paralysed.*
By God's strength someday I will be free.
When that day comes I will be filled with joy.
This I know.
I haven't walked from the day I was born,
On the warm backs of my parents and brothers and
sisters
I can go anywhere.
This I know.
I am unable to speak.
I cannot speak gossip
Or speak harsh words.
This I know.
In the midst of sorrow and pain
There is joy and happiness.
In the midst of this, I am alive.
This I know.
       Kumi Hayashi, Japan, from Oceans of Prayer (NCEC)

Friday November 4   **HEBREWS 11.1-10**

The obedience of faith

Old Testament characters had not received the light we have in Christ. But they took God at his word and demonstrated instant obedience. Paul saw that God accepted their 'righteousness'. Their faith was an attitude of soul through which developments of the unseen future became actual. To them, faith was an encounter with God. A taste of God's goodness enabled them to trust God. They looked forward to God's promise, rejecting the temptation to turn back. Faith and obedience are 'two sides of the same coin'. We need a clear inward vision of God the almighty and all powerful that we may trust him and obey.

✳ *God, give us light to know your will,*
courage to obey your will
and a heart to love your will.

For personal reflection or group discussion

Reflect on the hardest experiences of your life and how much you have been helped by God's presence.

Make a list of new and difficult challenges that face you as an individual and your local church. How do you think your faith may have to change and develop to tackle them?

ACTION

Think of a costly action you have felt challenged to do but have avoided. In God's strength, go out and obey God's will.

GOD'S LASTING COVENANT

Notes, based on the Revised English Bible, by

Michael J. Townsend

Michael Townsend is superintendent minister of the Hudders-field Pennine Methodist Circuit in Yorkshire (UK). He is a regular contributor to theological journals and a book review editor.

'Covenant' is not a word we use in everyday speech. Dictionaries offer suggestions like 'treaty', or 'agreement', though we do not tend to think of our relationship to God in these terms.

Biblical covenants embody God's special relationship with people. In some cases, as with Abraham and Moses, the Jewish nation is indicated. In the covenant with Noah, all creation is involved. Our theme ends with the 'new covenant' which God has made through Christ and here, supremely, the offer is to all.

Let us reflect:
I trace the rainbow through the rain,
And feel the promise is not vain,
That morn shall tearless be.

George Mattheson

Saturday November 5   **GENESIS 9.8-17 ***

God makes this covenant with Noah and his descendants. As the only human survivors of the flood (Genesis 7.23), they symbolise the whole of humanity, while 'every living creature' that come out of the ark indicate that God promises a new relationship with the whole creation.

The sign of this covenant is to be the rainbow, which according to tradition, was unknown before the flood. The writer of the story sees the rainbow as a reminder to God, rather than to Noah and his descendants (verses 15 and 16). The Hebrew word for 'bow of war' is the same as for 'rainbow'. The flood is interpreted as a consequence of God's anger against corruption and evil. But the bow of war is transformed into the bow of hope. All God's creatures may now live in the consciousness that mercy and love are at the heart of their existence.

✳ *Gracious God, you care for everything you have made and hold us all in your love.*
Open our eyes to your presence and to the 'rainbow of hope' in our suffering.

Sunday November 6   GENESIS 18.1-15 *

It was not only Sarah who laughed! Abraham did the same when God told him that he and Sarah would have a child (see Genesis 17.17). As Genesis tells the story, the couple had been waiting twenty five years for God to keep this promise. The covenant revealed to Abraham – when he was called to leave Haran and set off on a journey to an unknown country (Genesis 12.2) – was that God would make of his family a great nation. Each passing year had made its fulfilment, humanly speaking, less likely.

Yet, quite literally, God had the last laugh. Their child was called Isaac which means 'God laughs'.

This strange story shows how the whole of humanity would be blessed through this unlikely couple. Abraham and Sarah were chosen, not only to experience God's blessing for themselves, but that others might be enriched by the fruit of their obedience. This is the manner of God's covenant: God calls so that, through those who respond, new life and hope may reach others. But without obedience God cannot get started at all.

✳ *Pray that those whom God calls may not keep the blessing to themselves but share it freely with others.*

Monday November 7   ROMANS 9.1-9 *

Paul writes here under the stress of strong emotion. A loyal Jew himself, he cannot, in his heart, understand the opposition to the gospel he has encountered from many of his own people. This rejection causes him such agony, he would even be willing to be separated from Christ if such a thing would benefit those Jews who do not believe.

As we saw in yesterday's reading, God had made a covenant with the whole nation. Yet many, by their unwillingness to face new challenges, were not recognisable as 'children of Abraham'. Paul knows that God's promises cannot fail (verse 6), even if our reactions to it make it appear that they had done just that.

Christians have sometimes assumed that God's promises were simply transferred from the descendants of Abraham to the Church, but Paul does not say this. Instead, he re-defines the nature of the covenant. It is now no longer restricted to any racial group, but is open to all the 'children of the promise', those who share the faith which Abraham showed. What might be the equivalent of that insight for today's church?

✳ *Give thanks for the wonder of the gospel.*
Pray for those who refuse to receive it.
Offer to God your willingness to share it.

Tuesday November 8   LUKE 3.7-14 *

At what point does the living faith of a community begin to suffer from 'hardening of the arteries'? That is not easy to answer but we can learn to recognise its signs: for example, when members of the faith community begin to rest on achievements of the past instead of seeking renewal of tradition in the present.

This takes various forms, depending on Christian denominational background. Some cling to a particular form of worship, insisting they cannot find God in any other. There are others for whom particular church buildings provide the only place where prayer can be valid. Others proffer the faith of their parents or the ecclesiastical achievements of grandparents as evidence of their own faith, like those who said, 'We have Abraham as our father.' These are just some of the ways in which people, whatever their tradition, evade the challenge of personal response to what God is doing in their midst.

God's covenant with us is to be renewed in the personal faith and action of discipleship in every generation. Only so does it remain a living relationship bringing blessing to the world.

✳ *Jesus, are we really like that –*
following in our father's footsteps
without a thought for the real meaning of things?
Do our Synods and structures so constrict us
that the heart has gone out of our message?

Then lead us by the hand
in our true Father's footsteps
so, clothed in your righteousness,
our lives, committees and churches
become your community on earth.

                                        URC Prayer Handbook

Wednesday November 9 LUKE 11.33-41 *

All God's gifts, even the covenant relationship, can be corrupted and go bad God gives us light, but we can – and do – turn it to darkness. This happens when religious tradition becomes an end in itself, insisting always on 'the right way' to do things. This was the point of the harsh rebuke Jesus offered to the Pharisee who was surprised that Jesus had not engaged in the usual ritual washing before a meal. Excessive concern about the correct performance of religious observances is no substitute for living justly, as those who are full of light.

It is a harsh lesson but a necessary one. It might be a salutary exercise to think of some things in our own religious tradition which we value greatly but which, if we are honest, are always in danger of blinding us to the wider issues of justice and truth in today's world.

✳ *Lord of renewal, help us in the practice of our faith*
to recognise those things which are at the heart
of our relationship with you and those which are not.

Thursday November 10 ROMANS 5.12-21 *

Today's reading is part of the contrast Paul draws between the kingdom of death, symbolised by Adam, and the kingdom of life which comes in Jesus. The new covenant made through Jesus does not merely overturn the old order – whereby human beings were captive to sin and punished by death – though it certainly does do that. It makes of us a new creation. In John Ziesler's fine phrase (in his commentary on Romans), Paul 'sees Christ as inaugurating a new way of being human'. This is because the new covenant is all about human beings being remade in the image of the Son of God who is, in turn, the pattern of what God always intended us to be.

A famous atheist once said he would believe in Christianity when Christians began to look more redeemed. People made in the image of Christ, with his love, gentleness, compassion, forgiveness and openness represent a new way of being human which the world desperately needs. It is for this reason especially that we should set no limit to what our covenant God can do in our lives if we permit it to be so.

✳ *Reflect on the new life that has come to you through Jesus. Give God thanks for all that it means.*

Friday November 11   **HEBREWS 8.1-6 ***

The early Christians knew that their religion was both new and not new. It was new because, in Christ, God had created a covenant relationship both decisive and final. It was not new because the relationship incorporated elements of what had gone before and was the last of a series of such covenants.

In today's reading, the author uses two pictures to make the point -

● The old covenant was administered by earthly priests who had to keep on offering their sacrifices. The new covenant is administered by Jesus the great high priest, who has offered himself once and for all.

● The old covenant was exercised in the Tent (and its successor the Temple) which was only a copy of the heavenly sanctuary. The new covenant is offered from heaven itself, because Jesus the high priest is at God's right hand.

None of this is easy for us to understand, because we may not naturally think in such terms, but the main thrust is clear. What God has done for us in Christ is once and for all; it never needs to be repeated.

✳ *Thank God for the self-offering of Jesus.*

Saturday November 12   **HEBREWS 8.7-13 ***

For the writer to the Hebrews, the old covenant depended too much on externals. Jeremiah, however, had caught a new vision (Jeremiah 31.31-34) which the writer to the Hebrews quotes to show how the new covenant in Jesus moves us in new directions.

● God's truth becomes the inward motivation for living (verse 10b). This is demonstrably superior to a religion which relies on external observances.

● Our relationship to God is personal and intimate (verse 11). This knowledge of God and God's will is the basis of a religion involving the whole personality.

● Forgiveness of sin is something of which the believer can be assured, not because the correct religious ritual has been performed, but because we have trust in Jesus, the bringer of the new covenant.

So the theme of covenant comes full circle. We began with God's covenant with all humankind (see notes for November 5).

The new covenant which has been inaugurated in Jesus is offered to every human being. Those who respond to it find a quality of relationship with God which can only be described as a new creation.

✳ *Quietly examine your own relationship to God and measure it against what God offers in the new covenant.*

For personal reflection or group discussion

Read Jeremiah 31.31-34 and reflect on how much we hold in common with the Jewish community today. Covenant is still fundamental to the Jewish Faith and way of life. What are the implications of our covenant with God as a church?

ACTION

Find out something about how Christians can give practical expression to the covenant with Noah and his descendants by caring more effectively for our planet.

HOPE NEVER DIES
(JEREMIAH 31-42)

Notes, based on the New Jerusalem Bible, Good News Bible and New English Bible, by

Desmond Gilliland

Des Gilliland is an Irish Methodist minister. He served as a missionary for four years in China and eight years in Hong Kong. He has been a Chaplain to the universities of Dublin and secretary of committees on Social Welfare and World Development and is now retired.

Jeremiah's ministry, like that of Jesus, ran counter to the ideas of religious and political leaders of his day. They believed that their God (with some help from Egypt), would save Judaea from Babylonian conquest. Jeremiah believed the victory of Babylon was inevitable and that they must accept this and find their destiny in the inner kingdom of covenant with a righteous God.

He saw that the Judaean delusion of being clothed in the military protection of Yahweh was naked self-deception. In denying this, Jeremiah appeared to them to be unpatriotic, defeatist and insulting to God. In reality, he loved his country passionately and spoke of what God saw as best for his people.

For rebirth and resilience, blessed be God.
For hunger and thirst to see right prevail, glory to God.
For all who speak out for truth, let us praise the Lord.
For all who triumph over their bitter conditions, Alleluia.
For all who risk their lives and reputations for the gospel, thanks be to God!

South Africa, Methodist Prayer Handbook

Sunday November 13   **JEREMIAH 31.15-22**

Hope for prodigals!

What an amazing eight verses! Verse 15, 'Rachel weeping' refers back to the nation of Israel taken into exile by the Assyrians a century before and never heard of again. With a similar catastrophe about to overtake Judaea, Jeremiah poignantly identifies with that grief of Israel. In Matthew 2.18 this verse is recalled to express the grief of the powerless at a meaningless massacre. For Jeremiah, as for Jesus, God's love was at the centre of all suffering, as it is today:

> With mewing sound, like a tiny kitten
> the refugee baby has gone;
> Rachel again with grief is smitten
> and Christ is the centre of all,
> the sorrowing centre of all.   *D.G*

Israel is then depicted as

● **a prodigal son** (verses 17-20) and God as the loving Father,

● **a prodigal daughter** (verses 21-22a) – 'Come home, Virgin Israel . . . How long will you hesitate, rebellious daughter?'

Verse 22 presents a puzzle. The English translations vary greatly. Peake's Commentary suggests that it is a copyist's comment on the novelty of Israel being both son and daughter:

> 'For the Lord has created a new thing on the earth: a woman will play a man's part' (REB).

This was 'inclusive language' 2,500 years ago!

✳ *Lord, forgive us prodigals.*
Set us down with Jesus in the midst of the world's sorrow
and renew your covenant with us and ours with you.

Monday November 14   JEREMIAH 33.1-13

Prisoner of Hope

In this chapter, Jeremiah, a biblical predecessor, was in prison, still proclaiming the certain fall of Jerusalem and the need to make terms with the Babylonians. Today's passage is from the Book of Consolation (Jeremiah 31-33), so called because Jeremiah saw beyond destruction to a new era of restoration. He lifted the whole situation out of the context of shallow optimism or tragic defeat into a larger context in which ultimate victory lay neither with Babylon nor Judaea, but with the unchanging will of God, whose name I AM overarches all history. Even Old Jerusalem is still a name of power!

> The ancient city still draws pilgrims
> to churches, and mosques, and the old Wailing Wall,
> and 'Next year in Jerusalem' is the heart-cry
> of Jews who may never get there at all.

Jeremiah, however, evisaged a purified Jerusalem, drawing pilgrims to God and the New Jerusalem of God's peace.

* **Lord, help us in our own Jerusalems**
  to sort the transient from the real
  and become prisoners who hope in values that abide.

Tuesday November 15   JEREMIAH 33.14-26

Hope fulfilled in God's way

This passage does not occur in the Greek translation of the Hebrew text, which means that it was probably not in the original Hebrew but added as a later comment. It develops in detail the vision of a restored Judaea and Israel, and prophesies a messianic King of David's line. God's covenant with the people is movingly declared to be as sure as the laws of the universe itself.

This is a resounding promise of religious and political restoration. We need Jeremiah's corrective insistence that the covenant is two-sided and depends, like all true nationalism on the **quality** of the nation's life. As the Irish poet, Thomas Davis (1814-1845) says,

'Freedom comes from God's right hand, and bears a noble train,

And **Righteous** men shall make our land a Nation once again.'

Restoration did come in God's own way in Jesus, who did not re-establish national and religious independence but brought a new covenant and a Kingdom that transcends the kingdoms of the world.

* **Then learn to scorn the praise of man,**
    And learn to lose with God;
  For Jesus won the world through shame,
    And beckons thee His road.   *F W Faber*

Wednesday November 16   JEREMIAH 34.1-7

Hopeless?

The book of Jeremiah is a treasury of 23 years of the prophet's sayings and doings. It is not a chronological account. 'No one can pretend that Jeremiah is an orderly book' *(The Torch Bible Commentary)* and Martin Luther wrote, 'We must not trouble about the order . . .' For example, this chapter concerns the last days of Zedekiah, while the next chapter goes back 14 years to the reign of Jehoiakim *(see the table of events)*.

Today's verses prophesy doom. Are those who warn us that we are destroying the earth's environment actually prophets of hope, if only **we** will listen?

✳ *Teach your children what we have taught our children, that the earth is our mother. Whatever befalls the earth befalls the sons of the earth.*

Chief Seathl, American Indian

TABLE OF EVENTS IN THE LIFE OF JEREMIAH

640-609BC Reign of King Josiah – call of Jeremiah to be a prophet

609BC King Jehoahaz who was deposed by Egypt after only three months.

609-598BC King JEHOIAKIM – Vassal of Egypt for four years and of Babylon for seven years. He then rebelled but died before the Babylonian armies arrived.

698BC King Jehoiachin reigned for three months and surrendered to the Babylonians. He was taken into exile with 10,000 leading citizens – the FIRST EXILE.

597-587BC King ZEDEKIAH appointed by Babylon, but later rejected Babylonian control. Jerusalem was beseiged and fell in **586BC** – the SECOND EXILE.

586BC Gedaliah was appointed Governor. He was murdered by the Judaeans who then fled to Egypt taking Jeremiah with them. Jeremiah died in Egypt.

Thursday November 17   **JEREMIAH 34.8-22**

Hope defiled

All Jews were members of the covenant people, so it did not seem right that Jews should hold other Jews as slaves. Yet if someone had a debt which he could not repay, he and his family might settle it by serving as slaves for not more than seven years and then be freed. But the rule of only seven years was not well observed.

In the siege of Jerusalem, as pressures increased, slaves became an irrelevant luxury. They were a burden to feed and needed to be free to fight the enemy. So Hebrew slaves were set free by royal command. It was done out of mixed motives, but slave owners made much of their piety in this 'virtuous deed'. When, however, Egypt made a move against Babylon and the siege was temporarily eased, the slave owners went back on their promise and took their slaves back again. It was a nauseating act of hypocrisy and greed.

Yet how typical is our own tendency to vow good deeds when in trouble and to relapse when the trouble passes.

✳ *Lord Jesus, remind us that consistency in love and justice*
is the only true test of greatness in your kingdom.

Friday November 18   JEREMIAH 36.1-19
A hopeful response
Here, we have moved back 14 years into the fourth year of King Jehoiakim. Even before this, Jeremiah had spoken in the Temple about the fate of Jerusalem and of the Temple itself, and had been threatened with death. Another prophet, Uriah, who had prophesied the destruction of Jerusalem was in fact put to death, even though he had fled to Egypt. Little wonder, then, that Jeremiah was forbidden to speak again in the Temple. So it fell to Baruch to write down the prophecies and to read them to the crowds which had come to the Temple for a special fast-day.

The leaders of the people were impressed and disturbed by the content of the message and decided that the scroll should be presented to the King and read in his presence. They wisely told Jeremiah and Baruch to go into hiding!

The reading of the scroll in the Temple was a very important occasion. When the Scriptures are read in church or privately, is it a great occasion for us?

✳ *I am puzzled about which Bible people are reading when they suggest religion and politics don't mix.*
Desmond Tutu, South Africa

Saturday November 19   JEREMIAH 36.20-32; 45.1-5
Written, irrepressible hope
Chapter 36 tells a very dramatic story. Yet the Layman's Bible Commentary declares, 'Chapter 36 is one of the most important passages in the whole book. In the annals of prophetic writing it is unique.' It not only records the beginning of one book of the

Bible, but, in today's passage, foreshadows the long record of savage opposition to the written Word, the suppression of the actual script, and the danger to its authors. It records the tenacity of the inspired prophet in producing another copy, and in chapter 45 tells of consolation for the scribe in his weary labour. The whole history of the Bible and the way in which Jews and Christians became people of the Book is there in embryo, down to IBRA readings of this very day.

✳ *Lord, we thank you for the Bible:*
its inspired writers, faithful scribes,
translators and distributors.
May we be among those who daily meet you in its pages.

For personal reflection or group discussion
Reflect on the life of your own nation. Which aspects of its future are threatened? Where do you see signs of hope?

Sunday November 20   **JEREMIAH 37.1-21**

A gesture of hope misinterpreted

Jeremiah had paid good money for a piece of family land in the occupied territory of Benjamin as a pledge of confidence in the future (Jeremiah 32). The Babylonians temporarily lifted the siege to deal with an approaching Egyptian army, causing an unfounded hope that Jerusalem would be spared. Jeremiah rejected any such confidence, but saw the lull in the fighting as an opportunity to visit his plot of land and reaffirm his faith in a positive future. Paradoxically, he was arrested while leaving the city as a suspected deserter, flogged and put in an underground dungeon. The King did not dare to interfere, but could never ignore Jeremiah. He consulted him privately, and again asked what was really God's word. The answer was the same message of doom, unless the city surrendered. The King rejected the message, but gave the prophet decent prison quarters in the palace grounds.

In China, those who had seen hope for themselves and their country in the Christian message were often regarded, like Jeremiah, as 'running dogs of the foreign imperialists'.

✳ *Do we love our country enough to reject popular false gods of materialism, and suffer for it?*

Hope from a stranger

Jeremiah's reprieve was short-lived. To the desperate – and brave – garrison, his counsel of submission was infuriating. The leaders went to the king and demanded that no leniency be shown to the seemingly defeatist prophet. The weak king gave way again and Jeremiah was flung into an empty storage well to starve and die.

Rescue came in the unlikely person of an African palace slave, a Sudanese eunuch who risked his life by telling the King that this was no way to treat a holy prophet! In his quiet way, Ebed-melech was one of the precious non-Jewish heroes of the Old Testament. Fortunately the weak king overruled his advisers and Jeremiah was hauled out of the pit. Ebed-melech was not only brave, but gentle and considerate. He provided old clothes as underarm padding, lest the ropes should chafe the emaciated armpits of the holy man!

✷ *Jeremiah (39.15-18) promises that Ebed-melech would be favoured by God. In these days of African famine, can we redeem that promise by generosity of brave proportions and gentle love to Africans and others in the pit of starvation?*

A dialectic of fear and hope

There was real empathy between Jeremiah and the weak but good-natured king who asked again for the counsel he was too timid to accept:

'Advise me once more. Hold nothing back.'
'The truth, Sire, could mean my death.'
'No! That I swear; not by my hand
nor the ill-will of others. Fear not, speak true.'
'The truth then, the very truth of God is this.
If you would be truly strong, truly yourself,
truly the king and father of your people,
reject the fiery men of pride and war.
Set all pomp aside. Go out with inner dignity.
Surrender to the king of Babylon's men.
So may you save from fire the city you love,
its children, men and women from the sword.
Resist and all things will be lost:
the city, its people and the Temple of the Lord.'

Not strong enough for valiant self-abasement,
the troubled monarch sadly shook his head.
Yet, true to that inner gentleness,
he kept his sworn promise to the prophet
of safety in the palace of his own guard,
until the city of Jerusalem fell.

✴ *Grant to us, Lord, the blessed courage of the peace-*
makers in putting others' welfare before our own fear
and pride.

Wednesday November 23   JEREMIAH 39.1-18
End of hope?
Stubborn, self-centred in their belief that Yahweh was a national
war-God, the beleaguered garrison did not lack courage. For
one and a half years the Judaeans held out against the might of
Babylon. The wall, the Temple and their own misguided faith
made them brave. But when these failed, and the Babylonians,
in 586BC, poured through the breached wall, resistance was
futile. They fled and were pursued. The leaders were captured
and killed. Weak, tragic, good-natured Zedekiah saw his sons
executed, was blinded and taken in chains to Babylon.

The city and Temple were looted and burnt and the city walls
demolished. The population, apart from the poorest, were
deported to Babylon. The remnant behaved like bewildered
wasps buzzing round their plundered nest. We are left with
Jeremiah, sad survivor of his own predictions, still, one
imagines, lonely, isolated and misunderstood. But he sought out
Ebed-melech and promised him safety.

In Babylon, among the exiles, as we shall see, faith grew and
hope survived.

✴ *We raise our voices in prayer*
through the bars, boldly
believing that there will be an answer
as our people awaken.
Edicio de la Torre, Philippines © CAFOD

Thursday November 24   JEREMIAH 42.1-17
Another hope dashed?
Gedaliah, a good, moderate man was appointed governor of the
conquered state. He was based at Mizpah, on the borders
between Judaea and Israel, instead of among the ruins of

Jerusalem. Jeremiah was with him there, no doubt mentally picking up the pieces out of which a future for his people might yet emerge.

There were still those who could not come to terms with defeat. Ishmael, a proud hot-headed man of royal blood, utterly rejected a governor appointed by Babylon. With a gang of bitter young royalist officers, he murdered Gedaliah and his entourage and took others captive.

A regular, responsible Judaean force rescued the prisoners, and Ishmael and his gang fled to Ammonite territory. But even the moderates were terrified by probable reprisals by Babylon and planned to escape to Egypt. Before going, they called once again on Jeremiah to tell them what God would have them do. Unlike Zedekiah, they pledged themselves to accept the verdict, whatever it was. The prophet advised them to stay and face the future in their own land and be God's people there: to go to Egypt would be disastrous. Despite their promise, they rejected his guidance and took him with them to Egypt against his will.

✳ *Jeremiah, like Jesus: gentle, loving, unbreakable.*
BEHOLD THE MAN.

Friday November 25   PSALM 137

Hope in Exile

Jeremiah's warning of disaster in Egypt was fulfilled. Babylon overran Egypt. The Jews who fled there seem to have degenerated into an idol-worshipping community with little sense of destiny as the people of God. Jeremiah died, or may have been murdered there. The other exiles – those deported to Babylon – did not lose their identity.

● They kept their intense nostalgia, expressed in this Psalm, for their homeland – a feature of Jewish life ever since.

● They joined the earlier group of Judaeans, exiled at the beginning of Zedekiah's reign, already established in Babylon.

● Much of the Old Testament was collected and written down there and, deprived of homeland and Temple, they became the people of the Book.

● They formed small synagogues, 'congregations', to take the place of the Temple.

● They followed Jeremiah's advice to live as good citizens of Babylon and became a settled community and a respected minority.

● Because of their good standing, the Persian king Cyrus allowed them to return to Judaea to resume their national and religious life. In them, the tradition lived. It has been said that Israel's true work only began when, to the superficial eye, she ceased to be.

✳ *Death is the supreme festival on the road to freedom.*
Dietrich Bonhoeffer

Saturday November 26   LAMENTATIONS 4.1-7: 5.15-22
Hope never dies

Lamentations is not attributed to Jeremiah in the Hebrew Bible, but the five laments so vividly evoke the feelings of the people after the fall of Jerusalem that the book became firmly linked with Jeremiah in the English versions. The vision of hope gleaming through thick darkness is certainly akin to Jeremiah's faith and witness.

The first four laments (meant for reciting), are written with consecutive letters of the Hebrew alphabet for each verse. They are still used in synagogue worship on the ninth day of the fifth month (in which the destruction of the Temple is lamented). To read Lamentations is to enter into the sorrows of the world. For Jeremiah, as for John a later prisoner (Revelation 1.8-9), God is the 'Alpha and Omega', the A to Z of human life and history. In that alphabet, HOPE NEVER DIES.

✳ *We ask for faith*
to celebrate even while we mourn
knowing that death and prison
are already signs of a people's struggle
for freedom and life.
Edicio de La Torre, Philippines © CAFOD

For personal reflection or group discussion
Write your own A to Z of hope for your community and the world.

ACTION
Become a 'Kingdom spotter'. Like Jeremiah, let us discover the truth and apply it in our daily lives and social context.

ADVENT 1

HOPE THROUGH DAVID'S DESCENDANT

Notes, based on the New Revised Standard Version, by

Alan Greig

Alan Greig is minister of Kintore Parish Church near Aberdeen (UK). He was previously minister of an Ayrshire congregation before serving for seven years as a Church of Scotland missionary with the United Church of Zambia.

After the tribes of Israel settled in the Promised Land, each tribe was basically independent from the rest. This meant that there was no central political control and no obvious way of working together in times of crisis. Demands grew for the tribes to be ruled by one leader – a king.

The anointing of David as king of all Israel at Hebron marked the completion of this change-over. Only David and his son Solomon ruled over the united kingdom of Israel, but their descendants were to reign in Judah for about 400 years. Even after the end of the monarchy, the Jews believed that one day they would be ruled by one of David's descendants known as the Messiah. Advent, the four weeks before Christmas, is the season when Christians prepare to celebrate the coming of the Messiah.

> *Father, I praise you that the coming of Jesus*
> *was your planned way of making me your friend.*
> *Thank you for the living hope I have in him.*

First Sunday in Advent, November 27   2 SAMUEL 5.1-12 *
King David

Choosing leaders is an important task for the citizens of any democracy. The policies and qualities of the leaders chosen will help to determine the future. The choice of David as king of all Israel had two immediate, but long-lasting, results.

Firstly, by uniting the twelve tribes under one leader, Israel was able to consolidate its position and achieve secure borders. In choosing David, the elders had found an able soldier and leader whom they also believed to be the Lord's choice. The reigns of David and Solomon, his son, were later regarded as the 'golden age' of Israel. Hundreds of years later, the chosen people hoped for another leader like David.

Secondly, this enlarged kingdom needed a neutral capital city, so David captured Jerusalem, which lay between Israel and Judah, and established his headquarters there. It was to become the centre of Jewish religion. Today, 3,000 years later, the city of Jerusalem is holy to the followers of Christianity, Judaism and Islam.

✳ *Father, we pray for the peace of Jerusalem.*
May it become a place of reconciliation
for Christians, Jews and Muslims.

Monday November 28   2 SAMUEL 7.1-16

Who will succeed David?

A thousand years after his death, the Jews hoped for a descendant of David to rule them. Why? The hope was firmly based on God's promise.

Those of us who live in long-established democracies take it for granted that when a national leader dies, there will be a clear way of appointing a successor. Equally, we expect a smooth hand over of power if a government is defeated at the polls. This had not been the case in Israel. Saul's death in battle had led to a period of uncertainty and weakness. Through the prophet Nathan, God revealed to David a **principle of succession** that was to provide relative stability for Judah for hundreds of years. The principle was simple – they would be ruled **forever** by David and his descendants (verse 16). The northern tribes did not accept this after the death of Solomon, but Judah did and was ruled by David's descendants for over 400 years.

Later, when Judah was ruled by an occupying power instead of its own kings, its people remembered God's promise and looked forward to the day when the Messiah, David's descendant, would rule them.

✳ *Hail to the Lord's Anointed,*
  Great David's greater Son!   *James Montgomery*

David's prayer

David had every reason to be proud. His reign had provided peace, security and prosperity, and God had promised an important role for his descendants. David's response was prayer, in which we note the following important features:

● **Humble amazement** at what God had already achieved in his life (verse 18).

● **Thanksgiving** for the promise of future blessing for his descendants (verse 19).

● **Acknowledgment** of God's greatness and uniqueness (verse 22). In David's day, people believed in the existence of many gods. While David recognised that Israel's God was special, the Jews realised later that there is only one God.

● **Calling to mind** God's wonderful deeds in the past – the Exodus, the covenant (agreement) at Sinai and the settlement in the Promised Land (verses 23,24).

● **Petition** for the promise to be fulfilled, so that God's name would be glorified forever (verses 25-29).

Is prayer a part of our daily life or for emergencies only?

✳ *Lord God, like David, I can hardly believe that you love me.*
Because of your great salvation in Jesus Christ,
you alone are worthy of praise.
Bless my family and help us to do your will.

Jesus – David's descendant

By the time of Jesus, there was widespread anticipation among Jewish people that the Messiah, David's descendant, would soon come to restore their fortunes. Oppressed by Roman colonial government, they longed for a great king like David to lead them to freedom. Matthew probably wrote his account of Jesus' life for a Jewish community in the hope of persuading it that Jesus was the Messiah. By opening his Gospel with a detailed family tree of Jesus, Matthew wasted no time in establishing that Jesus was directly descended from Abraham and King David. In Jesus' coming, God fulfilled the promise made to David.

Many of the names will be unfamiliar to us, especially those covering the period from the exile in Babylon to Jesus' day, because little is known about that period. The names remind us that God's promises are often fulfilled through the lives of ordinary people like ourselves. The family tree of Jesus contains the names of people who, despite their failings, were used in God's plan of salvation. God wants to use us too!

✶ *Lord, here I am.*
Help me to be useful to you,
for Jesus' sake.

Thursday December 1   1 CORINTHIANS 15.20-28 *

Eternal hope in Christ

Most Jews did not accept Jesus as the Messiah because he failed to meet their expectations. Their ancestors had trusted David who went on to achieve a period of peace and prosperity for Israel. Despite his pedigree, Jesus did not liberate them from Rome. After Jesus, nothing was changed. Or was it?

Paul was certain that Jesus had achieved something more wonderful than a temporary military victory. This certainty was based on his firm belief that Jesus had been raised from the dead. The rising of Jesus was a sign and guarantee of the resurrection to eternal life of all believers (verses 22-23). Paul teaches that someone trusting Jesus becomes part of the body of Christ, and will undoubtedly share in all his experiences, including resurrection.

Death and evil have been conquered by Christ once and for all. Death is not the end, but the completion of earthly life and the beginning of life in God's presence. What a wonderful hope!

✶ *Make Christ's victory over death the focus of your prayers.*

Friday December 2   MATTHEW 21.14-17

Hope for the needy

When Jesus visited the Temple there were mixed reactions.

Religious leaders were **annoyed.** When David captured Jerusalem, it was said that the blind and lame would not be allowed to enter the Temple (see 2 Samuel 5.8). A thousand years later, the blind and lame came to Jesus in the Temple and he did not turn them away. He welcomed them and healed them after driving out of the Temple those who had been exploiting the poor when they came to offer sacrifice.

The children's reaction was **praise.** They acknowledged Jesus as Messiah and called him Son of David, and Jesus saw this as a fulfilment of Psalm 8.2.

This incident should encourage the Church, not only to minister to the weakest and most vulnerable in society today, but also to listen to what they have to say. It is vital for the Church's witness that it does not act like an exclusive club, but as a community where all are welcome and valued.

✳ *Lord Jesus, you have clearly stated*
that when we minister to the needy, we minister to you.
May we not fail you by failing them.

Saturday December 3   LUKE 23.35-43 *
Hope through the cross

Within days, the praise of the children in the Temple was replaced by the mocking of soldiers, onlookers and a criminal. The word 'Messiah' had become a title of derision. From a human point of view, it seemed that the power of evil had defeated Christ's way of self-giving love.

In the midst of sorrow, Luke reveals a brief conversation between Jesus and one of the criminals between whom he was crucified. Somehow, this convicted man sensed that Jesus was the victim of a grave miscarriage of justice. He believed that Jesus was different and expressed, in a simple way, his belief that Jesus was King (verse 42).

The cross is a mystery. Through the death of Jesus, God dealt **once and for all** with human sin. In a wonderful way, a hopeless situation was transformed into a proclamation of God's love for the world. By trusting Jesus, the condemned criminal was given eternal hope. By placing our trust in Jesus, David's descendant, that hope can be ours too.

✳ *Lord Jesus, Son of David,*
thank you for the great hope you bring to this life
and for the life to come.

For personal reflection and group discussion

Make a list of people in your community who need a message of hope. Read again Matthew 21.14-17 and Luke 23.35-43. What message comes across to you most clearly? How could you use this?

ACTION

Visit someone in your community who is finding life difficult and share the advent message of hope.

THE WORD OF GOD

Notes, based on the Revised English Bible, by
Gordon Jones

Gordon Jones is a retired Methodist minister who has served in West Africa and the United Kingdom, and has worked with the Richmond Fellowship for Community Mental Health.

The Scriptures, for both Jews and Christians, are often called 'The Word of God' because they speak directly to people of faith in every time and place. On the surface, they are the words of people – with their cultural prejudices and ignorance. We need to judge what we read by the standards of Jesus and be guided by the Holy Spirit. At a deeper level, for those 'who have ears to hear', they carry God's message to our generation.

> *Gracious Spirit, teach us*
> *a real love for the Bible.*
> *Show us how to take it*
> *out of its dust jacket*
> *and into our hearts and souls;*
> *how to carry it joyfully*
> *from the lecterns and pulpits of our churches*
> *back into the wide open spaces*
> *of your everyday world.*
> *Guide us on the great voyage of discovery*
> *it urges us to make*
> *towards the things that are eternal.*
>
> *URC Prayer Handbook*

Bible Sunday, December 4 **LUKE 4.14-21 ***

An important part of synagogue worship was a reading from the Law or the Prophets. Jesus was asked to read from Isaiah and he chose Isaiah 61.1-2a – a message of hope, spoken to the Jews just after they returned from exile in the 6th century BC. Jesus saw them finding fulfilment in the Kingdom he had come to proclaim. 'This,' he was saying, 'is what I have come to offer – good news for the poor, liberation and healing.'

Think of your own nation, or others that you know who are in political turmoil, and imagine what these words mean in those contexts. Notice that Jesus omitted the words: 'and a day of vengeance of our God'.

Jesus' listeners were impressed at first (verses 22-30) and then their admiration turned to hatred when Jesus showed that what he offered was not only for them but for all people. Here is an example of Jesus re-interpreting the words of Isaiah. What Isaiah had only partially understood, Jesus made clear – God's offer of liberation and healing for all peoples.

✳ *Father, help us to take your message to all people, especially those who are victims of poverty, violence or oppression.*

Monday December 5   **ROMANS 15.4-13 ***

Paul wrote this letter to prepare for a visit he hoped to make, though little did he realise that he would come to Rome as a prisoner to be tried by Caesar! The prospect of preaching the gospel in Rome was important to Paul, so he set out its basic truths: that we are saved from sin, guilt and hopelessness, not by trying to obey the Law but by accepting in faith the grace of God. This, he was convinced was God's message, not to one nation, but to the whole world. This was the message of Jesus (in yesterday's reading). Paul quoted the Scriptures to support his message: Psalm 18.49 (in verse 9), the Septuagint translation of Deuteronomy 32.43 (in verse 10), Psalm 117.1 (in verse 11) and Isaiah 11.10 (in verse 12). So, says Paul to Christian readers who are all too ready to see those with whom they disagree as being outside God's plan of salvation, 'God's word of universal salvation is at the heart of the Scriptures!'

Do we set up barriers against people who do not conform to our ways and beliefs? Are we like those who looked askance at Jesus mingling with prostitutes, Samaritans and 'sinners'?

✳ *Think quietly about verse 13. Pray that the qualities mentioned there – joy, peace, faith, hope – may be ours, taking away our fears, barriers and lack of love.*

Tuesday December 6   **ISAIAH 55.1-11 ***

Some Jews had been exiled in Babylon for nearly fifty years, but Babylon had just fallen to the Persian King, Cyrus (539BC).

These words are full of exultant hope, encouragement and challenge. Out of a background of suffering, God's word comes like water to the thirsty (verses 1 and 10). God, out of everlasting love for them, keeps the covenant. God's thoughts and ways are not like ours – often revengeful or despairing: they are infinitely more compassionate (verses 8-9).

We find that God's word is not empty, but fulfils God's loving purpose (verse 11). Isaiah was speaking to a people who had suffered greatly. It may have led many to assume that God did not care for them. This, says Isaiah, is not so. God is involved in people's suffering, shares it, shows its purpose and a way through it. Suffering remains a 'problem' for us all. But God does not behave towards us as an over-indulgent parent. Instead, God intends us to grow into mature, free persons (and in this world that involves suffering).

This word of God is constantly heard as we read the Bible – in the history, the prophets, the life, death and resurrection of Jesus. The value of reading the Bible regularly is that God's word becomes clearer. Do we hear it? How do we respond?

✱ ***Lord, thy word abideth,***
And our footsteps guideth;
Who its truth believeth
Light and joy receiveth. *Henry Williams Baker*

Wednesday December 7 1 THESSALONIANS 5.16-24

Paul wrote 1 Thessalonians after his friend Timothy had told him of the successful outcome of Paul's recent visit to Thessalonica. Verses 19 and 20 speak of two activities to which it seems the Thessalonians had not given much attention – 'inspiration' (which may refer to speaking in tongues) and 'prophetic utterances'. Paul goes on to say in verses 21 and 22 that they have to be 'tested', for speaking in tongues may be meaningless emotionalism and prophetic utterances may not always contain a message from God. The question we must always ask is whether they come up to the standards of the teaching and example of Jesus.

There is a parallel here in the way we read the Bible. To accept the literal truth of every word is dangerous. There are some parts which most certainly misinterpret the mind of God. Look for example at Leviticus 24.20 and then at Matthew 5.38-39. Jesus rejected the Old Testament demand for revenge and so do we. The Bible should be read critically, trying to get beneath the details to what we can discern as the word of God and what is not. This is 'testing the spirits'.

✳ *For some people, the words 'the Bible says' are the end of the search for truth; for others they are the beginning. What are they for you?*

Thursday December 8   ZEPHANIAH 3.4-18 *

Zephaniah was prophet in the 7th century BC, when Judah was victim of much invasion and many priests and leaders were corrupt. Zephaniah speaks of God's anger. It is a frightening and challenging passage to read. It reminds us that the message of the prophets was not all comfort (nor was the preaching of Jesus). The word of God is often a challenge. And yet it is not a negative, hope-destroying challenge. The stern Zephaniah ends on a note of joy. Those who respond to the challenge, change their ways and accept persecution will triumph in the end. They may be few – a 'remnant' (verse 14). They will show that God's wrath is the converse side of God's love and offer both the challenge and comfort of God's word to their community.

You who read these notes, you are part of the 'remnant'. It is for you to continue to proclaim the word of God to your society worn down by many evils.

✳ *We are called to proclaim the word of God to the world. Pray for guidance that we may do this in our own neighbourhood without fear and with humble confidence.*

Friday December 9   PSALM 119.89-96

Psalm 119, is a prolonged cry of joy at God's law. The Psalmist may not have been thinking of the Torah. He sees that God teaches the law and so to know and keep the law is to seek God and discover the joy of knowing and loving God.

The law is often called, 'Your word'. It is not a threatening word; it is a guiding word, full of promise. In this reading, God's word is shown to be everlasting, the power that created and sustains the universe. It is a delight to the writer, even though obeying it may bring persecution from enemies (verse 95). This is the Word of God we find in the Bible – in its history, its law, its hymns and in its supreme revelation in Jesus. No wonder our delight is in reading it daily!

✳ *Come, divine Interpreter,*
  Bring us eyes thy book to read,
Ears the mystic words to hear,
  Words which did from thee proceed,
Words that endless bliss impart,
Kept in an obedient heart.   *Charles Wesley*

Saturday December 10   PSALM 119.105-112

The Psalmist knows the difficulties he will have to face when he is obedient to God's word – God's Law, but he is determined to continue to be obedient. He reaps his reward now: the joy of loving God, living in God's presence and experiencing a fulfilment of life which comes through obedience.

The word is a light. Like a lamp at night, it shows the path ahead when we feel lost. The Bible shows us the way to live. It shows the pitfalls and dispels the frightening shadows. The light of dawn promises a new beginning after we have fallen. It opens our eyes to the nature of God.

All this comes from our reading the Bible carefully, critically and, above all, with our eyes fixed on Christ who called himself 'the light of the world'.

✳ *Your word is a lamp to guide us and a light for Our path.*
  Grant us inner vision, great light of life,
  that we may awaken to your will for us,
  and be alive to our part in your work in the world.
                                          Church of South India

---

For personal reflection or group discussion

What passages would you recommend to someone reading the Bible for the first time, a lonely person, a frightened person, a child bereaved of a parent? In a group, share with one another reasons for your choices.

ACTION

Discuss with a few friends how you may encourage others to become regular readers of the Bible.

ADVENT 3

THE FORERUNNER

Notes, based on the Revised Standard Version, by

David Bridge

David Bridge is minister of the Epsom Methodist Church and chairs the British Methodist European Affairs Committee. He has written a number of books, the most recent being **Letters to Rebecca**, *a dialogue between an agnostic undergraduate and a Christian friend.*

When Jesus sent out his followers on their first mission, Luke tells us (Luke 10.1) that their purpose was to visit towns and villages where Jesus was to go and to prepare the way. This is a perfect description of the missionary task. It is not our job to convert people. If we do, they are in serious trouble for they will become like us. Only the Holy Spirit can convert people to God. Our role is to help them meet Jesus and be open to his Spirit. So we are all forerunners, preparing the way for the coming of Jesus. John the Baptist was in a special sense a forerunner.

> *Almighty God, we praise you*
> *that in your love for us and for all people,*
> *you come to meet us in the person of Jesus.*
> *We praise you for the life of your Spirit*
> *who speaks to us in many ways and reveals your truth.*
> *Grant that as we study your word,*
> *your Spirit may speak to us and through us to others.*

Sunday December 11   **LUKE 1.5-25 ***

Not one but three messengers of God are described here:

● The first is the angel **Gabriel**. Biblical writers frequently speak of angels when they want to describe direct communication from God. Gabriel evokes awe and wonder. This is the authentic reaction to God and we must never allow our relationship with God to become too cosy.

● The second is **Zechariah**. He evokes puzzlement. He has a message to give to people waiting for him in the outer court of the Temple, but cannot give it because he is tongue-tied, as we often are when we try to speak to others about God.

● The third is one who will grow up to be known as **John the Baptist**. He will evoke change, healing relationships and converting the ungodly.

We are called to be messengers of God. Like these three, our task is to help people experience a sense of awe, to find words that they may understand and to make them aware of the Spirit of God who changes lives.

✳ *Think of people who have been messengers of God to you.*
Are there those to whom you might be a messenger in a similar way?

Monday December 12   LUKE 1.57-66

Throughout the Bible, great importance is attached to the choosing of a person's name. Names conveyed a message about a person, or at least about parents' expectations of their children. Isaiah gave his sons names which amounted to a short sermon (see Isaiah 7.3 and 8.3 for example) and one can only hope they found shorter nicknames for everyday use! A new name, given later in life, often indicated a change of lifestyle or status. When the birth of Isaac was announced (Genesis 17.15-16), his mother's name was changed from Sarai meaning 'mockery' to Sarah meaning 'princess'. His father's name had earlier been changed to Abraham meaning 'father of a multitude'.

When Jesus gave Simon the fisherman a new name, Peter meaning 'rock', it indicated Jesus' expectation that Simon would become a changed person. It was a sign of God's confidence in him.

The friends of Zechariah and Elizabeth assumed they would simply follow the customs of the past in choosing a name for their infant son. But God was about to do something new and so the baby would have a new name. John means 'God is gracious'. His birth was a sign of God's love about to be revealed in the birth of Jesus.

✳ *God, you show confidence in me,*
allowing me to call myself 'Christian'.
Help me to become worthy of such a name.

In a sense, the story of John the Baptist is told in reverse in Luke's Gospel. Later this week we shall study chapter 7: John was in prison but sent some of his disciples to see if Jesus was the Messiah, the one about whose coming he had spoken to the crowds by the Jordan. Jesus gave these disciples a message to take back to John but we are not told what he made of it. Indeed Jesus commented, before he knew John's reaction, that the least in the kingdom of God would be greater than John.

The story in chapter 1, however, encourages us to believe that John was persuaded by the message his disciples brought and that he recognised Jesus as his Lord. It is inconceivable that the stories of John's and Jesus' births would have been so intertwined and that Zechariah could declare such a prophecy about his son, if this were not so. The ministry entrusted to John, to 'lead people to salvation through knowledge of Jesus' is a ministry to which the church is called today. The content of this ministry is also as described: to enable people to worship God freely, to know forgiveness of sin, to live in light rather than darkness and to discover the way of peace.

✳ *Father, when the story of my life is told,*
may it be found to intertwine with that of Jesus.

Wednesday December 14   **LUKE 3.1-6, 15-20**

The message of the preacher contains both comfort and challenge. Part of the meaning of the Hebrew word for salvation is 'having room to move'. So Isaiah, who lived in a country where travel was not easy, envisaged the Messiah creating a level plain out of the rough terrain of his homeland. The slaves who sang, 'When I get to heaven going to put on my shoes – going to walk all over God's heaven,' were expressing the same longing. This was easily recognisable as good news.

But there was also a word of challenge and John did not hide it. The Messiah comes to separate the wheat from the chaff and to destroy what is worthless. Some welcomed the comfort but were not able to accept the challenge as John was soon to discover. His call for repentance and justice threatened those in authority and they had him arrested.

We may be tempted, as we try to share our faith, to offer the comfort and hide the challenge. It is a temptation we must resist. Only the authentic word of God has power to save.

✳ *May I be always open to the challenge of the good news and, when it proves costly to be a disciple, may I remember the sacrifice of Jesus.*

Thursday December 15　　　　　　　　LUKE 7.18-23

In prison, John was anxious to confirm that the one he baptised in the Jordan was indeed Messiah, God's chosen one.

It is interesting that when John's disciples met Jesus, they spoke in a kind of code rather than use the word Messiah: 'Are you the one who is to come?' Only someone familiar with the scriptures would know that this phrase referred to the Messiah.

In reply, Jesus did not answer yes or no, but invited John to recognise in the things he was doing, authentic signs of the Messiah at work. Until Palm Sunday, Jesus did not make an explicit claim to be Messiah. There were so many different expectations current in the Palestine of Jesus' day that had he made such a claim early in his ministry, people would not have listened to him, so strong were their preconceived ideas.

Words are not neutral things; they have many associations bound up with them. We would be wise to follow Jesus' example and communicate as much by what we do as by what we say.

✳ *Lord Jesus, may nothing I do drown what I say about you.*

Friday December 16　　　　　　　　LUKE 7.24-30

In Jesus' day, there were groups of devout Jews who found it impossible to practise their faith in normal society and so formed communities in which they could live a simple life and devote themselves to prayer and the study of the scriptures. Their motives were similar to those who formed Christian monastic orders centuries later. John the Baptist seems to have joined one of these communities, but he was also a missionary who came from time to time out of the desert where he lived, to invite people to take their religion seriously and make a fresh start. He baptised those who responded to his preaching as a sign of their new beginning. Baptism had been practised by other groups for various purposes, but John was distinctive in offering baptism as a sign of repentance.

Asked for his opinion of John, Jesus had no hesitation in affirming John's ministry as the work of God. At the same time he must have hoped that, in the light of the report his friends would take back, John would recognise him as Saviour. We should value godly qualities in those who do not confess themselves to be Christians, while at the same time praying that they will be led to recognise Jesus as their Lord.

✳ *Father, may I be open to signs of your life in all people,*
yet able to share my faith in Jesus,
the source of eternal life.

Saturday December 17   LUKE 7.31-35

Jesus draws a contrast between his own lifestyle and that of John and in so doing, tells us about himself. When the Gospels show Jesus at leisure, it is often at a party or a meal table with friends. In these informal moments, Jesus comes close to people. He does not criticise John for his austerity; the targets of his anger are those who make no response to God in any way. He remembers seeing children playing at weddings and funerals and noticing that whichever they choose, there are always some who do not want to join in. It does not matter, Jesus says, if you respond to God's call by cutting yourself off from worldly pleasures or by enjoying them. What matters is that you make a response instead of sitting on the sidelines. For then you will discover God's Spirit in your life.

The task of the messenger is not to persuade people to change from one style to another but to invite them to live in the power of God's Spirit.

✳ *O God, may I accept people*
who express their devotion to Christ in different ways,
as I myself hope to be accepted.

For personal reflection or group discussion
Are there any vital elements missing in the message of salvation in Luke 1.73-77? Does the Church today neglect the message of judgment which John describes in Luke 3.17? How would you communicate this theme?

ACTION
Think of and find another person you might help by sharing your faith with him or her.

ADVENT 4
CHRIST COMES

Notes, based on the Good News Bible, by
Simon Barrow

Beyond the tinsel of the Christmas season, there is the abiding promise that 'God is with us'. When we read the birth narratives in the Gospels, we naturally look back from what we already know of Jesus and his coming. Many of our readings this week start from an entirely different perspective: two periods of great testing in the history of Israel when faith was stretched and the hope of a Messiah began to take shape. Looking back to these glorious dreams of God's kingdom described in the writings of Isaiah and Micah, it soon becomes clear why Matthew and Luke were so influenced by those promises. We, in turn, can see the significance of Christ's birth in a new, challenging light.

> *God of mercy and judgment,*
> *who alone can exorcise the powers that grip our world:*
> *give us wisdom and patience to recognise your special*
> *gift*
> *in the one who gives us renewed hope:*
> *Jesus the Christ.*

Sunday December 18   Isaiah 11.1-10 *
New hope for the world

In times of upheaval, dare we hope for a better world? Isaiah did – but not because he trusted human beings or their institutions. Prophesying from the capital of Judah, Jerusalem, (740–700BC), Isaiah warned Ahaz (his weak, unprincipled king) that attempts to appease Assyria, which had already subjugated Syria and Israel, would only lead to disaster. But all to no avail. Israel was destroyed and Ahaz found himself paying protection money and building altars to foreign deities.

Against this backdrop, Isaiah rekindled the hope of all who put their trust in God, not superpowers. The royal line of David, crushed and broken, will yield a new Messiah. The qualities of this coming king (verses 2-5) stand in deliberate contrast to the faithless vacillation of contemporary rulers. In the new age of peace with justice, relations among people (verses 3-4) in the natural world (verses 6-8) and between people and God (verse 9) will all be restored.

From the seeds of Judah's despair comes a promise of God which is at once local and (verse 10) global. For us, in an equally troubled world, it points to Christ, who carries for us all the hopes of God's new dawn.

✳ *God of life, may your wise Spirit enter the hearts and minds of all who are caught up in the brokenness of our world.*

Monday December 19   Matthew 1.18-25
God in the ordinary

There is something incongruously matter-of-fact about Matthew's story of the birth of Christ. Yet the truth it decribes is breathtaking. God comes close to us not in power and might, but in the fragile form of a Galilean child of obscure parentage.

But there is also a deliberate link with the long-cherished Jewish hope of a Messiah (a chosen one of God) in the royal line. First, Matthew describes Joseph as 'a descendant of David' (verse 20) and precedes his account with a genealogy linking Jesus to Israel's foremost King. The intention is not to present an exact family tree. It is God's purpose which binds the faithful together, more so than blood.

Second, Matthew reads the birth of Jesus through the words of the prophet in Isaiah 7.14. His use of the word 'virgin' (verse 23) represents a Greek translation of Isaiah's Hebrew term for 'a young woman of marriageable age'. The one born is God's own, a sign and seal that 'God is with us' right at the heart of our lives. God's breaking into human history has been revealed!

✳ *Loving God, give us faith and courage to receive your Christ into our hearts and into our world.*

Tuesday December 20   Luke 2.1-7
God's purpose at work

Like Matthew, Luke emphasises the prophetic nature of Jesus' birth and royal lineage. Bethlehem, too, is noted as the birthplace of King David. This child will be a sign for the nations. How stark, then, is the scene of the Messiah's birth. Not only is he born outside a royal household, he is even denied the dignity of a simple lodging . His true worth goes unregarded, a portent of things to come. God's way is achieved by stable and cross rather than by palace and throne.

The crucial point in Luke's story is not just that God is at work in Israel's faithful, but that the promise of God became true because of an action of the occupying government.

Caesar Augustus was not, in fact, governor at the time Jesus was born. Perhaps one of Luke's sources mistook his name for that of Saturninus, whose census is well established. In any event, Luke shows that the Roman authorities have become unknowing accomplices in an event of saving significance which stretches far beyond their influence. God's redemption draws in even those who do not own it. It is for everyone.

✳ *God of the whole world,*
help us to bring your Christ-like love to all in authority.

Wednesday December 21   Luke 2.8-20
A footstool of heaven

It is vitally significant that the first people to recognise Jesus and worship him were shepherds. Untrained in religion and unskilled in theology, shepherds fell outside the orthodox fold because their demanding jobs made it difficult for them to fulfil traditional religious observances. Yet they knew the truth unswervingly when it hit them. Jesus was going to make all the difference in the world, and the fact that he was to be found lying in an animals' food trough caused them, of all people, no concern at all! There are other important hints in this story of Christ's destiny and purpose. For Jesus is the one who will tend the battered sheep, search for the lost ones and go outside the fold in search of those beyond Israel's flock. He will even sacrifice his life for those he loves.

And then there is Mary, remembering and pondering. She it is who carries in her thoughts the action of God among the lowly. In a world of busyness we are apt to forget, to overlook, to ignore. The gift of those who pray and reflect is that they help all of us to remember what is important, and why.

✳ *God of surprises, give us grace and courage*
to stoop low enough, that we may find heaven there.

Thursday December 22   **Isaiah 45.22-25 ***

Salvation is at hand

In 587BC, Jerusalem was totally destroyed by the Babylonian armies. The city's inhabitants were unceremoniously deported to Ramah and key opponents of the occupying power were executed. The majority were then sent to Babylon where they were to remain in exile for 49 long, hard years. Sadly, occupation, murder and the creation of refugees is not just a thing of the past.

But the writer of these chapters saw other forces at work - the Persians and their king, Cyrus. The wheels of history would turn again and a worshipper of gods other than Yahweh would bring deliverance. This must have been a strange promise for a people trained to reject all foreign deities.

Through it, however, they learned a vital lesson. God is always bigger than we think and God's purposes reach far beyond our imagination. It is something of this awe-inspiring vision which these verses seek to capture. God's saving love is for the ends of the earth. Oppression and hate will be wiped away. Even when all signs seem to be pointing the other way, there is a firm promise to hold on to. A promise which we see fulfilled in the coming of Christ . . . for all.

✳ *God of stable and cross,*
   may we and all your children be free
   and the whole earth live to praise your name.

Friday December 23   **Micah 5.2-4 ***

Promise and judgment

Micah was a contemporary of Isaiah of Jerusalem. It seems he may have been a city elder of Judah (cf Jeremiah 26.18). His message agrees wholeheartedly with Isaiah about the need for faithfulness in times of both prosperity and trial.

The book of Micah thunders with judgment against false prophets, the mistreatment of the poor and (verse 3a) impending national disaster at the hands of Assyria. But it also sings tenderly of God's mercy and deliverance (verse 4). And this, ultimately, is where Micah stood strong. For he too shared the growing vision of a time of universal peace under God (verse 5), and the advent of a new king in David's line.

It is to this overriding hope that our passage returns. The words about Bethlehem, least among the towns of Judah, are quoted prominently in Matthew 2.6 and John 7.42 in connection with Christ's appearance. Like Micah, Jesus started from the premise that loyalty to the loving will of God brought judgment against human deeds and human institutions. But the final victory is always of love.

✳ *God of fire, cleanse and heal us of all that destroys,*
   and show us your endless mercy.

Christmas Eve, December 24   **Isaiah 49.8-13 ***

A time of restoration

At a time when much of what we call 'The Holy Land' is still torn by division and conflict, it is salutary to read the words of Isaiah concerning the longed-for restoration of Jerusalem (538 BC) after years of exile in Babylon. Just as the people of Israel are chosen, not for their own sake but for the sake of the world (cf 49.6), so the promise of deliverance points towards a covenant with all peoples (verse 8). Here, the echoes of Jesus in the Gospels become louder still. Verses 9 and 10 remind us of several passages in Matthew and Luke's Gospels, not least Luke 4.18. Verse 11 alludes somewhat to the spirit of the Levitical Jubilee, the time of equalisation when land was supposed to be restored to its original owners. It has parallels in Luke 3.4-5. The image of the highway through the mountains is one of levelling, as the Lucan passage makes obvious. Our resting point, as we await the Messiah, is one of comfort and joy. God will visit and redeem those who live in darkness.

✳ *God of hope, nourish us with expectation*
   as we wait on your chosen one, Jesus Christ our Lord.

For personal reflection or group discussion

What difference does the form of God's self-disclosure in Christ make for us, our church, our world?

What is distinctive about the vision of God's Kingdom in the prophets and in the stories of Jesus' birth?

ACTION

Decide what thankful gifts – of time, effort, resources – we will offer to God as we celebrate Christ's coming.

CHRISTMAS
TIME FOR REFLECTION

Notes, based on the Good News Bible, by
Akuila Yabaki

*Akuila Yabaki is a Methodist minister from Fiji serving in Britain
with the Methodist Church Overseas Division as Area Secretary
for Asia and the Pacific.*

We take time this week to reflect on God's greatest offer, the gift
of fullness of life in Jesus Christ: his coming and saving work.

● Christ is the Word of life for humanity and the whole universe
which is held in bondage by the powers of darkness.

● Jesus, the presenter of God's message of salvation, is
himself the message: the good news for all nations. His coming
represents the dawning of a new age when God, who has both
power and grace, brings hope and change to all people.

● Certain essentials and discipline are required of those who
seek to live in Christ's way. Light and darkness cannot go
together. For instance, the inward life of prayer is essential to
defeat the powers of darkness.

● Life cannot continue as before.

O God, so great was your love for the world,
that you gave your only Son for us.
Ground our belief so firmly
in the mystery of your Word made flesh,
that we may find in him victory over evil,
for he reigns,
now and forever.

Christmas Day, December 25   **JOHN 1.1-14 ***

The Word of life

Much of what we do at Christmas time is about personal
relationships: relaxing with friends, family gatherings, sending
cards to loved ones far and near. Christian faith is linked with
fellowship and Christ is our Companion, Brother and Friend.

But fellowship has both light and darkness. At the heart of
Christian worship there is a meal and it takes place behind an

empty cross and an empty tomb. John's Gospel brings out the confrontation between light and darkness. Evil is not just in our hearts, but is cosmic and inherent in the whole system of the universe. The saving of humanity is part of a greater reality – the conquest of evil which holds the universe in bondage. Jesus is God's word for the saving of the whole cosmic order. We are challenged to think on a large map.

God's compassion and creative power are displayed in Jesus' actions, words and life. Our own lives are both nourished and judged by the Word and this calls for attentive hearing. In a talkative world, we need to learn to be silent and to listen so that we can truly hear. We will then move from hearing into communion with Jesus, the Word made flesh.

✸ *O holy Child of Bethlehem,*
  Descend to us, we pray;
  Cast out our sin, and enter in;
    Be born in us today!   *Phillipps Brooks*

Monday December 26   TITUS 2.11-15 *

Strength to respond

Seldom do we find a passage so clear about the moral power of the Incarnation. The grace of God dawned upon the world in the birth of a child: in the life, death and resurrection of Jesus. This event is the bedrock of the Christian life.

This message is 'naught for our comfort', but for all humanity, and there is an assurance at the heart of the Christian faith which empowers us to speak the truth with boldness and love in grateful response to God's self-giving.

We have freedom to say 'No' to ungodly behaviour and to offer to God that which is due – a life fit for God's service. The young elder in Crete is exhorted to exercise the full authority of Christian ministry in teaching, encouraging and sometimes rebuking. We need to recover this sense of moral authority: fearlessness in taking risks in order to see right prevail.

The coming of Christ is an act of grace and brings hope to a troubled world. Hope is about a new way of looking at things. Clearly, the blessing of Christmas is that God offers us a new way to follow: the way of the Saviour, Jesus Christ, who gave himself for us.

✳ *Forgive, cleanse and renew us.*
  Implant and nourish
  your love of justice in our hearts.
  Make us passionate in the cause
  of those who cannot speak for themselves.
  Give us the will to be advocates
  for the most needy of your people.

Edmund Banyard, from *Turn but a Stone (NCEC)*

Tuesday December 27   ISAIAH 61.1-4 *

Power to serve

Jesus, in the synagogue at Nazareth, made explicit claim to fulfil this prophecy (Luke 4.18-21). He saw himself anointed in the Spirit of the Lord and his entire ministry, in words and action, brought good news to the poor.

Still, today, in many parts of the world, the poor cry out from situations of oppression, illness and imjustice, though these cries seldom appear to have been heard. The biblical faith is a challenge to existing powers, secular or religious, and exposes them for what they are.

Power used the right way will produce results and benefits for the weak in society. But it begins with a deep sense of call, of being sent to proclaim, to declare, to bind up, to give. This sense of being sent we must claim for ourselves if we are to be faithful to the ministry of Jesus. The spiritual and social are not separable but belong together. We must always find space for worship and contemplation and not allow the social agenda to run away with us in our day to day activities. Compassion and love for others always flow from a depth of spirituality.

✳ *To serve the present age,*
  My calling to fulfil; –
  O may it all my powers engage
  To do my Master's will!

Charles Wesley

Wednesday December 28   ISAIAH 61.5-11 *

Living the good news

The good news is that God moves to change human conditions – to restore those who have been denied their rights, to give honour and a decent standard of living to those subjected to shameful poverty. Good news is God acting, as always, to bring back wholeness into our lives. People from every nation will then joyfully answer in praise of what God has done.

We are people of our time: we have a picture of God moving on the fast lane with us in clock time. But verse 11 sounds reassuring: God's saving work is likened to seeds sprouting and growing in the garden. God is likened to a gardener, tending the growth at a pace different from ours. There is hope here. So often, we feel powerless, dispirited and enraged by verbal assurances from politicians who achieve so little towards making the world a better place. But we can take time to be at peace within ourselves: less bustling activities and an alertness to God's way of doing things. God is Creator and Deliverer.

✳ *Lord of mystery,*
  let us feel your presence at the heart of life:
  we desire to find you in the depths of everyday things.
  Adapted from a prayer by Luis Espinal, a Jesuit priest
  murdered in Bolivia (Christian Aid Lent studies 1992)

Thursday December 29   **1 JOHN 1.1 to 2.1 ***

Christ the righteous

John makes the extraordinary claim that in Jesus God was seen and heard. Jesus, the Word of life, came to present God's message. There is a missionary urgency to tell it and experience the joy of bringing others into the fellowship of those who see God in Christ.

Christ is the centre of the fellowship. We come together at the cost of his own blood which purifies us. We come to the Lord's table, trusting in his mercy and 'not in any goodness of our own'. The presence of others is essential because true fellowship is always a living encounter with Christ.

John had to deal with those Christians who claimed to be 'without sin'. Sin cannot be explained away, but sin is incompatible with God. There are those who seek to have 'the best of both worlds' which is impossible. Light is the sphere where God is and where life is to be found. To live in the glare of God's light is to have turned our backs on the way of darkness. But we are not left to our own devices. Christ has come. God loves the sinner and provides the remedy. Christ the 'righteous one' is with us and 'pleads with the Father on our behalf' (2.1).

✳ For to us a child is born,
to us a Son is given,
Alleluia!
All the ends of the earth have seen
the salvation of our God,
Alleluia!

Friday December 30   1 JOHN 5.13-21

Christian certainties

First, it is a privilege to approach God in prayer. Prayer is not so much asking God for anything as listening to what God has to say to us. This kind of prayer will get us through. We also name people before God with their needs and present difficulties. Jesus has opened the way and for his sake we have confidence that God hears our prayer (verses 13-15).

We can be certain that the evil one no longer has total hold over us. We may have bouts of temptation, but Christ our defender is stronger than the evil one. There is liberty to remain outside in the darkness and beyond the scope of forgiveness, if we so wish. Such is the awesome responsibility of being free! The astonishing thing is that many people make decisions which lead to death (verses 16-19).

We can be certain that Jesus is true God, and the way to eternal life; he has come into the world so that we may know God. There are those who would say that one can be good without belief in Jesus as the Son of God. John's reply is that apart from Jesus there is no real understanding of the truth and no power to live by the truth.

✳ Come, Lord Jesus,
come and make us real.
Free us from the grip of evil.
Make us new in mind and spirit.
Fill us with the energy
and the joy
of forgiven people,
for you alone are our hope,
you alone can save us.
                    Edmund Banyard, from Turn but a Stone (NCEC)

Matthew's Gospel ends with the worldwide mission of the Church: the great commission to go and make disciples of all nations (28.19-20). And it begins with the infant Christ worshipped by Jews and Gentiles alike.

Different traditions have presented the magi as astrologers and wise men. The rising of a star was often associated with the birth of great figures in history.

Herod was an ambitious puppet king under Roman authority who hoped universal recognition and honour. But the magi, bringing gifts from their nations, saw greatness only in the Christ child who later taught that true greatness is the way of humble service.

The adoration of the magi fulfilled the promise that the nations would bring their worship to their Redeemer King. The mission of the Church has for years been perceived as sending and giving. More enrichment could be ours today when, like the family of Jesus, we receive with humility and gratitude the gifts of other nations and cultures. Christ came for us all.

✳ *Love, like death, has all destroyed,*
Rendered all distinctions void;
Names, and sects, and parties fall:
Thou, O Christ art all in all.   *Charles Wesley*

For personal reflection or group discussion

What challenges have come to you from this week's readings? And what are the main insights and challenges that have stayed with you from this year's themes? How will you carry them forward into 1995?

ACTION

Take time to affirm all that you believe about God – God's creative power, compassion and justice – and find new ways of service to others in word and action.

SCHEME OF READINGS FOR 1995

Themes are based on the new Lectionary (JLG2) and include again the study of some books of the Bible.

1. Living sacrifices
2. A living community (1 Corinthians)
3. We shall overcome (Exodus 1–15)
4. Signs of the Kingdom
5. LENT – Strength to resist
6. LENT – Who is Jesus?
7. LENT – The way of suffering
8. EASTER – Risen!
9. Bread of life
10. People of God
11. ASCENSION AND PENTECOST – God's Spirit in the World
12. Building a nation
13. Reaching out
14. Building bridges
15. What are our motives?
16. Looking at time
17. Pictures in the Psalms
18. Strength to forgive
19. The power of the Gospel (Romans 1–8)
20. Peace with justice
21. Pray for peace
22. All is sacred
23. By faith (Genesis 12–22)
24. Questions of citizenship
25. ADVENT – Hope for all
26. ADVENT – The prophetic word
27. ADVENT – Prepare the way!
28. ADVENT – Joy to the world!

Gospel for the year: St Luke

Order your copy early

Encourage at least one other person to read the Bible daily and to order a copy